Angling on Lomond

Mr Edward Cochrane, then 83 years old, with the record Loch Lomond salmon of 44½ lb, caught in 1930 on a trolled blue and silver minnow off the Stables, Ross Priory, on the Claddich shore.

By courtesy of Harry McVinish

Angling on Lomond

Bill McEwan

With a Foreword by
BILLY CONNOLLY

ALBYN PRESS LTD · EDINBURGH

To My Kin,
whom I sometimes recognise on shore leave.

Printed by Anchor Press Ltd, Tiptree, Colchester, Essex from composition by Alacrity Phototypesetters, Banwell Castle, Weston-super-Mare, Avon, and published by Albyn Press Ltd, 2, 3 & 4 Abbeymount, Edinburgh 8

Line illustrations by Tony Steers
All photographs, except where indicated, are by the author.

Contents

List of Illustrations

Colour Plates

Black & White Photographs

Diagrams

ERRATA

The fold-out map of Loch Lomond is to be found inside the back cover and not, as indicated in the text, within the body of the book. The captions to the line drawings of salmon and sea trout on pages 153 and 154 should be transposed. The head and tail shown on the right are those of a salmon, and the drawings on the left are characteristic of the adult trout family.

Introduction

I SHOULD never have bought a house, least of all the one I'm supposed to live in. It stands on a little hill on the outskirts of Glasgow, and from an upstairs window I can't see Loch Lomond. Then why mention it? The answer is that as I gaze out forlornly I *know* that infernal loch is there, quite unjustly, and *I* am not!

No, I can't see the loch from upstairs, but I can't forget it either. Toothache has been said to be "the hell o' a' diseases". It surely is but there's a much worse one. Early symptoms are to be caught watching the trees in the garden sway slowly in a rising breeze, their leaves rustling in sympathy, as masses of grey cloud head toward Loch Lomond. You, on the other hand, are heading to work, aware of the fine wind but not the city dust — perfect conditions for the bob fly. Even when skies are blue and the world says, "Oh, what a lovely day," you think, "Good God, the sun's right in their eyes." Suddenly, in Gallowgate, a salmon rises and you come back to earth. Then come the inward lies. "Probably be a gale down there. The loch'll be like a millpond." Any lie will do to calm the torment only an angling diehard will suffer.

We fishermen occupy a different world from that of ordinary mortals. Our thoughts are not like theirs, and even our weather is different. For us, having caught this disease, there is only one remedy — to get down to the loch and stop the moping. Maybe then the sane people among us will have some peace — at least until we come back!

Scotland has hundreds of lochs and rivers that are justly famous for their fishing, but Loch Lomond is unique. To some people it is a symbol of all that is Scottish, an area of incomparable beauty celebrated in poetry and song the world over by homesick exiles. To others, for not every lover of the outdoors is an angler, it is a centre for hiking, climbing, boating or simply somewhere one can escape to when the pressure of "toon" life becomes too great. But to the visiting, and often unenlightened, angler its beauty can soon pale as he scans the sheer vastness of it. At this stage he could be excused a natural desire to abandon the fearsome challenge, his tackle becoming tinier by the minute and the task a torment. Where, and just how, to start is the problem and, having witnessed the many comings and (mostly) goings of visiting anglers, my prime reason for writing this book was to supply some of the answers, whereby much of the great surface water can be eliminated as we loiter, like the fish, in its more rewarding highways and byways. These vary little from season to season, and there are some unfailing spots where fish can almost be guaranteed to skulk.

Each week throughout the game fishing season I drive a mere twenty miles to fish on the loch. Others, from home and abroad, travel hundreds of miles to reach the same magnetic stretch of inland water. On its shores, over a great many years, I have met people of practically every nationality. It is, therefore, not without some guilt that I admit to few reciprocal visits to the home waters of other anglers, being continually occupied with the expansive puddle on my doorstep.

As the biggest area of fresh water in Britain, Loch Lomond fittingly contains the largest variety of fish species to be found in any one loch in Scotland. This includes perch, pike, powan, eel, flounder, minnow, loach stickleback, roach, brown trout and the big two this book will largely, but not exclusively, deal with — salmon and sea trout. These last two "bonnie fechters" have kept me and others fully occupied for many absorbing years. Quite often, the angler in search of the coarse species cannot understand our total preoccupation with the game fish. It is easy to see his point of view, but perhaps not fully taken into account is the very restless, almost nomadic nature of the Scot, and what appears to be yet another national pastime: that of keeping on the move and searching enormous areas before success can be fully savoured. Unlike the coarse angler, who fishes in a somewhat static fashion befitting his prey, the Lomond game angler is always on the prowl, and God has seen to it that he has enough water to search! It follows that instant success is not *too* easily come by, and it is probably through much aquatic travelling, enduring atrocious weather in the process, that he builds up a fund of game fishing facts and habits that need constant testing and revising. Sometimes, in the process, a fish is caught!

Although the loch gives great pleasure to a great variety of people, some satisfied to cover it at high speed, I feel it is the angler

10

in his more leisurely-paced craft who gets to know it best. He will probably have been out from early spring, when Ben Lomond wears its snowy cap, thereafter enjoying the changing scene until all he catches are the autumn leaves. Even in our materially-minded society, money cannot buy the many delights the loch can offer and, as a victim of the particularly virulent strain of angling disease which attacks Lomond men (and women), I neither require nor seek a cure.

This book, then, is the fruit of many years of enjoyable battling with the loch, yet I agree with the feelings of a well-kent loch angler of yesteryear that success is more likely to come to the angler who is in sympathy with the loch and its surroundings. It pays to go out on it, never *at* it. A word of advice on another aspect of the loch is worth noting! It can behave like a lamb and, if you willingly gambol along with it, all should go well, but in the grip of a north-east gale, it is more like a lion. Never take it for granted. When all is said and done, I cannot better the summing up of Jock Scott:

> If you have no knowledge of your water, what an appalling amount of time you waste! Life is too short to spend precious time fishing in spots where salmon are not. To the earnest fisher the loch is not a place that affords lounging facilities. In my view it is a place for the really hard-working angler, *for there is more to be learned where a loch is concerned*; river pools are speedily learned by heart. Not so the loch and, to the writer, therein lies its fascination. I would not give tuppence for the easy water, give me the difficult lake and I am content.

In apt response, the Almighty apparently gave us Lomond and an abundance of problems to go with it.

In this book I set out to do what I do every year — to discover Loch Lomond all over again. In passing, I hope to enlighten the newcomer to some ways of tackling, but never completely solving its many angling problems. I hope I may include yet another slant for the local's armoury, realising he knows a fair bit about his loch already. Such is the extremely broad content covered in tackling our largest angling surface, the text (forgivably I hope) to some extent presumes that the reader has at least a feint knowledge of what a wet fly is and how to cast a short line. Whereas the latter may appear a simple enough task in print, it is an art which the writer still constantly strives to perfect. You are very near Loch Lomond fish in a drifting boat, and they should only be disturbed when they realise, too late, that the fly they have just taken reached them in the sneakiest way possible . . .

11

In the text, many words and phrases of local origin appear, as if to create further chaos amongst the many dialects heard on the shores, with increasing frequency each season. A few are unique to Lomond, so that, since we are trying to solve angling problems and not create them, it has been thought desirable to include a form of translation under "Loch Lingo", a glossary, at the end of the text. Calamitous it would be to provide a visitor with a salmon at the end of his line and then find that he *disnae ken whit tae dae aboot it!*

A Word from
Billy Connolly, Angler

I FIRST met Bill five years ago when I moved house to a village near Loch Lomond. Deciding to do something about my long time hankering to take up fishing as a hobby, I asked some of the locals for information and, from all sides, Bill's name kept cropping up. Some suggested that, due to the wholesale slaughter he conducted on the loch, he should have swapped his car years ago for a hearse. Others felt that he studied his prey so intensely that his skin was developing a scaly look and his hair wasn't silver by accident.

The night I met him is clearly etched in my memory, somewhat embarrassingly, and I'm sure he will recall it in hilarious fashion. The season had just finished on Loch Lomond and Bill had been sea fishing on the Clyde estuary. Waxing lyrical about a new lightweight rod and a mammoth fish he had landed with it, I was invited to inspect the amazing properties and deceiving strength of this weapon which he regarded almost with reverence. Slightly nervous, in spite of being assured it would take "more strength than you've got" to damage it, I was told to take hold of the tip. "Now just hold on while I put some steady pressure on," he urged. I did — *and promptly halved it in two!*

I think all of his rods must be a little battle weary, none more so than the big long fly rod he uses on the loch. I stopped wondering, even doubting, if such length was an advantage when two interesting things happened a few days from the end of the season. *I* caught my first loch salmon on it (he found an obliging fish) and when I kindly lent him it back he hooked a big fresh fish whose one desire was to hide under the boat all day. But no problems. He used that big wand to keep the fish away from the boat and saved it hurting its wee head on the planks.

His sideboard at home isn't cluttered with cups and trophies. Twelve bottles of whisky stare at you — all prizes for catching big sea trout on Loch Lomond. The labels have got wee notes on them telling where and when the fish were caught. I was alarmed to find all the bottles were full and, at the same time, discover his big failing. He won't open them for anyone!

In this book and any time I'm out with him, he manages to make that great loch seem wee'er than it really is. He goes right to where the fish are, which saves petrol and search parties out looking for types like me.

A blank day or bad conditions never seem to dishearten him: he's already planning the next attack. Maybe no-one's told him about other lochs and rivers but, if they have, he still prefers to stay where he somehow belongs — fishing on Loch Lomond, and as hard as he can at that.

What a fearsome and vast subject he has tackled, without going over the top of his "wellies". I'm certainly glad that he did and so will all who join him in this much overdue and enlightening angling approach to big bad Lomond. After years of reading turgid, boring books on angling, it is especially delightful to find one which has humour without detracting from the subject matter.

No-one has better knowledge of the loch and how to fish it than Bill McEwan. No-one admires this more than me.

Aquatic Visitors — A Plea

As you buzz or sail around the loch, enjoying your well-earned summer holiday, spare a thought for the many log-like objects you will notice drifting freely down the shores.

There will be men aboard these boats and they will appear to you to be "swishing" long poles at the water. They are fly fishers — a peculiar breed — and they too have paid their financial dues. In return for their money, they expect to lift out of the water, with these poles, fish. Although you may think that they drift aimlessly — and I have no doubt you will sometimes be right — they are, in fact, trying to get themselves and their boats blown, by the wind, over these unsuspecting fish in the water, *ahead* of them. If you and yours proceed towards them and across the water they attempt to fish, the closer you get the more chance you have of hearing curses which I cannot repeat here. And you're on holiday...

It's a huge loch is Lomond and yet, to this day, I am constantly amazed at how many boats, *at such cross purposes*, can arrive at precisely the same spot at the same time. No-one catches anything but an earful!

Boats trolling on the loch suffer just as much, yet they can easily be recognised for what they are by their slow pace, the protruding rods and their fondness for patrolling the shallow shoreline. Like others, I have had all three baits and lines severed by the propellors of "whizz kids" in planing boats, as they pass dangerously and devastatingly across our transom wakes. An expensive business — for us!

Anglers are usually a most friendly lot and, candidly, many "incidents" happen without the visitor intending any offence whatsoever. I merely try to explain what all these boats are doing, no matter how aimless they may look from a distance! A slight alteration in course, giving them a decent berth, won't cost you much and they'll be able to go on about their business. Thank you.

A Note to Female Anglers

Difficult as it might be for the male angler to be honest, I think it can be fairly admitted that we incur the wrath of the opposite sex quite enough with our worn-out, lame excuses for persistent absence as we selfishly pursue what many consider to be a hard-bitten, all-male pastime. Certainly, I have no wish to increase rightful female objections by the obvious text wording which, for ease of present-ation, assumes the potential angler to be male. Not all loch anglers, by any means, are male and, since 1927, quite unchallenged by the humble majority, a lady has reigned supreme on the loch. She can be found in "Existing Records"!

1
Loch Lomond:
Sticking to Facts

A Few Preliminaries

LOCH Lomond is the largest area of fresh water in Great Britain, covering 27.45 square miles; shaped like a long triangle, it narrows sharply and becomes considerably deeper beyond Rowardennan. There is a liberal scattering of islands and islets at its widest part, the "bottom end". A mean depth of 623 ft has been recorded, and the areas of real interest to the angler, the shore and island depths of 5-10 ft, are a mere fraction of the total size.

The Loch and surrounding countryside are of world-famed natural beauty and anglers fishing the "road shore", a long stretch of fishable shoreline between Firkin Point, above Inverbeg, and Tarbet, during the summer months often have the accompaniment of considerable traffic noise and the "greetings" of camping shore dwellers and day visitors who will assail them from many a hidden perch with small, and sometimes not so small, stones. These usually miss the boat, but I have heard some very interesting exchanges between anglers, seeking peace and quiet, and visitors, seeking excitement!

On one occasion, two friends and I drifted the shore in a wind you rarely get — the one which blows parallel to the road shore — and a gentleman kept pace with our drifting boat, firing at us questions like, "There ain't any fish there, are there? What'll you catch here, then? Are these worms yer throwin'?" and so on.

A short, lively battle with a 3 lb sea trout answered his questions, in part.

When we last saw him, he was kicking quiet blazes out of the toes

17

of his boots and, back towards us, was unaware that we were then prepared to answer some of his questions...

The Bottom End

A man could spend his entire life fishing the "bottom end" of Loch Lomond. He would be a satisfied man. Not only would he be able to fish for practically all of the species of fish our loch contains, but he wouldn't have to travel as many aquatic miles in seeking them out as the more northerly fisher who faces the challenge of the "tap end".

Although the main area of the loch is the bottom end, busier and entirely different in character from the "tap", one complements the other beautifully, and if either had to dry up the loch would certainly never have the same appeal.

The lower basin is comparatively shallow, and this is of great importance to the salmon fisher, whose concern is a creature with a strong preference for depths of about 4-8 ft. That's where *Salar* will most often be caught, as he restlessly appears from time to time in an eager, "taking" mood.

There are times, in long hot spells, when fish will be taken in the deeps, where they cruise to relieve the boredom of their over-familiar shallow lies. Fish caught in deep water, though, are the exception and it would pay the beginner to stifle his excitement when "slunging" fish are to be seen leaping and cavorting in the deeps, as the King of Fishes will. Remain in the correct depth of water, fish steadily and cover every inch of the drift: the salmon will arrive, sooner or later, under your rod and ready to do business. To tackle the problem by chasing after every fish seen to rise, or swirl, in deep water will result in a terrible waste of effort and valuable fishing time.

The bottom end has a distinct advantage. Since it is so broad an area, it receives a better supply of what the tap end often lacks — wind. An added bonus is that there are a variety of fish-holding spots which will suit the wind in practically any direction. If you examine the map and direct the wind to blow from the north-west, say, you will see that this wind suits Inchlonaig, Inchfad, Inch-murrin and many other drifts. Reverse the wind to the south-east and you might cover Inchmoan, Inchcruin, Darroch, Buccinch and/or other drifts to suit. The wind can blow from practically all around the compass and, fishing the lower basin, you will seldom fail to find likely drifts.

Just to illustrate how lucky we are, try to picture Loch Lomond without any of its famous islands. A look at the map will clearly show that a great percentage of the game fish linger around the island shores from mid-season onwards. If we hadn't the islands, only the main shoreline would remain and, apart from the loch being grossly overfished by anglers concentrating there, both trolling and fly fishing, much of the charm (and many of the fish) would vanish at once.

Another vitally important feature of the bottom end is that a run for shelter during a sudden squall need not be quite so frightening with so many islands in the vicinity. It would pay the novice to think twice about long crossings in unsettled weather. The loch can behave like a lamb, but when black lines appear on the horizon, start planning for sanctuary. To illustrate one of the real dangers, it is all too easy to feel comforted by the very closeness of the Endrick Bank as you drift it in a steady breeze from the north-west. When this wind rises and the boat tends to drift too fast, in no time at all there can be spindrift, terminating in gigantic rolling waves crashing on the rocky shores of Claddich. The return journey, into the wind, can be trying in the extreme.

Thankfully, it doesn't happen often during summer, but many times near the end of the season, when the loch is high and the wind roars through the island trees, I have had to remain ashore for long periods before timing departure during a lull.

In spite of the foregoing, many of us have managed to catch fish in what look like utterly hopeless conditions from the shore. Again, we have the islands to thank. Around some of their corners, the wind can be doing as it likes, whilst we fish out small nooks and crannies in more stable conditions. I recall a howling gale from the north, when I drifted alongside other boats in the comparative serenity of the Geggles, fishing *out* from the island shorelines, and catching sea trout in "another world". Little wonder one often hears an unlucky boat admire another's catch and remark, "Were we fishing in the same loch?"

Most anglers react in much the same way when Loch Lomond is mentioned. "You'll know the Endrick Bank, then? Now, there's a great drift!" The Bank is unique in an angling sense, being probably the best-known feature of the bottom end. It holds salmon, sea trout (not so many), pike, perch, eels, and the odd roach shoal, near the river mouth. It can be a busy zone indeed but, lest newcomers are attracted to the inviting grassy shoreline, it should be pointed out that, like many of the island retreats, it is well protected as a Nature

Reserve and caution should be used in going ashore there at all, unless in dire emergency. The wildlife is prolific and under constant watch, and I, like many others, prefer it that way.

There are many farms whose lands sweep right down to the shoreline, especially at Boturich, Claddich and Strathcashell. Good relations between the angler and farmer should be maintained and not abused by entering fields, lighting fires or camping without permission.

Goodwill is extended freely by many farmers, but only through thoughtful behaviour on the angler's part. The western shore of the loch has many places of interest, from Balloch upwards. The Bear Park at Cameron House is much visited, and I could lose myself for days upon end in the well-maintained natural history museum founded by the late John Colquhoun at Rossdhu House, near Arden. This is the residence of Sir Ivar and Lady Colquhoun. Sir Ivar is Honorary President of our Loch Lomond Angling Improvement Association, and takes a keen interest in its affairs. From Bandry Bay to Luss is picturesque indeed, albeit the waters are comparatively barren of game fish. Drifting, as I do, the shorelines of the bottom end, I am continually reminded of the real dangers of swimming in the loch, without local knowledge, and of the regular drownings involving first-time holidaymakers. Should swimming be attempted, likely spots should be chosen with great care. Even at those will be the hidden menaces of the sudden, steep shelves where the shallows end and the black depths begin. Temperature drops can be critical and the onset of cramp a real peril. At the very least, always have company when tempted, and keep to the shallows. Attempts to rescue someone in difficulties can put more than one life at risk, and it must be emphasised that strangers should heed the warnings of locals. They have seen tragedies not easily forgotten.

If you keep the foregoing advice in mind, you will discover that the bottom end of the loch has nothing but pleasures to offer.

The Tap End

I imagine that, many years ago, setting out from Balmaha to attempt to fish the shores of Rowchoish would have been considered well-nigh impossible. To the present-day angler, it is fairly common-place, and the journey there and back well within the day's schedule, with plenty of time for the inevitable "drum-up" (brewing of tea) amidst the grandeur of Craigroyston slopes, or perhaps even as far north as Inversnaid.

The "tap" end has no set starting place, but I would personally feel to be "down the loch" anywhere below Ross Point.

Rowardennan is a good base for fishing up the way and many an adventurous jaunt have I had fishing out from there. The great snag, ever present, is the constant fear of losing the wind, the loch being so narrow in parts, and subject to local valley winds which can make solo drifting extremely difficult. I have, on a very vew occasions, managed to drift from Rowchoish Bay to Ptarmigan Lodge, with a minimum of correction strokes at the oars, but conditions rarely permit this.

Due to the very nature of the shoreline, a method similar to that used in fishing the Endrick Bank is preferable, with the boat being corrected and lowered by means of the oars to suit the varying contours.

The waters can be crystal clear, and such is the sheer beauty of the surroundings one can forget that the big city is not far away. It feels like Norway, Sweden and Canada all combined, and yet it must have that something special since it attracts visitors from the very countries mentioned. There is no substitute for the Bonnie Banks, world-wide.

Lately, there have been murmurings of new roads and water scheme projects which, if implemented, would result in the unspoilt being spoilt, and one of the decreasing number of places where Nature still reigns supreme would soon know the sound of rubber on tarmac. In the circles in which I move, such events are deplored, and in certain quarters we are accused of being selfish in our ways. I have no intention of entering into a political debate, so suffice it to say that yet another step would be taken to mar yet another bit of beauty.

For the time being, though, the tap end remains as it always has been and on returning to the little haven of Balmaha it seems a busy place indeed, after the solitude of Rowchoish. It is then I feel on "shore leave", with the big city and the demands of a small business calling for attention.

When fishing the shoreline above Rowardennan, you will notice longish patches where the rock plunges deep into the water, with black depths below. Such areas rarely produce salmon. They would appear to prefer the more gradual shallows, in clean shingle, and overall the shore is more inclined to this pattern.

There are plenty of hill burns and, from the Grey Mare's Tail on Ben Lomond, they cascade down into the waters below in a

21

spectacular way when the rains come. A flood at the tap end has to be seen to be believed, and I have been present when logs the length of the boat bobbed all over the place. The odd dead sheep, or even cattle, as I saw off Luss in 1976, can puzzle the angler, as they bloatedly float into view, usually feet upwards.

Rowardennan has plenty of atmosphere, especially during the summer, when it is a positive hive of tourism, with city day-trippers, climbers, youth hostellers and the multitudes who come from far and wide aboard the *Maid of the Loch.*

Inversnaid, a good distance north, attracts similar interest and, apart from a picturesque little harbour, has a modern self-service eating place. It cannot be said that the humble angler is the main cause of its prosperity, since his modest meal is usually aboard, tucked away in wee plastic bags.

Anyone attempting to fish these waters, out from Balmaha, say, should ensure that plenty of fuel is aboard, as there are few places for filling up in this area. Tarbet, on the western shore, has handy facilities in this respect, not too far from where your boat lies on the shore. It is a nice in-between distance for topping up the outboard fuel tank.

The entire eastern shoreline from Rob Roy's Cave, just above Inversnaid, can be fished right down to Rowardennan, or "the Roo", as it is known locally. Some of the best-known banks or points are at Culness, "Dirty Dicks", the shore opposite Tarbet and above, Rowchoish Bay and rocks, Rowmore and Ptarmigan Point. Every little outcrop of rock, where the shingle is clean and the depth about right, can bring the surprise you seek.

The western shore, from Tarbet down, known as the road shore, can be a fruitful drift, with the somewhat strange company of passing vehicles of all descriptions. It fishes in patches and for some reason, of late has not held the fish it used to. Again, perhaps not so many boats bother to find out the current state of affairs, preferring the longer and more rewarding eastern shore stretches.

Several parts where the shore wall rises from the loch, especially around the Firkin Point area, are well worth a drift and my last good fish taken in this district was off the lone oak tree which stands on the shore at an acute bend of the road.

Ardlui, and the hotel, is the most northern port of call, and yacht chartering appears popular nowadays.

Some seasons ago, when the hosts at Rowardennan were Mr Bill Porter and his wife Carol, the nets had some fabulous nights. I

called in one evening, proud of a fly-caught salmon, to be shown by
Bill to the door of the large cold room. When the door was opened,
fish almost spilled out on to the floor. I muttered something about
"*One* on the *fly*", etc, but it fell on deaf ears! I have stood watching,
and often assisted, the nets being drawn there and, other than
concluding that these fish are the most "settled" in the world, can
find no reason for their total lack of response to the fly or troll.
Perhaps the odd one has been taken, but this bears no relationship
whatsoever to the number of fish occupying these lies. To me, it
seems ill distributed and the angler doesn't get his fair share!

For sheer variety of surroundings, Loch Lomond seems unequalled, but without the tap end the picture would never seem
complete and it is always with great pleasure that I point the boat in
that direction, knowing that fish, even as far travelled as they are,
will possibly still have lice on their flanks. They're always a step
ahead of us.

The Islands

The number, size and shape of Loch Lomond's islands seem to have
been determined by the Great Man Above, who also provided Ben
Lomond as an ever-watchful caretaker.

Minus the same islands, the panoramic beauty of the loch would
still be impressively vast and it would remain, in the light of cold
facts, the largest area of fresh water in Great Britain. But a gigantic
sheet of water, thankfully, is not everything, and the pattern, and
much of the character, of the loch seems to have been schemed to
perfection by the location of the many and varied islands. Our game
fish appear to think likewise, as they use the shallow shore waters as
resting-places throughout the season, albeit disturbed from time to
time by boats — mostly of the fishing fraternity.

If you look at the loch from above Balmaha, at the pier, or better
and higher still, from the nearby Conic Hill, a chain of four islands
faces you, extending in an almost straight line from Balmaha to
Inchmurrin, and lying in the original path of what is commonly
referred to as the great Highland Fault. (See map of the bottom end
of the loch on p 00.) Once upon a time, it appears, the four islands
were the summits of a small range of hills, stretching across to the
western shore; the only loch then was the shallow area to the south,
which eventually overflowed into deeper valleys and gigantic
caverns, northwards.

Alas, the islands fall short of perfection as far as the greedy angler

Taken at sunset from the Conic Hill above Balmaha. Off the south-west tip of Inchfad, just below the disappearing sun, nestles Darroch

is concerned. If he had his way they would hold fish all round their shores. With very few exceptions, practically none of them do. There are islet exceptions which will be given attention in the following angling summary.

The summary begins with the islands near the angling base areas of Balloch and Balmaha.

ABER ISLE (Isle at the river mouth) A fairly old central lake dwelling with extremely dangerous rocks all round. Quite often, this tiny island retreat is first stop for a "drum-up" (brewing of tea) by anglers who have set out for the day, trolling from Balloch. Small though it is, the bird and plant life is prolific, and it is well protected as a Nature Reserve, as the notice board proclaims. Seldom do I manage to finish a snack without sharing the remains with two swans which sneak up, regularly, at just the right time.

No matter from what direction Aber is approached, it remains very dangerous round its shores and engines should be throttled down a good safe distance away from its menacing little approaches. Over the years, I have witnessed visiting craft sailing, apparently carefree, to grind to a standstill over its disaster zones.

Aber is often sought as an angling bearing by those fishing the Endrick Bank nearby, and the location of several good fish-holding holes on the Bank trolling route can be determined by the position of Aber off the bow or stern.

I have seen fresh fish rising all round this islet, losing their sea lice in acrobatic leaps, as they arrive in the loch by what seems to me a short cut across the deeps, before settling near the river mouth whose scent they have unfailingly traced. These fish are then great "takers", and it pays to ignore their leaping state and remain in the right depth of water, on the bank, where the same fish are likely to arrive sooner or later. The area around Aber Isle, certainly, has produced many a cruising fish, but I have little reason to believe they are anything else. In the same shallow, but weedier, depths can be found the odd pike, which are seldom too far from the river mouth area.

For all its size therefore, Aber Isle is much referred to by the angling breed and merits more than a little space. Too often, when asking where a salmon was caught, comes the reply, "Off Aber," the answer sometimes covering a strangely vague area!

CLAIRINCH (The flat isle) A dense little island, off Balmaha, again with a wealth of plant life adequately protected by the Nature Conservancy Council. A small shingle shore, facing Balmaha, is much used by visiting craft, mostly those of anglers, and as many as eight boats have been seen drawn up on its limited little shore. The area of water between Clairinch, Aber Isle and the River Endrick mouth has yielded many a fish and it was off the eastern shore of Clairinch that the tragic "daymare" was recorded (see Chapter 11). There is a small point and reef at the south-west tip, worth a brief fly drift, and the very short shoreline there has produced salmon, sea trout and brown trout, mostly in the course of flood conditions. A friend and I formed the opinion, as we landed all three species in somewhat amber-coloured water, that these fish had just paused there before crossing to the river mouth and ascending as the heavy waters decreased.

The island is of strictly limited fly fishing significance, in spite of occasional catches.

INCHCAILLOCH (The isle of old women) It owes its name to an ancient nunnery that existed on the island and is often visited during the summer by boat parties from Balmaha. A nature trail exists and there is a large sheltered bay at the south-west tip, called Port Bawn,

25

where safe anchorage is available and limited camping is allowed. To the angler, the entire island can be mean indeed. It seems an eternity to me since I heard of or took part in fair catches off its northern shoreline, mostly on the troll. A rocky reef is shown on the map as a brief fly drift and, in the past, I have caught the odd salmon and some very fresh sea trout; but of late it has been fairly quiet. "Caillie" can have its years, but nothing like as often or as good as some smaller, less likely-looking islands. Having said that, it should be trolled diligently from its Balmaha end, after the small jetty, towards the east tip of Torrinch.

TORRINCH (The tower island)   It is so named because of the face of sheer rock that rises about 100 ft from the loch, on the west side of the island. With the exception of Inchmurrin, the islands on the line of the Great Fault do not appear to fish today nearly as well as some years ago. In 1975 I saw a heavy salmon landed on the troll in the water between Inchcailloch and Torrinch. Perhaps if more fly fishing were attempted, by more boats, results would be different, because in the past its shoreline on the northern side held many a salmon. Off the bluff rock at the north-west tip, I have caught good sea trout but, funnily enough, more success came my way off a small, rarely mentioned reef of dangerous rock opposite Torrinch, known as the Skerry. To finish the day, I stopped at the north-west tip off this reef and in double-quick time landed a 5 lb brown trout and three thickset finnock, all to the dap. However well I have done in this area, the return trip always yields a blank, as if the fish only rested there for the briefest period before perhaps crossing the loch to more likely lies. Follow them we must!

CREEINCH (The tree island)   Like Torrinch, it does not appear to hold the fish for any great length of time, barring at the jagged end rocks, again at the north-west tip and a good distance off it. Usually, after finishing the Inchmurrin drift and heading back to Balmaha, this spot is worth a call, especially when the black nebs (young adult sea trout) are in.

INCHMURRIN (St Murren's island)   This is the biggest island on the loch, some 1½ miles long, and is probably the best known and most talked about. Apart from its excellent angling significance from mid-season onwards, it is much visited by boat parties from Balloch and loch anglers in general. One undoubted good reason for its popularity is the licensed hotel, run by Mr and Mrs Tom Scott, who also provide holiday chalet accommodation, which must be

26

booked well in advance. Tom farms part of the island, apart from attending to hotel duties, and is kept very busy indeed. Absolutely unbelievable is the sight of a huge cock salmon, beautifully mounted and cased in glass, which hangs on the lounge wall. One would immediately assume that the giant fish of some 36 lb had been caught by a regular off Inchmurrin, or on some part of the loch nearby. No such story can be told, because the guilty party was Tom himself, who caught the brute on what I think was his first outing on the River Tay, with one of his first casts. I keep telling him I have risen bigger ones, just off his doorstep on the loch!

As seen on the map at the beginning of this chapter, the entire north-western shoreline can be fished and, in the case of the fly or dap, this can provide endless drifts if the wind blows at all parallel to the shoreline. As with Inchlonaig, I have on many good fishing days remained there for the entire duration, with rewards aplenty. I should say that the best, or most concentrated part is the last third of the shoreline, facing the Creeinch/Balmaha direction, and the salmon and sea trout caught there are legion. At the very end of this part is a large rock on the shoreline, which should be drifted fairly close in and then the boat allowed to drift on and outwards into what appears to be too deep water, off the pretty sandy bay. Although I cannot pinpoint it to a square yard, there is an excellent lie there and I have often been surprised by the freshest of fish taking at the very end of the day. The grassy slopes of this bay have sheltered many a tent but permission should first be sought from Mr Scott at the hotel.

When Inchmurrin is good, it is very good. I tend to start giving it a call from late June onwards. In August 1977 my son wearied of holding the dap rod, but he must have been driving a fish quite mad, anyway, because a 6½ lb sea trout took when I fished the fly "correctly". I could hardly share with him the bottle of Ballantines received, but a cash transaction was arranged there and then!

The same entire shoreline can be trolled, somewhat deeper than the fly depth, and on indifferent days there is always present the temptation to visit the hotel, only to find that many have thought likewise, and sooner. The grave error in these visits is that the true wind cannot really be seen as it blows down the other, fishing, side of the island, and many linger too long!

The "Murrin" will fish to the last day of the season and I presume, rightly or wrongly, that the fish which rest there are bound for the river Endrick.

27

Up the loch from Balmaha is a flat island with a house and jetty clearly seen at the south-east tip: this is Inchfad.

INCHFAD (The long island)   It is both farmed and of very important angling significance, being easily reached in a short crossing from Balmaha. Off the house and small jetty is a weedy stretch where I have seen and caught pike, on my own admission, without trying, but the remainder of the island has salmon and sea trout from quite early in the season until the back end. Powan also seem particularly fond of its shores, and it was off a fence which enters the loch waters at the north-east tip that I caught two by fair means, and in the mouth, while fishing for something different. A splendid drift is to commence, with a wind to suit, off Darroch and across the short north-west shoreline until the corner point of the island is reached. This can be deadly water indeed and amongst the many sea trout it holds, be ready for the rise of *Salar*, who is also greatly attracted to the area. The point just mentioned should be crossed with great care and concentration, ready for the rise of either species.

An absolutely mad fish, more out of water than in it, performed in front of our very eyes one day as we drifted to the point. I believe now that its crazed state might have been due to a lamprey or wound, but although it put a great bend in my rod for a few seconds, its visit was craftily brief.

The entire island shore can be drifted from this point to the north-east tip, where large sunken boulders lurk. It was here, at the very end of the drift, that Mrs Leckie-Ewing caught her 36½ lb salmon on the fly, a record to this day.

Although a wind blowing more or less parallel to the shore can be the most convenient, I have cause to remember an onshore blow on a day when most boats preferred to drift across the top of the island, in the open waters, towards Darroch. We elected to fish Inchfad, and started a series of short drifts directly below the large barn which can just be seen behind trees at the north-west end. With dap and fly going well, four fish were boated in no time at all, the smallest 5 lb and a grilse, the other three sea trout from 5-8 lb. A tidy little gathering which, I must admit, took us by surprise.

On the troll, the centre bay must be watched for heavy weed during the summer, but towards the back-end many boats encircle the entire island by this method, since occasionally fish appear nearer this time at the south-east end.

The Royal Mail boat Marion *skippered by the late Mr Alex MacFarlane*

EILEAN DARROCH (The isle of the oak) The ancient tree still survives. Nearly all who visit the loch have a soft spot for this quaint "fairy" islet. Around its limited shores are to be caught the finest salmon and sea trout in the loch, and to do it best, the oars will often be required. It sees a lot of trolling boats round its corners and puts up with many a picnic but, given a good rolling wave on its little shoreline, some of the biggest fly-caught fish have succumbed to the stealthy angler who treats it with the undoubted respect it deserves.

A fairly long crossing can now be attempted, to complete fishing part of the lower basin, so that the boat can be headed to the western end of Inchmoan, arriving at Inchgalbraith.

INCHGALBRAITH Ruins of the old Galbraith stronghold remain on this tiny islet, which can hold sea trout and the odd grilse nearby. But, before describing one of the longest and most popular drifts on the lower loch, I will mention two largish islands of little angling significance, regarding game fish at least. Should I err in this respect, I should welcome indeed any angling secrets these islands have withheld for so many, many years.

INCHTAVANNACH and **INCHCONNACHAN** are rarely mentioned in the angling context, but they are beautifully tree-clad islands in their own right. The *Maid of the Loch* has a tight manoeuvre at the narrow Inchtavannach straits, opposite Bandry on the main shore. There is a short stretch of shoreline on this island, on its southern shore,

29

where a house and jetty stand, which has produced fish in a limited way. Likewise, I know of at least a few fish taken off the south-east rock and shingle shore of Inchconnachan. Rarely do I permit them a visit, more often — if mistakenly — preferring other drifts.

We could now start the long and well known drift from near Inchgalbraith, at Inchmoan.

INCHMOAN (The peat island)   I can personally vouch for its boggy inland area, whilst exploring during the "doldrums". From this area is a nautical short-cut to anglers who wish to dash up to Inchlonaig, or further north, in search of winds that do not exist: the boat can be taken through narrow straits, where a tufted, grassy mini-islet sits, between Inchmoan and Inchtavannach, proceeding between the latter island and Inchconnachan and emerging, if lucky, facing towards Luss on the left and with Inchlonaig ahead and slightly right. Beware the perils of the rocks off Luss. Some are marked, but bad weather has hidden some from view with dire consequences. Of late, I have noticed foreign guests fishing with floats amongst the reed beds in the "short-cut" and must fairly conclude that they seek coarse fish, such as pike and perch, amongst the weedy channels.

Our main drift, then, will start around Inchgalbraith and over the longish reef opposite, at Inchmoan, drifting from there to a shallow area preceding the first of two of the best known points on the loch. After the large sweeping bay of golden sand the shoreline ends at a point, again with a boulder on the shore, which is known as the Short Point, and the boat can be drifted to pass it fairly shallow. A series of drifts can be attempted in this area. The point itself is rounded, to enter a sweeping bay which again terminates in another equally famous mark, the Long Point of Inchmoan. Provided that oars are used and the area is not too busy, this point can be drifted repeatedly at varying depths. I would not attempt to list the numbers of salmon and sea trout caught here or hereabouts. This is one of the best drifts on the loch from quite early in the fly fishing season.

It is almost superfluous to mention that, of course, the area can be covered on the troll in the same fashion. After the point, Inchmoan sweeps slightly northwards and is nearly, but not quite, linked to Inchcruin, where there are very narrow shallow straits. People and, quite often, deer can be seen wading from one island to the other. The area enclosed by the "Moan" and the "Crin" is a lagoon known as the Geggles and, on days when the wind doesn't suit elsewhere, fish can be caught, mostly sea trout and small brown trout, on the fly or very small trolled Mepps.

INCHCRUIN (The round island)   Very aptly named since it can, in fact, be fished almost all round. Starting at where it almost touches Inchmoan, it can be drifted, or the boat rowed, in a south-east direction, then almost due east to the Ladies Point at the farthest eastern tip. A large rock sits on the shore (I often wonder who puts them there) just before the point and, on its good days, which are fairly numerous, a more yielding drift could not be wished for. To the newcomer, there will usually be plenty of fly fishing boats in the area just described, and the lines of their drifting pattern could easily be followed. To the south-east of the Ladies Point, at Inchcruin, there lies a short and usually visible rocky reef with a white marker post on it. On the post is usually a gull, scanning the fishing potential of "Little Ireland".

LITTLE IRELAND   I am not sure how it got its name. It certainly isn't emerald green and it would not be an Irish joke to come into too close contact with it. But the fish are in touch and sea trout can abound in its vicinity. The joke should be on them.

The tip of Inchcruin can be rounded, at the Ladies Point, where a sheltered sandy bay, abounding in firs, is often sought for the inevitable "drum-up". A small hut stands on a brief outcrop of rock and frequently sea trout linger nearby. The shoreline of Inchcruin can fish, spasmodically, past the jetty and house on the shingle shore. It is here that I have frequently been startled and once knocked down by our big turkey, the capercaillie (*cappercailzi*) as it moved from under the overhanging boughs! From the shore, continuing on the same line, the boat will reach a solitary large rock, described in our dap fishing day in more detail (Chapter 6), and the end of the best fishing would be the short stretch of shore from the rock westwards. Off to the north-east is a small, heavily wooded island called Buccinch.

BUCCINCH (Isle of the he-goats)   Thankfully, none exist today to interrupt regular visits to its little shoreline and home-made jetty, at the south-west tip. This part can be full of surprises, especially late season, and I have managed to save many a blank day by casting around the shingle tip hereabouts. Salmon and sea trout are commonly caught, but it has provided me with some of the best brownies for size and condition that I have ever caught on the loch. One of nearly 5lb put two sea trout of the same weight almost to

31

Two fresh run sea trout, 4 lb each, and a brown trout of 4½ lb (bottom). Note the start of a small kype on the brownie. August fish on size 8 flies: a Priest (top), a Haslam (middle) and a Dark Mackerel. Off Buccinch

shame, such was its girth, colouring and general neatness. I am also certain that the biggest brown trout I have ever risen, in atrocious conditions, came off the very small and little mentioned islet, nearby Ceardach.

CEARDACH (The smithy) This lies off Buccinch, to the east, and I can still remember rising my largest brown trout ever, easily double figures, to a Dark Mackerel on the bob. I got a long, long look at its markings before it lazily rolled away from the fly. From this islet, looking northwards, can be seen the "fishless" side of a marvellous fishing island, Inchlonaig.

INCHLONAIG (Isle of the yew trees) Legend has it that they were planted on Robert the Bruce's orders, to supply bows for his army. The islands are all so beautiful, each in its own way, that I find it almost impossible to name a favourite, but if forced to make a choice I should probably put Lonaig near the top of the list. As an angler, you are as good as your last fish, and a favourite island usually has a strong connection with the size and numbers of fish landed from its shores. Inchlonaig has been extremely fair in its distribution of fish to downhearted anglers. From July onwards I approach it with high hopes and have seldom been let down other than by reasons of bad weather or on days when the fish are rising nowhere.

It can be approached on the troll from either side of Strathcashell Point, from where you cross to a small but popular sandy beach which ends in a cluster of rocks. Then you pass through the eastern bay water, which tends to be a mixture of sand and weed, and continue past the point, in a northerly direction, before turning and trolling the entire north-western shoreline, perhaps a little on the deep side. Possibly more fish are caught at Inchlonaig on the fly or dap due to the fact that trolled baits are easily fouled on its somewhat erratic bottom contours.

If approached, with the fly and/or dap as the attractors, from the western tip, opposite Luss, the outcrop of rock at the extreme end can be fished quite close in, and should the wind be kind and blowing from the direction of Luss and its valleys, the boat can fish the entire shoreline, very similarly to Inchmurrin as a drift, with depth being the controlling factor. The Mid-Bank, about the centre of the shoreline, holds major fish aplenty, salmon and big sea trout. It has been especially kind to me in relation to the latter species and again, in 1978, provided a "Ballantine" sea trout of $10\frac{1}{4}$lb. As related under the dap (Chapter 6), I left behind its bigger brother!

As a long island drift, I have to admit that in certain favourable conditions it has held my attention for an entire day, which is contrary to my usual tendency to visit less rewarding and more difficult to fish drifts.

A small but perhaps useful pointer is that the location of Lonaig can be most useful on days of indecision when we cannot appraise the situation and decide whether to go up the loch or return to the bottom end. If the boat is slipped out a little distance from the eastern shore, the weather near both Ross Point and the Ladies Point can be fairly estimated.

From lovely Lonaig, looking to the north, will be seen the Ross Point area and two islets called the Ross Isles.

THE ROSS ISLES   The outer one has never matched the inner for sheer angling success. It can be fished all round, given the wind to accommodate, but herein lies one of the greatest difficulties in fishing this deadly little zone. Many, many times I have had to give up as the wind gusts down with great force, *but in too many directions*, from the surrounding valleys and glens. There are days when the boat has been treated like a mere spinning top and the shores sought regularly in an attempt to restore sanity. For all that, round the area of the inner Ross Isle has supplied game fish, quite often covered in sea lice, and when the wind does buffet with unfortunate regularity there are many little bays nearby to provide shelter. At the very mention of the inner isle, I am prompted to make a bold and rash statement. I do not think that there is any similar little bit of water on the loch which has provided so many shallow-lying fish, given relatively undisturbed water. I recall a few salmon, from 12-20 lb, being hooked from lies which appeared to be more on the shore than in the water.

A further advantage in fishing this area is that the weather can be seen much further up the loch and the hopefully rewarding trip thus attempted. In doing so, a small isle will be passed opposite the Rowardennan Hotel, the Hen Isle.

THE HEN ISLE   You can almost be sure that the progress of your boat and its selected course, as it passes, will be watched with more than a passing interest! The nets, from the hotel, operate off the western end of this islet, sometimes with staggering success. When the netting is poor, you can be sure it was your boat that "scared them a' away". I have never caught a fish there, nor unsettled them, so it seems appropriate to cease our island fishing jaunts the same way as we started out — fishless.

ISLAND WILDLIFE   It would be difficult to leave the islands without some mention of the wildlife. Since I endeavour to concentrate on the fish life, I shall not sorely try the ornithologist nor attempt to deal fully with the abundance of subject matter that exists on the loch and the famed Endrick Bank.

Some years ago, there was much ado about a rare bird spotted on the bank. Next day, it was confirmed in the daily press that a pink and beautiful FLAMINGO had landed near the river mouth and — as with the osprey — the event was talked about in hushed whispers, but *everyone* whispered!

As you leave Balmaha Bay in the early summer, the chucking JACKDAWS will follow you out, as you head for Inchcailloch, and they will follow you in, as you head for Balmaha.

Rarely will you round the Black Rocks, after Manse Bay, without nesting KITTIWAKES protesting your presence. When rounding many other points, if you are first on the scene, the lazy HERON will let you get quite close before its large, droopy wings remove it in an ungainly fashion to another private fishing perch. It is my confirmed belief that this bird should be charged an annual fee, like us, since as an angler it has us all beat. The bird, I believe, has minute glands just above its feet and when it stands so motionless at the river's edge, it secretes a fluid into the flow which gradually attracts small fish to its hovering bill. We, on the other hand, seem to go about it the hard way!

Like years of yore, 1978 saw good catch figures coming off the loch, and perhaps I was not alone in noticing a big increase in the number of CORMORANTS throughout the season. A good sign, maybe, since they feed on small fish. For some reason, I don't much admire these birds myself, being indifferent to their looks and skin-diving plumage. Smaller, and with much nicer markings, is the MERGANSER, with the same type of serrated fish-holding bill. I have seen many females with their broods while fishing above Ptarmigan Point. Nearer "home" again, many SWANS on the Endrick Bank can give you an idea of depth, so vitally important, as they "stand on their heads" whilst feeding, and the MALLARD DUCKS in Balmaha Bay are a most tame and friendly little lot, keeping visitors and regulars alike constantly amused.

Fishing on the bank, I am always delighted to see my favourites, the TERNS, SWALLOWS and SWIFTS. For sheer mastery in the air, they come into the "Spitfire" class and to watch the terns, or sea swallows, at work as they hunt flies or small fish is quite absorbing. They are lucky birds to me, since more than once as I have looked skywards at their graceful antics, a reel has screeched as if the salmon knew I was not paying enough attention!

BUZZARDS are common on the loch and, like the eagle, they can be spotted soaring with large outspread wings for what seems like an endless time. A friend and I once witnessed an amazing fight between a lively young buzzard and a heron, the latter being harassed almost out of the sky. Crows also seem partial to altering the cumbersome flight path of the heron, given the slightest chance.

The same friend and I were fishing Mill o' Ross Bay one year when a little TUFTED DUCK appeared, playfully surfacing near the boat. He disappeared and I remember, so grim was the fishing, that I mentioned I wouldn't even have minded a "touch" from the little duck, to relieve the boredom. As I cast my flies astern, when moving off, the line tightened with a queer spluttering on the surface. Our little friend had granted my request and gave us a good laugh before gently coming off.

There seems no end to the variety of birds on the loch and, apart from waterhens, coots, wagtails, the finches, jays, curlews, dippers and oyster catchers, there are many others.

If, as you drift some of the island shores, you spot a slight, quick movement in the gorse with a flash of white or light brown, it will doubtless be ROE DEER. They are quite common on several of the islands and can often be seen crossing from one island to another, on foot or, occasionally, swimming.

A little more frightening can be the odd occasion when you are at the tap end of the loch, in the Craigroyston area, and stumble into a herd of WILD GOATS. If on foot, it appears wise to "freeze", when they will go on about their business. Some can look suspiciously fierce and I prefer to carry on my conversations with them while I am afloat!

Some islands have BRER RABBIT but, as far as I know, none exist on Inchcailloch due to the presence of stoats and weasels, the latter seldom seen by me.

There is one visitor to the loch which is never welcome. I believe it is rated as a fish, since it has gills and can swim. There the resemblance ends because, to me, there appears no justification for its existence. I can see no merit or function whatsoever in this little horror. It's an aquatic parasite and passenger which adheres to our gamest fish, boring into their prize flesh and obtaining a free journey into the loch at the same time. I refer, of course, to the eel-like LAMPREY. If it is a fish, it's a pseudo-fish, and a poor imitation at that.

In the course of fishing the loch I have landed many fish with the tell-tale lamprey wounds on parts of their bodies. The subject of wounded fish deserves a chapter on its own, but there is no doubt in my mind that a fish, so injured, will snap at the first bait or fly to appear in its vicinity.

I have often seen the lamprey rise to the surface with the hooked fish and only let go at the very last minute. On several occasions they have come aboard, the greed in them so great that they remind me of the bloated rat which cannot leave the foodstore alone and loses all its instinctive fear in the process. Like most of the eel family, they cling to life until the last and even when they appear to be dead can come back to life, fully recovered. To try and find the one which has

36

The holes in this 22 lb salmon are the work of the lamprey. (The troll, Golden Sprat, the Claddich shore)

dropped off and disappeared between the floorboards, into the bilges, is almost a lost cause. I am quite sure there is *still* one in my boat somewhere! I do hope there doesn't exist a "Protect the Lamprey" society, because I have it in me to sympathise with all God's creatures, all *but* the lamprey.

At the Stables, on the Claddich shore, I hooked and landed a beautiful salmon of 22 lb. It was perfection in shape, and I still retain a picture of myself, holding it up in the bow of the boat. What it doesn't show is the other side of the fish, which had two fresh and ugly holes drilled into it by our little lamprey friend. One hole was much larger than the other, as if the creature had taken its choice of the tastier flesh. What with lampreys, seals, nets and anglers, it's always a marvel to me to see the large numbers of fish which survive these manifold hazards and eventually reach their spawning redds.

To end this little island interlude, I will, perhaps, someday find the anglers who suffered the same fate as I did while trolling on the loch one spring, near Aber Isle. The outside rod stopped solidly into a mammoth object and although it moved ever so slightly when all my strength was applied, I gave up and backtracked, reeling in all the while. Four blackish objects surfaced, pointing upwards, from a weaving mass of grey hulk. Incredibly, I was into my first and far from fresh-run *sheep* and, as I recovered my composure, I found it impossible to recover the bait. As I cut through the line, the dead

37

animal turned bloatedly and three silver flutters gave away the fact that my experience had been shared with others. They were Toby baits!

I cannot, however, imagine that the day will come when either the famed Abu or Hardy company will wish such a picture for their "Halls of Fame". How sheepish can you get!

FOOTNOTE TO THE ISLANDS

There will come a day when you will tend to associate almost every island with cherished memories of the safe shelter they provided on some of the loch's notoriously "black" days. As you cross the open waters and one of the sudden and nasty squalls, with its short hard waves, arrives, driving you to seek shelter, it will invariably be to one of the islands that you repair, glad of its very nearness.

There will be days when, for reasons of bad weather, few boats will be seen where you expect to find them — afloat — but they will be drawn up safely on the shores of one of the many retreats.

You will almost know, as these havens become familiar to you, if someone has been there some hours before, and yet the signs of their visit may only be slight. A log you were happy to recline against last week has been moved, just a little, but enough no longer to suit your outstretched body. A dry patch of grass, oblong in shape, stands out, telling you a camp has only just been broken. Often, amid well-formed loch fireplaces of stones and boulders, embers will still glow, and you will inwardly bless the departed as you re-kindle the flames. The shingle or sandy shores may still show fading pawprints, reminders of your best friend's last gallop ashore there and, as he finds his bearings again, he may well recover his chewed piece of branch as it lies lapping at the water's edge.

Some of the small island sanctuaries are not quite so obvious, but you will have them, sensibly, in the back of your mind as the weather worsens. It should scarcely be necessary to remind you that you should leave them as unspoilt as possible.

The Rivers

The main rivers running into or out of the loch are the Rivers Leven, Endrick, Fruin, Falloch and Luss Water. The first three will be of most interest to anglers, and since this book deals mainly with the loch, I will of necessity keep details brief. I would have little doubt that, at the time of writing, there seems justification for the rivers to be dealt with more comprehensively in the form of another book.

The River Leven is fairly short, winding its way through a somewhat industrial belt from the Firth of Clyde to Balloch, where it unites with Loch Lomond. Up that same wee river swim our salmon and sea trout, to enter the loch, where they will idle the time away — if left alone — until the back-end, when lots of rain will enable them to run the streams and rivers of their birth.

The entire Loch Lomond fishery, including the rivers and parts of the estuary, is controlled by the Loch Lomond Angling Improvement Association, the Secretaries being Messrs R. A. Clement & Company, 224 Ingram St, Glasgow G1 1HH, and daily or weekly tickets can be had from them or lochside stations such as Balmaha and Balloch.

At this stage, I should perhaps mention that whereas the Leven does not compare scenically with the Tay or Spey, or other expensive rivers in Scotland, it does — like many other short connecting rivers — produce the most beautifully-shaped salmon and grilse I have ever seen. I go as far as to say that I have seldom seen their equal for shape, condition and proportions, and all to be had for a most modest fee!

The Leven opens for business on 11th February, and eager loch anglers always await its early catch reports. The local angler will readily show you where to cast your Yellow Belly, Mepps or fly, and in the last few years the river has fished well indeed. Likewise the Fruin and Endrick, late spate rivers whose first floods flatter to deceive but improve as the season draws on. By late October, these rivers and many of the loch burns have high stocks of fish, the majority of which have remained indifferent to the multitude of flies and baits presented to them by me and hundreds of others who pursued them on the loch.

The Big Nothing

Loch Lomond is unique in many ways and, amusingly, so is the boat-to-boat method of communication used upon it — our veritable Ministry of Silly Signals! A "regular" can instantly tell a newcomer by his failure to respond to his signal, and unless the visitor learns fast, he will not usually be invited to swap messages again.

The fingers and hands "speak" a most comprehensive language, and I have not seen its equal on any other loch in Scotland. Once mastered, it is a very quick method of signifying success or failure and it can also communicate the various moods of boat crews.

Basically, when trolling, it is the rule that boats approaching each other will pass port-to-port. This should be learned early in one's career, thereby avoiding harsh words or ill-feeling. It does maintain some order and, apart from being very easy to accomplish, there is usually plenty of time to guide your boat on the correct path, to avoid fouling the other boat's lines.

A sort of pregnant pause precedes the signalling as each boat debates who will "open the batting". Let's assume that you wish to know how the other boat has fared. Simply catch the eye of the man at the tiller as your craft are about to pass, and hold out an arm in front of you, rotating both hand and arm in a swift series of large circles; in other words describing the letter "O" by hand. This means, "I have caught nothing — how have you fared?" If your large "O" signal is returned, then the other boat is just as clever as you, and has caught nothing. Between boats on poor fishing days this is the only signal you will need!

If, however, the other chap replies to you by extending his hand, showing only one finger, it means he has one fish. Do you want to see it? Of course! You then go through the imaginary motions of grasping a fish by the wrist of the tail and raise your hand, in that position, a few brisk times. This will get the necessary result and a fish will be held up and shown to you.

Still not satisfied, you will want to know its weight. You then raise both hands, with all fingers extended and palms facing the other boat, and extend them several times. If the fish is, say, 14 lb, the captor will show both palms to you, i.e. ten fingers, and then one palm with only four fingers showing. Simple. You will usually know, or have to guess, the species, but if over 10 lb in weight you can be almost sure it's a salmon.

Communications can break down under the slight complication of two boats approaching each other when they *both* have fish. Neither boat, of course, will signal the big "O" and the suspense can be quite electric as the crews stare each other out, anxious for the deadlock to be broken by the recognised signal. Someone has to give way eventually and, unable to contain their joy, one boat will proudly raise and display their fish, only to be outdone as the other raises *two*. One-upmanship at its very best!

On the troll, monotony can sometimes set in and, if the fishing is quiet, a weird variety of signals can be transmitted. The head resting on folded hands means, "So bored I could sleep"; a standing posture, with the angler flaying his body with his arms, "Cold, isn't it?" There are ways of notifying a fish lost, and where, and also if someone in a group of approaching boats has a fish, etc. A brief chat with a "regular" will do no harm, if you are puzzled in any way.

Just a word of caution. When signalled to show your fish, be careful that you don't hold it up and then drop it — on the wrong side of the gunwhale. It has happened, and in a slippery instant is undone the work of hours, maybe days, or, if really dogged by bad luck, years.

I once went to the trouble of catching a 4lb sea trout, and when washing it clean at the side of the boat, in the middle of the loch, let it slip from my grasp. You get no prizes for that. But by far the gravest event of this nature happened to a fellow angler from the bay. Having caught a beautiful 12lb salmon, fate decreed that, some hours later, he was to return it from whence it came. When he was showing it to another boat, it slipped from his grasp, struck the gunwhale, and preferred to return to its more natural environment, although by now a bit handicapped, rather than remain in the comfort of the boat!

Don't believe what anyone says about dead fish *floating*. If it's yours, or was yours, be sure it will sink like a stone!

Playing Safe

We may fish different waters, you and I, but I'll warrant our reasons for taking up the sport are not all that different. Fishing should be fun and practically everything associated with it a source of great, sometimes deep, enjoyment.

Like all outdoor pursuits, however, there is always the ever present risk of dangers, great and small. Who hasn't, at some time or another, slipped getting into or out of the boat, or even inside it? I admit to having insulted my catch in the worst way possible by standing on its slippery body, but I did not remain standing for long.

Flooded river banks present their own perils and I suppose one could go on endlessly pointing out the hazards of our outdoor sport. At least a basic knowledge of first aid, then, should be at our fingertips, even if it is only to help treat them for frostbite. Having mentioned it, the elementary cure for this unlikely malady afloat is not to rub the affected part, or parts, but to apply hot breath until feeling is restored and maintain heat by using the warmth of armpits or crotch, if this is practicable.

I recall applying much self criticism after a regrettable incident on the banks of the river Endrick some years ago. An angler, suffering from a heart condition of which I knew nothing, needed my help to net a heavy salmon. As he knelt to remove the hook, he gasped and fell back in what I took to be a faint of some sort. It transpired to be a fatal heart attack, confirmed by a doctor who was fishing just below us. I attempted mouth-to-mouth resuscitation but reflected later, with much remorse, as to whether I had done everything possible and correctly at that. As it happened, no action of mine would have saved the situation, a fact confirmed by the doctor there and then. Needless to say, I think it befits us all to know the drill and I briefly summarize it, as follows:

Clear the airways; remove false teeth; see that the neck is straight and the tongue checked for blockage. Turn the victim on his back and move his head back, with mouth facing upwards. Hold his jaw open and pinch the nose of the victim. Place your mouth in an air-tight position over his and blow rapidly and forcefully until his chest cage begins to rise. Remove your mouth and, keeping the victim's mouth open, let him exhale the air. Repeat, trying to maintain a regular rhythm of 15-20 inhalations a minute. Continue until the victim's breathing has been re-established, or otherwise. If the rib cage does not rise when you blow, check for any obstruction, even dirt, in the airways. If the fingernails are blue he is not getting enough air.

It may be a cheerless subject, but should a precious life ever be saved by this basic knowledge what more could one ask?

Cramps should be treated with warmth and massage to the affected parts and swallowing a few grains of salt can help. A sprained or twisted ankle will be helped by not removing the boot, which can act as an excellent splint: merely loosen the laces a little. If footwear has to be removed, use cold compresses and bandage firmly to reduce the swelling.

Fishing with a hot sun burning the back of one's neck can have fairly serious after effects, so cover up accordingly.

Snake bites are fairly uncommon in Britain but the reaction of a disturbed adder, who is possibly more surprised than you, has been known to happen in the wilder parts of the Loch Lomond area and places like it. Panic will promote more danger than the bite itself. One or two aspirin and bandaging tightly on the heart side, followed by rest and the eventual call for an ambulance by whatever means possible will bring about the solution. There is only one poisonous snake in the British Isles and that is the adder or viper, so when you see one give it a wide berth and watch where you are walking.

Watery problems will naturally give the angler most of his troubles, hence the mouth-to-mouth directions which, although hopefully they will never be needed, it befits us all to learn.

For the time being, my ever present problem afloat is serious indeed: trying to light my last cigarette in a gale ridden downpour, six miles, of course, from Nowhere.

The Loch Lomond Angling Improvement Association (LLAIA)

Our precious fishing waters, including the loch, the rivers, burns and certain estuaries, are controlled and protected by the Loch Lomond Angling Improvement Association. Daily, weekly and annual permits are granted by the same body, the Secretaries of which are Messrs R. A. Clement & Company of Glasgow.

The vigilance of the LLAIA bailiff force, headed by Mr Neil Gillies, is ceaselessly put to the test each year as they tackle the unenviable job of seeking out poachers, day and night, patrolling the waters of the loch and banks of the rivers, inspecting permits and keeping an ever-watchful eye on illegal nets and pollution. Major tasks indeed, and we owe our thanks for the fortitude with which they tackle them. The Clyde River Purification Board works closely with the Association, and there is constant checking on all aspects of pollution.

To combat the ravages of the disease ulcerated dermal necrosis (UDN), a hatchery and restocking programme was adopted, with some success; but one of the many problems has recently been illustrated when, from an order of 200,000 salmon-eyed ova, only 75,000 could be fulfilled, and even these were disappointing at the hatchery stage. The Association now has its own hatchery and in 1978/9 45,000 salmon-eyed ova made good progress, free from disease and with low mortality.

Apart from the AGM, there are newsletters throughout the season, containing matters of great interest to members. A few years ago, in the spring, was welcomed what seemed to be a new breed of sea trout to the ends of our lines. They were (and are) magnificent fish, deep in the shoulder and small in the head, and again the end result of the diligent Association programme.

There are approximately a thousand members, each entitled to the letters LLAIA after his name — qualified and fortunate beings indeed!

R.A.Clement & Company, C.A., 224 Ingram Street, Glasgow G1 1HH. Tel. 041 221 0068

HEAD BAILIFF

Mr Neil Gillies, 5 Buchanan Crescent, Croftamie, Drymen. Tel. Drymen 362

Tackle Dealers

There are no tackle shops on the shores of the loch, but the dealers listed below in Glasgow and the surrounding area carry extensive stocks of angling equipment. Most of them also sell daily and weekly permits for fishing on the loch.

Lawrie Renfrew, 514 Great Western Road, Glasgow 12
John Dickson & Son, 18 Royal Exchange Square, Glasgow 1
Arthur Allan, 3 West Nile Street, Glasgow 1
Anglers' Rendezvous, 24 Parnie Street, Glasgow 1
William Robertson, 27 Wellington Street, Glasgow 2
Tausney's Sports, Anniesland Cross, Glasgow, and Clydebank
Caurnie Pets & Tackle, 105 Cowgate, Kirkintilloch, Glasgow
Cafaro Bros., 140 Renfield Street, Glasgow 2
James I.Kent, 2380 Dumbarton Road, Glasgow 14
Ian Tyrell Sports, Dumbarton and Helensburgh
Batchelor's Ironmongery, 157 High Street, Dumbarton

Angling Permits

Permits for an entire season, and for shorter periods of time, can be obtained from:
The Loch Lomond Angling Improvement Association, 224 Ingram
    Street, Glasgow 1. Telephone: 041 221 0068

Daily and weekly permits can also be obtained from the following addresses on the Lochside (an asterisk shows that boats can also be hired):

*Macfarlane & Son, The Boatyard, Balmaha
Strathcashell Camp Site, Nr Balmaha
*Inverbeg Hotel, Nr Luss
Colquhoun Arms Hotel, Luss
*Ian Thomson, Thistle Cottage, Luss

*J. Sweeney, Balloch
Marine Marina, Nr Balloch
Inversnaid Hotel, Inversnaid, By Aberfoyle
*Rowardennan Hotel, Rowardennan, By Drymen (hires boats only
   to residents)
The Clachan Inn, 2 The Square, Drymen
The Buchanan Arms, Drymen
The Winnock, The Square, Drymen

Other Useful Addresses

Loch Lomond and District Tourist Association, Information
   Centre, Balloch, Dunbartonshire. Telephone Alexandria (0389)
   3533

Mr J. Mitchell, Senior Warden, The Loch Lomond National Nature
   Reserve, 22 Muirpark Way, Drymen

2

Speed Bonnie Boat –
Getting Under Way

MINUS the bagpipes, drams and ballyhoo, the fishing on Loch Lomond and the River Leven starts on or around 11th February each year, when the salmon and sea trout begin to ascend the river to what they think is the safety of the loch.

They are usually given a few weeks' grace as, one by one, boats are made ready to patrol the shores from early March onwards. It is normally during this month that the first salmon makes its last mistake and falls victim to the troll. News of this capture soon circulates, details are recorded for the annual angling report, and heads start peeping out of windows and wondering. Signs of life increase, smells of varnish grow ever stronger and sounds of hammering swell as more and more boats are made ready, until, by late May, the great offensive has well and truly begun.

Planning, the secret of almost any successful campaign, starts with the scanning of a map and decision upon lines of attack, coupled with surprise weapons to lure the enemy into making blunders, while you are made a local, if not national, hero. The maps have been carefully prepared, after many years of conflict, and with the text will help to provide you with the two main items of essential information: where to start and the method to use.

Venturing out in March, there is only one way to begin — the troll. There is great fun to be had in the preparation, as you fuss with this and that, and the loch will appear virgin as you set out in the knowledge that the great fish are "in" and have seen few, if any, baits. *Yours* will be the one they want!

Note: Let me say straight away that I have absolutely no commercial attachments with the tackle industry. I can, as a result, write freely about gear, just as I find it or would like it to be.

Clothing

The old Scots saying, "Ne'er cast a cloot till May's oot," scarcely needs repeating, and attention to small details of personal comfort can make or break your first day out. Plan for arctic conditions! I am a great believer in the *layer* method of dressing up for the loch, to suit the piercing winds and occasional snowstorms we can enjoy at the season's start. On top of thermal underwear go two pullovers of varying thickness, then a light fishing jacket under the main exterior coat. In the unlikely event that you become too warm, you can take clothing off, but it is sensible to be clad adequately for bad conditions in the first place. Even in mild weather, you should always have an extra layer of clothing with you, in case of a sudden deterioration and drop in temperature.

Loch Lomond, apart from testing our powers of endurance from time to time, will also test to the full any type of waterproof garment. Whereas the river angler can to some extent keep mobile, thereby shedding some surplus rain, or seek the sanctuary of nearby bridges, trees or cars, the loch man has no such choice afloat. Sheltering ashore, during anything but the heaviest continual downpour, can often result in forfeiting the chance of an excited fish.

It is no place for gossamer-light polyurethane-coated nylon garments, with their tendency to billow before clinging to the undergarments in a saturated fashion.

I don't believe I have ever come in *completely dry* after a rainy day on the loch. This would indeed be a feat, as we are dealing not only with rain falling from above, but with spray and sheets of water which will find the slightest chink in our armour. Wet hands must, at some time or another, enter pockets depositing water in the process.

It is interesting, therefore, to record that my state of dryness and general comfort improved no end recently by using an inner insulated garment, "Tog 24", which became unavoidably damp around the wrist area but did not cause any great discomfort. A big asset are the four large pockets wherein my customary bits and pieces remained dry for the first time in ages. It seemed odd, indeed, not to suffer the drudgery of emptying sodden pockets of liquid cigarettes

47

and rusting fly hooks and the like. The outer coating of this jacket is of fairly rugged material, the inner of a delightfully warm pile fabric called Teklan, and I believe the makers are presently considering the design of a garment with the angler's need very much in mind. The pile, incidentally, does not "pill" (gather into little woolly balls), rupturing the smoothness and effectiveness. The makers are Textral Manufacturing Ltd of Preston.

For extreme conditions early or late in the game fishing season and ideal for the winter Pike angler, Tog produce a first rate one-piece insulated suit. Straight away, my eyes went to the zip, especially the bottom end. Once bitten anglers, who have perhaps tried one piece suits which are very definitely made in one enclosed piece, will appreciate the near hypothermic state one can reach in peeling off layer upon layer of clothing when performing a vital daily necessity afloat, only to meet with almost insurmountable opening and closing problems. The Tog zip, being two-way and extremely fine, minimises heat escape and, testimony to this garment's supreme comfort is my great reluctance to cast it off and suffer the numbing effects of "normal" temperatures when they come along. The suit is also a boon when camping, doubling as pyjamas and solving the problems of a sudden extra-cold night or damp down sleeping-bag filling.

"If it wasn't for our waders, where would we anglers be?
    Not nearly so damned uncomfortable and cold below the knee..."

Somewhat similar to the immortal words of our local bard and keen angler, Mr Billy Connolly, yet expressing an angling dilemma, it must be admitted that waders and "wellies" are not the best foot warmers in the world — especially to one seated in a loch boat for perishing hour upon hour. Tog "wellie warmers" are knee length, unlike the many insulating sockettes available, and if they have a slight snag it is the thickness of the glowing pile, but a size bigger than normal in waders (a fairly normal angling precaution) takes care of the problem.

Someone once said, "You can always tell British anglers. They all wear these sticky fishing coats." It is certainly true that jackets, coats and trousers made from oiled Egyptian cotton are still very much part of the angling scene, both in heavy duty and lightweight versions.

The name Barbour is perhaps synonymous with this type of protection and, to my mind, this firm have excelled themselves with their latest fishing jacket, the "Northumbria". We can no longer bemoan the lack of pockets: it has *eight*, some of them cunningly conceived without the need to unfasten everything to enter. A non-conductive wading strip is incorporated at the bottom, which will be greatly appreciated by loch anglers wading to their moored boats, and the material itself has a much drier and more durable finish. To complement the "Northumbria" jacket here, at last, is a *zip* — a real one. It is made of substantial, heavy brass (double ended, of course) and must rate as the chunkiest Rolls Royce of zip fasteners, well in keeping with the general thoroughness with which the jacket has been designed. Maybe now we can look forward to shedding rain sodden clothing at the *waterside* rather than continuing the struggle at home, at the *bedside*, cursing seized zips as only a seasoned angler can.

Perhaps it is fair to say that such jackets tend to become stiff in cold weather and sticky when warm, the latter state often being the disguised cause of nylon casts floating when they should sink. More often than not this occurs when the garment is new and the impregnation has not had a chance to develop a "shine". Again, reason enough for the ever-present bottle of detergent. The makers' intention is to keep *us* dry, however, using an extremely durable material which can be re-proofed from time to time, with adequate pockets to suit the angler's needs. Thousands can't be wrong.

Amongst the plethora of wet-weather gear, sales of which must have rocketed over the past few "summers", has emerged what I and fellow outdoor types welcome as the wonder material of the future — Goretex. At present it suffers from the same drawback as carbon fibre used in rod-making — cost. This will rightly deter many, but I live in the eternal hope that many of our space-age materials, with their magical qualities of lightness and efficiency, will sooner or later stop frightening our average incomes, currently at full stretch coping with minor needs like food, heat, rates and petrol.

Goretex seems finally to have solved a good many problems, the main one being wet from within — condensation. The fabric has a nice supple feel to it, quite unlike any other material I have experienced, and it is both lightweight and warm. Apart from the clothing applications, manufacturers are already using it for single-skinned tents, groundsheets, etc. Much weight is shed, but not at the expense of insulation. I will not elaborate on the rather complicated construction of the fabric other than to mention that it is full of minute holes which do not permit rain to enter, but allow body vapours to escape.

Goretex was pioneered by the well-known firm, Berghaus. I have blessed the hood of their "Sirocco" jacket on days when survival afloat depended largely upon dryness and comfort around the neck and face. This extremely well designed hood has two features I applaud: it extends beyond the face, supported by a very light and flexible wire frame which can be bent to form a suitable visor, and it offers very little restriction when the user wishes to turn his head around. The latter avoids the "black-out" which results when the head moves *inside* a normal hood, which can lead to one's failing to see the imminent big wave and the dangers it presents.

When we started dressing up for the loch, at the beginning of this chapter, I advocated the layer method of keeping warm. However, the ideal would be a single garment which would both insulate one from the extreme cold and, at the same time, be completely waterproof. Until recently I should have imagined all such garments to be, of necessity, weighty — until wearing one, again from Berghaus. They have taken the Sirocco a stage further with their Igloo jacket by using an entirely new insulating material — Thinsulate. As the name implies, this filling is extremely light yet has many times the heat retaining qualities of material twice or three times as heavy. The outer material is Goretex and the result is an unbelievably light, waterproof garment which dries out extremely rapidly. Complete with their unchallenged hood, I have rarely felt so warm and comfortable. It is a rare experience to feel clad for the summer and yet suffer little ill effect amid the icy blasts of winter.

One firm, already well known in the backpacking and mountaineering world, is now catering for the angler's needs as well. Rohan, of Skipton, North Yorkshire, are currently producing sets of clothing incorporating Goretex in some of the garments. This firm has done much to smarten the image of the outdoorsman, though this is incidental to their main aim: the production of clothing to suit a well-studied purpose. Why should we anglers still look like refugees from the dustbin when our backpacking cousins revel in functional beauty? Apart from jackets, this firm produces "Trotters", lightweight trousers with a much-needed high waist.

Peter Storm, well known suppliers of foul-weather clothing (our loch supplies the weather) now offer us a great advance in proofed wool sweaters. The wool fibres are treated with the new Peter Storm W1 Proofing which gives a water-repellent surface to the wool without affecting the natural absorption and removal of water vapour from the body via the core of the wool fibres (this being the difference between wool and other fibres). It is claimed that this treatment will last the life of the garment and I must confess that, having acquired one of their sweaters at great speed, I can vouch for the unaccustomed dryness of the wearer. This firm intend applying the same treatment to hats, socks and woven fabrics for trousers and other apparel which should be great news for anglers the world over. And others who get damp, too!

My longest-lived fishing jacket was made by the firm of Henri-Lloyd, and, when I finally put it aside, the stuffing had literally been knocked out of it. We shared a lot, that faded jacket and I. Testimony to the material (heavy nylon backed with neoprene) is the fact that I continually discover it being used by professional instructors in outdoor pursuits who vitally need both waterproofness and toughness. The high neck, zip and hood are excellent in the "Glencoe" jacket, to name but one of this firm's products.

When selecting an outer garment, regardless of material, keep in mind that your business afloat is mostly conducted from a seated position which will not permit quite the same air circulation or drying out facilities afforded the more mobile river angler. Choose, therefore, on the big side. While you do not want to glide skywards by means of an over-roomy outer structure which catches every little gust of wind, there is nothing worse than being so tightly encased that your every little movement brings groans of protest from the seams and zips of the outer shell. This applies particularly to waxed or oiled cotton heavy-duty jackets which are liable to shrink, or to any garment prone to sealing in body vapours. Whereas neoprene coated nylon has excellent waterproofing qualities, it serves best afloat when provided with a quick means of ventilation such as a double-ended zip to admit the drying air.

Recently came the welcome rediscovery of the PVC cape, or poncho as it is called today. Folded up it takes little space, and by undoing a few press-studs you can make it into a useful ground sheet. I admit to being almost fanatical in seeking out gear which serves a double purpose, and this item is high on the list.

Climbers, backpackers and others using up more energy than the average angler choose their clothing with great care although their choice may vary considerably, depending upon their individual reaction to the many materials available. Faintness, feelings of nausea and general weakness often result from sealed-in, ill-chosen garments. But, again, we anglers *must* be different: we have simply got to *look* the part, whatever that might mean...

It is abundantly clear that most manufacturers have come to realise the need for inner garments which match up with the more robust and windproof outer. Most fishing jackets nowadays have optional linings, some with press-stud fittings.

Perhaps it's my imagination, but after a wet and windy day on the loch, garbed with impenetrable materials, one part of the anatomy does not realise it is supposed to be bone dry like the rest of the body: the part you sit on. Absolutely waterproof (that much abused word) trousers must complete the fishing suit. PVC or a modern mixture still seem best.

In addition to completely waterproof clothing, I have found one item essential. Given the choice between a normal fishing hat and a hood, it would always be the latter for me. As it is, I use both: a softish hat with fold-down ear muffs, and an enveloping hood — preferably one firmly sewn or welded on to the jacket. With a warm scarf, or towel, round the neck and the drawstring up really tight, there are days when the bitter weather almost seems to be happening to someone else.

Little wonder that the well-insulated loch man is easily spotted in the local inn. After only one wee, light refreshment, beads of sweat appear as he takes on the appearance of being in a sauna!

Don't Forget

Against the brief time it takes to hook and land a fish — or visit the local fishmonger — the preparations involved seem on a par with Scott's, as he made ready for the Antarctic. If all the fishing gear I have seen being emptied out of cars and loaded into boats were piled together in one vast heap, we'd have another mountain at Balmaha — much higher than the Ben!

Final checks usually start the evening before the jaunt, although some leave it later and others bother little at all. Sprats and their correct mounts, baits, hooks and new nylon should all have been seen to, and petrol and oil both collected and mixed beforehand, or *en route*. The vital bread and rolls, camera and films, newspapers and dry towels (plural) all go into multitudes of polythene bags.

Since tackle shops are virtually non-existent on the loch shores, a visit should be made beforehand to a well-informed local or city dealer. A brief list of dealers is given at the end of Chapter 1. A tiny box of swivels, lying shamefully unused on his shelves, is of little use when you need them most. You'll always forget something, and in my case it's often a major item, which brings me to a most dreadful personal confession which was neither mentioned, nor admitted, at the time.

A few years ago, early in May, I arrived minus my vital bait tackle box. Instead of the tragedy I deserved, the reward was the first fish of the season, caught on the fly. A well-planned affair, indeed, considering trolling was *the* method at the time and the baits rested safely in their box on the floor of a cupboard at home. The fly rod was with me, however, and a few casts from the previous season still hid in a jacket pocket along with a small clear plastic box containing some assorted flies. On went a size 6 Claret and Blue and in came a forgetful 11 lb salmon. It had forgotten to be careful; I had remembered to be careless!

When the weather worsens, the river angler can always speedily repair to the sanctuary of the parked car or the fishing hut. Fortified by a flask, or by the more usual beverage, he can re-emerge when the sun blinks through again, fit to resume the challenge. On the loch, it's a different matter. Distances, plus the hefty outboard and associated gear, nearly always mean that when you have to come in it's for keeps. It is one of the minor tragedies of loch fishing that while you, having lost out to the weather, are preparing to wend your way home, others have timed their arrival to perfection and proceed to go out in the improved conditions and catch fish.

Some days, certainly, a wise man will read the signs of real hopelessness afloat and retire, to be tormented only very slightly by the decision, knowing full well the difference a day makes. But daily bread needs to be earned and not many can pick and choose their day off, so that being able to survive bad weather at the very *start* of the outing can be vitally important.

The loch has rightly earned a reputation for being subject to sudden and nasty changes in the weather. Too often, due to a sharp and short-lived response in the fish, which sense imminent rain, I have ignored the first few drops, mesmerised by the thought that the fish could go "off" at any minute. Much too late, on go the waterproofs to enclose sodden arms and rear end.

Other small items in the "survival" kit can be hidden away in spare oilskin pockets and some fads of mine include a cheap disposable lighter, bound in shrink-wrap film, a spare twenty cigarettes in a tin box (what an admission), spare dry mitts, an emergency wader repair kit, imitation chamois, a few choice flies and baits and umpteen handkerchiefs which I hand out freely to anyone who will listen to new excuses for old failings.

When sorting out clothing at the end of one season, I put my hand into a pocketful of weird glue. I had finally found the Mars Bar and spare candle!

Hiring a Boat

Since staying above the waves adds to your angling prospects, it is essential that you hire, own or borrow the right kind of craft.

Balmaha without boats would be like a loch without water but, apart from the eastern shore, the start could well be made from Balloch, Luss, Inverbeg, Rowardennan and other places where craft can be hired or trailed and launched from the beach. Do not, of course, forget your permit.

Wherever you start, the maps will guide you out, and it should come as no surprise to you to learn that you are close to a trolling route almost straight away. This is one of the real benefits of the map, since many a newcomer has sailed miles out of Balloch or Balmaha in search of the fishing grounds, only to learn that he could have been fishing, in the early season especially, almost the minute the outboard was started.

The problem should be tackled as you would a strange, unfamiliar car journey. Consult the AA — in our case, the Angling Areas! They are shown clearly on the maps, but 'phone boxes are scarce and breakdown facilities remote.

Balmaha has been my base for many years and I would suggest that, if new to the loch, the short walk to the pier or, better still, a little climb to just above it will give a good view of the lower basin. It looks, and it is, an enormously big loch but the fish, thankfully, don't need or use it all. To attempt to find them if they hid all over its entire length of 22·64 miles would result in more than a few lost boats, and a good boat is hard to replace! Rarely do we see the loch's entire area of 27·45 square miles, although a lot of the time I feel I've covered every square inch in search of a fish. Our salmon and sea trout use only comparatively small areas of the loch's bottom, depending on the water level and species sought.

MacFarlane & Son at Balmaha provide the ideal type of boat for hire, but it is advisable to book well in advance. To my deep regret Alec MacFarlane himself died suddenly recently — it will be hard for me and many others to imagine the loch without him, and with him has passed away more than a little Loch Lomond legend. For many years he delivered mail to several of the islands on the lovely little diesel-powered *Marion*. The sight of this unique wee vessel, with the familiar red funnel amidships, as she ploughed through the loch's worst weather, was reassuring indeed. The skipper was well known on the loch and spoke with authority and experience on practically any aspect of our great water. He endured anglers, rescued learners, recovered boats and overcame storms and anything you care to mention. He frequently appeared on TV.

Grandson Sandy, in spite, or perhaps because of, the constant sight of salmon and sea trout, makes no secret of his preference for pike! He fishes away at the weekends and during school holidays and, being familiar with the pike "regulars", he is acquiring a dossier which may put previous records at risk.

When it comes to hire boats and the general running of the boatyard, the section should really be entitled "See Jimmie", since the tireless Mr James Pairman and his staff do this very well from dawn to dusk in summer. There is no close season for Jimmie. Moorings need laying and recovering; boats must be launched and retrieved; varnishing and a multitude of other tasks have to be done. Jimmie also keeps day-to-day records of catches, weighing and entering fish in a book. In 1978 this book was particularly well filled, and by the end of the season Jimmie was complaining that he was "fair tired o' lookin' at fish". A good complaint, from our point of view! Many who have lost oars, rowlocks and the like owe thanks for his help.

Other centres for boat hire are Balloch, Luss, Rowardennan and Inverbeg. There are many boats available at Balloch, where the first salmon and sea trout enter the loch via the River Leven. The fishing for them starts, as at Balmaha, almost at once.

At Luss, Mr Ian Thomson, whose house is near the old pier, has several boats for hire and, with local aid, he runs a Loch Rescue service. Permits can be had, also, at the Colquhoun Arms Hotel in the village — once voted the "most picturesque in Scotland".

On the same shore, some distance northwards, the hotel at Inverbeg is owned by Mr Jack Bisset, who has boats for hire, and many foreign visitors have been attracted to this part of the loch.

Remaining lochside hotels are at Rowardennan and Inversnaid on the eastern shore, but 'phone confirmation would be wise regarding the hire of craft. At the head of the loch is Ardlui, where the same applies.

Safety First — Loch boats

On certain days I think it would be reasonable for large signs to be posted at lochside anchorages saying, "Loch closed today. It will get dangerous later on." No doubt we would still find an easy way to sneak out, but what really matters is to come back in.

A good sound loch boat is a help and here is a prize example of where money doesn't buy everything. A more expensive boat isn't necessarily a safer boat.

Every year sees a variety of really small craft out, some with just a single rod dangling over the end. Inflatables are very popular but they cannot seriously be expected to cope when it comes to fishing the loch in the adverse conditions it frequently presents. For sheer transportability on holiday, and as tenders, they are excellent, and there is no doubt that in calmish conditions they can troll in a limited way. But their main drawback, apart from being unable to take really heavy weather in safety, will become clear when you hook a 15 lb salmon. In six or ten feet of limited rubberised space it

The boat referred to on p. 57 which cost its owner £4.50 some twenty years ago. There are many craft lying about in a semi-disused state which are well worth a second look and a lot of labour. This boat sits low in the water and drifts true, with no skittish tendencies. The excellent Seagull engine is older than the boat by a good many years

is no easy matter to scoop it out with a trout net and then, while you remain seated, have it share the yielding floor with you, hooks and all! There are times when my own boat seems too small at 17 ft.

For many, many years the hire boats at Messrs MacFarlane's of Balmaha have received very worthy praise. They are due the same again. Each boat in this small fleet used to be named after a family of birds, and names like Plover, Partridge, Peewit and Wharp, to name but a few, come readily to mind. They still go out, and return, in safety, having placed their occupants in less danger than many in modern craft. These boats and those of the regular brigade of local anglers know the loch very well and, if they could speak, they would doubtless tell us how right they have been for the job. At times, I would prefer mine to remain silent!

A friend paid the paltry sum of £4 10s twenty years ago for a boat which lay at Balloch. It was brought to Balmaha and, although some of the planks might be rather "liquid", it remains one of the best-drifting fly boats on the loch.

If you intend both to troll *and* fly fish you will have to satisfy the requirements for the latter. Most boats can troll and are safe enough, but nothing could be worse for fly fishing than a skittish, fast-drifting or temperamentally-minded boat. Few boats are quite perfect in this respect, but the better ones are a joy to own or hire.

Boat Gear

Quite apart from the bung, there are several essentials to be carried in the true loch boat, and I give a few other pieces of equipment for added comfort.

ROD RESTS: A pair of rod rests are almost indispensable for trolling. Their basic double purpose is to hold the two outside rods securely, at the correct angle to the water surface, and create a necessary clearance within the boat for the angler(s) to move about freely. A boat can become mighty cluttered without rod butts criss-crossing near the anglers' feet, if they *have* to be wedged inboard, with the butts stuck into the floorboards. Most regular anglers make their own rod rests, fashioned to suit their own special craft, and these are, in most cases, almost permanent fixtures, with small plate recesses sunk into the gunwales. For the angler who desires transportability, the Japanese again have come up with an answer. I use a pair of their quick release rests which have broad thumbscrew fittings. They adjust to all but the thickest gunwale and permit

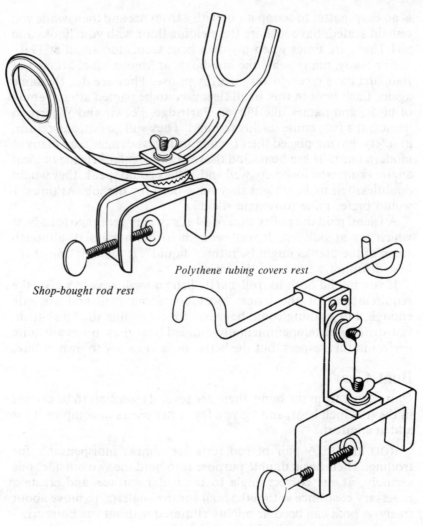

Shop-bought rod rest

Polythene tubing covers rest

Home-made Rod Rest
*This can easily be made from a G clamp
and a variety of odds and ends.*

Basic Rod Rests for Trolling or Bait Fishing

To avoid disfiguration of the boat, and for the sake of portability, use can often be made of the spare rowlock guides, and small blocks of wood placed to check undue movement under the pressure you hope they will receive.

58

various angles of tilt. Beware mounting the rods in a low slung position, relative to a *calm* loch surface: when a good wind comes up the rod tips will dip into the water, and so might you in trying to retrieve them! Many fellow anglers think the Jap rests look suspect and liable to work loose, but, having used them for many years with only one daymare (of my own making, possibly) I can only say they have never let me down. An added bonus with this type of rod rest is that, since I use comparatively short trolling rods, maximum "reach" is achieved since almost the entire rod length extends out from the gunwales. A final precaution, used by many, is to attach a small shock cord, which is hooked at either end, to both the boat and some part of the rod or reel which does not prevent the line from passing freely through the rod rings.

The sketches show the Japanese type (marketed by Shakespeare) and only one home-made version.

A BAILER will be needed to scoop out most of the loch from the bottom of the boat and put it back where it came from — quickly. I use a small brass pump as well but find a bailer useful so that all hands can be occupied and the job done quicker. To solve the problem cheaply, and make up a spare at the same time, get a gallon-sized square polythene bottle with cap and handle. Cut it diagonally in two — and you have two bailers! Make sure that the wee cap is still on or you will make little progress.

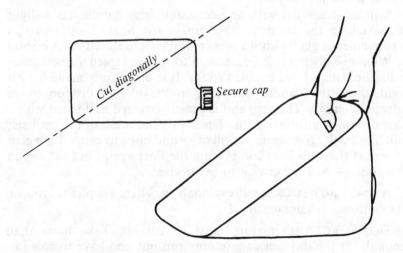

Cut diagonally

Secure cap

MAKING TWO BAILERS from a 5-litre polythene bottle

59

A NET for Loch Lomond should be strong and large, and the lighter the better. Avoid an orange mesh, for reasons explained elsewhere. Do not feel any guilt *whatsoever* about carrying a very large net. It won't be large enough one day. Just wait. To go out on Loch Lomond with an undersize trout net is adding to troubles you will get without trying.

Hardly mentionable is an incident in which I left the bay with a good net and, when it was most needed, found it wasn't there. On the Claddich shore, on a day of fine wind, I hooked a big and strong fish on the troll. Each time I engined it out, the boat was blown in again to the rocky shallows. Finally, as the big fish lay inert, I reached out for the waiting net which had been propped up, at the ready, resting against the gunwale. My hasty hand touched nothing. It had left. When I last started the engine up it must have overbalanced and slipped into the loch. The fish, a salmon, was exactly 20lb, and was luckily "tailed" out, by hand. My son and I searched the spot early the next day, without success, but when I opened the cover next time down, there was the net safely back aboard. A kindred spirit from the bay had spotted it and effected recovery.

A TAILER would have rendered the above story unnecessary! One now rests on the bottom of the boat, just in case, and is threaded also to accept a gaff head, which has only once or twice been used, on the lower jaw of pike.

A home-made net with an adequately long handle has a slight drawback in the room it takes up in the boat. I suffered this inconvenience gladly until a recent fatal visit to the city tackle shop of William Robertson & Company Ltd, where I spied the best semi-collapsible net I have handled so far. It is beautifully made from a rigid alloy, the handle extending in "Gye" net fashion to an adequate length. The grip end is plastic-covered and fitted with a pair of non-slip rubber grips. The depth and mesh of the net itself will handle the fish we all dream of — and hope to catch. I am glad to report that this item comes from the East again: but not Japan this time — North Berwick to be precise!

A SPARE ROWLOCK is self-explanatory. There are plenty lying on the bottom of Balmaha Bay!

The PETROL/OIL mixture must be correct. Take more than enough for the day out or you may run out and have to row in.

A SPARE PLUG, SPANNER, PLIERS, and SCREWDRIVER — at the

very least. A small MOLE WRENCH is the ideal "third hand" afloat and small PLIERS can double as disgorgers, although for this I prefer ARTERY FORCEPS. Take some wee coils of WIRE, Monel if possible. Although not obvious initially, amazing are its uses aboard.

A SPACE BLANKET is not essential, but mine has served so many uses I heartily suggest one. They are relatively cheap, made of strong, thin, laminated foil material, and keep even saturated bodies snug in an emergency. I once used mine on a visiting dinghy sailor who was caught out by one of the loch's notoriously quick rising gales and ended up clinging on to his upside-down craft. If you tie short pieces of nylon to the corner eyelets and fasten them to bushes or scrub, it can make a dandy wee beach shelter, windbreak or groundsheet. One side of mine is bright red, which is supposed to attract helicopters but also works well with bulls, which might make up for the excitement you have obviously missed afloat!

POLYTHENE BAGS of all shapes and sizes. Your bread or rolls *must* be kept dry or your day out will be a short one.

An old HESSIAN SACK. It's amazing how unfussy some anglers can be about keeping the fish corpse in good order during the course of the day. It matters more, of course, during the summer. One morning I saw a boat land a grilse right at the start of the day. I saw it again at night, in the bay, and, when the angler held up its poker-stiff body, I swear I heard it crack. The skin was wrinkled and parched, which is no way for a prime fish to end up — hence my reversion to an old method, in the absence of a good fish bass today. As we live in the Plastic Age you may find hessian sacks difficult to obtain. Do not use old coal sacks or you will get results opposite to those sought. Soaked overboard, the sack can be wrapped round the fish before storing it in the coolest and shadiest part of the boat. Let's hope that one day you need more than one sack.

A GAFF may be considered necessary, though I don't even like the *word*. When I was a mere youth, an incident nearly put me off fishing for life. On the River Inver a lady angler and her gillie were having some sport. Seven or eight times the fish was slashed by improper and mistimed gaffing strokes. The area around the stone she stood upon was bright red with blood. Some sport. Criticised I might be, but I reckon our fish give sport enough without us lacerating their beautiful flanks. Expertly done, and with extra-large fish, it can perhaps be excused and the mark go unnoticed. Personally, I'll find another way.

A PRIEST should go out with you on every fishing trip! The presence of one will be needed just prior to the demise of the fish. No need to apply to your local parish, as this is merely a short, heavy metal bar which is used to despatch the fish whilst still in the net. It is also a spider-type fly (a bit like the Butcher without wings or tail) and I've seen it do well on the loch.

A BUM-JOY may sound crude, but it is simply anything comfy to place yourself and guest upon while afloat. A Mini tyre inner tube has proved useful, but much better, today, are sheets of closed cell foam (CCF) stuck together. Neither these nor a Mini tube absorb water, but they do help absorb shocks to the posterior.

A small TRANSISTOR RADIO will give you weather broadcasts. Reverse the Loch Lomond forecast for real accuracy. You can also 'phone the local weather centre and a lady, who disguises her voice from time to time, will tell you what the weather is like where you are. On the loch I often disagree, and one day came fuming into the bay to tell her that the "light and variable" she had told me about nearly sank the boat! The line, alas, was engaged. Other anglers.

A spare coil of ROPE is very useful. If you are pulled up ashore and the wind is trying to buffet your boat broadsides, attach a short piece to the rear seat and the other end to a large stone, wade a few steps into the waves and drop the stone — and you will have peace of mind. One thing never missed on the loch is the tide.

A BALL-POINT PEN and SMALL NOTEBOOK are useful for recording any important information or bright ideas which come to you while afloat.

Take a few TOWELS, and hide one away for emergencies. I can't find one large enough for my tears some days. Cut into strips, they make good neck scarfs, and when tied around the wrists they help to keep the arms dry. Try casting without raising your arms, which is the only other way.

I should perhaps add that a firm in Wales, Cambrian Fly Fishers, know how wet we Lomondites get and so have produced cravats in towelling material. I told them that I could not cast without raising my arms, thereby collecting all the rain available, which — although handy for topping up the dram — is a bit uncomfortable to carry around. I also wrote to them about the WRIST SOAKERS previously mentioned, and they tell me that they are about to produce them.

A WATCH, unfortunately, has one major drawback: it will never

62

tell you the right fishing time. The weather, mainly the wind, should govern your angling hours afloat, and if you are used to regular meal times, prepare for changes of routine. One shouldn't spend the only windy hours of the day, when the fish are more likely to take, eating ashore.

FINAL CHECKS include ensuring that the rod top you have grabbed in a hurry fits your rod and not your boy's, since this error won't ease your problems six miles out from base. Don't forget a pair of SCISSORS. Your net should not have a hole in it. The greatest comedy I have ever seen was a salmon "whipped", rather than played, to the waiting net. It entered, swam out of the hole, and must have wondered why. Unless you have a four-stroke engine, remember to add oil to the petrol or you will need both a new outboard and bank manager. Finally, ensure that you don't arrive fully equipped and raring to go — on the wrong day!

Security

Boats, engines, general tackle, rods, reels, etc, are all expensive items, so it seems appropriate to conclude this chapter with a brief word on security. Theft has increased considerably in recent years and I have even heard of a captured fish being stolen.

Marking gear by scratching one's name on various items is common practice and helps, provided you intend to keep them indefinitely. There is a loss of value in any part exchange deal envisaged. An identity mark, known only to the user and located in an inconspicuous position, makes personal and police identification easire. Remember that chain is not a problem but only a minor deterrent to the determined thief.

Recording serial numbers, arranging more than adequate insurance cover, keeping your eyes open for any unusual happenings, discussing precautions and noting the habits of fellow anglers are all commonsense measures. Alarms for boats might also be considered, but not discussed openly.

A very interesting security product has come my way recently in the shape of the Volumatic security pen, and the price is modest considering what it offers. It is non-defacing and the mark is invisible except in ultra-violet light, facilities for which are now increasingly available to the police as an aid in tracing stolen property. All items marked can be listed in a personal register which, needless to say, should be kept in a place of great security.

3

Trolling

IT used to be called "trailing", which is really more apt, since you
trail behind you (in a boat, of course) fishing lines with baits
attached.

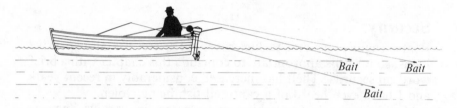

THE TROLL

Many people decry and detest it, pointing out the very real
damage it does to good fly water. Some troll all year and are
content, getting fish in the process. It is a splendid day out, amongst
the unsurpassed scenery the loch offers, with the possible bonus of a
salmon or sea trout thrown in.

I have no wish to be drawn into argument about the method other
than to say that I troll, fly fish and dap. There are times when one of
these methods is correct. Finding out *when* can take up the rest of
your life!

From the time when the loch opens for game fishing (salmon and
sea trout) in February, until late April, say, there is little doubt that
the troll is the method supreme and it will get the fish. And what
torpedo-shaped, fresh-run beauties they are.

Just to be out on the loch again, having prepared the tackle in
winter, is joy enough, but the main undercurrent of excitement lies
in two facts. First, the salmon and sea trout are expected to be big

64

Mr Jimmie Pairman, the Balmaha boatman, holding the author's 24 lb salmon, caught in the first week of June 1978

and will be in the pink of condition, fit to do battle with anyone who can provide what they are looking for. Second, the troll can be made to search the water deeper, and covers more fish along their routes as they enter the loch. So, be a purist if you will, but the fireside's not for me. Hail, rain, bitter cold and snow make life more interesting and the fish caught more worthily earned. You "live" the loch then, and to watch the weather slowly improve, week by week, until the fly is the method, makes for an interesting opening chapter to the events of the season ahead.

So troll — and enjoy it!

Loch Lures

Baits, at the start of the season, can be fairly large, reducing as the weather gets milder. For anglers who wish to troll all year round, small sizes at some time or another will be required.

On colour Plate 1 (opposite page 72), showing an assortment of lures, I have picked out some of the better trolling baits. There are others, of course, but those shown have earned their place and all have taken salmon. Sea trout, being more cunning in their ways, have avoided most of them save the Mepps and Rapalas.

I believe, personally, that if you reach the stage of fishing fine nylon and small baits you should be fly fishing anyway but, to contradict this statement, I have seen very good catches from the same small lures towards the season's end, when the fish are sometimes coloured (see Loch Lingo) and the excitement of spawning is upon them.

The sprat should be dealt with first and the baits viewed from top to bottom in the two columns shown.

A LIGHT GOLDEN SPRAT about 4 in long is shown, with the matching mount above it. The top mount is readily available from most tackle shops in a variety of sizes and, since sprats come in packets or jars, there is often a variance in length. It therefore pays to carry a few mounts size 4½-5 in, when a big offering is needed, and a selection of sizes from 4-2½ in, say.

The mounts themselves can be homemade or purchased as prawn spinning mounts, unleaded, and the barrel leads bought separately to give you a variety of weights. Too thick leads will present a problem when inserting down the sprat's body, ending up in a twisted misshapen object, which is what we are trying to avoid.

Often, mounts will come with three sets of trebles attached, whereupon I remove the top set at least by cutting through the wire near the retaining ring at the head of the bait. Two sets of trebles are plenty and I often resort to one, which invariably gives a better spin.

A small piece of copper fuse wire, the lightest possible, is always tied on to the rear of the mount, near the end treble, and twisted around the wrist of the sprat's tail to give a neat, compact appearance. When a fish takes, the fine wire breaks easily and, more often than not, when the fish is landed the sprat will have either disappeared or only the head area will be left, after the wrenching efforts of the fish to dislodge it.

A second, and smaller, mount is shown below the sprat; it

Books and catalogues contain a variety of well tried and tested knots. Like most anglers, I would find life afloat almost impossible without the blood and half blood knots. I would venture a tip for users of baits like the Rapala, which dispenses with the added iron-mongery of a clip swivel through the ring at the head of the bait. Use the tucked half blood but, when moistening before pulling tight, draw the knot up so that a small loop is left, with enough nylon protruding at the end so as not to create slip. The bait will wobble infinitely better and the fish will perform the ultimate tightening.

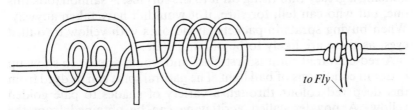

to Fly

The treble blood knot above is the tried favourite for joining two pieces of nylon. When tightening, moisten well, and end 2 can be left some 2-4 in long for the attachment of fly droppers. End 1 should not be cut off *too* close to the finished knot.

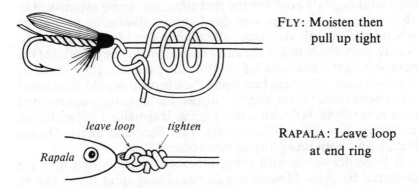

FLY: Moisten then
pull up tight

leave loop   *tighten*

Rapala

RAPALA: Leave loop
at end ring

contains more lead, enabling the bait to be fished deeper, or on a shorter line, attached to the "poker" rod (see Loch Lingo), and sunk deeper than a normal mount, in the engine wake of the boat.

At the season's end, I make it a habit to cut off the wire treble mounts and replace them using Alasticum wire and new treble hooks. If you cannot make a scratch in your nail with the tip of a hook, it is time to discard or re-sharpen it.

A point worth watching is to ensure that the end treble hook extends at least a little beyond the tail of the sprat. Better a small sprat on a slightly oversize mount than the reverse.

The sprat shown is the fairly common colour supplied both in jars and packets with a preserving liquid contained therein. Little as it might be, try to keep this fluid circulating in the jar or packet by keeping as well sealed as possible. Quite often, the addition of a little pilchard oil can assist (this also helps to check the strong odour of the preserving fluid), and I recall feeding out a sprat, so treated, and noticing a greasy film rising off it to the surface. A salmon took this one, but who can tell, for sure, if it wouldn't have taken anyway. When buying sprats in packets, avoid ones with yellow or dulled eyes, as these are likely to be old and stale.

A red-coloured sprat is first-class and would appear to show up better in conditions of bad light. The natural sprat can be dyed from this deep red colour through a variety of shades to pale golden yellow. A powder called acriflavine can be obtained from the chemist and combined with a modicum of formalin; many different shades, from dark reddish brown to lighter hues, can be produced, depending upon the mixture strength and the steeping times.

I can vividly recall seeing into the interior of a well-known and successful angler's boat for the first time, and being astonished to observe about twenty jars of dyed sprats, stacked in neat array around the side planks there, all securely fixed by rubber bands. Nearly every shade under the sun was present and he stated that the hardest to get right, and his most deadly, was a certain shade of "pinkish gold", the next best being dark brownish gold. Successful though the colour silver might be in metallic baits, for some reason I have never done well with a silver sprat. It remains a failure to me, something like the well-known fly, Teal Blue and Silver. On the loch, I find both unworthy of cast room.

A huge drawback with using mounted sprats is that they are devoured by kelts. Mounts are damaged and sprat losses can be heavy so that, when you need them most, your stocks are rock-bottom. Two excellent substitutes, indeed first choice for many, are the Rapala and Abu Killer, extremely realistic baits in sizes 5-3 in or less. Their added advantage is that, unlike the spinning sprat, their action does not tend to kink the line. I change the hooks on them, being careful not to spoil the ingenious built-in swimming action.

Below the natural sprat and mounts is an ABU KILLER, this being the middle of three sizes supplied. It has been doing very well of late on Loch Tay, so that it is currently enjoying a revival on our own loch, some colouring it to choice. It has more glitter than the similar baits below but the action must be checked, as usual, for swimming on an even keel. It has proved an extremely durable bait of its type and I have only lately dealt with a few old ones that visited, unfairly, rather rocky shallow water, thereby breaking the transparent diving vane. Being a fairly expensive bait, I took a fair amount of time over renewing this, using Araldite to complete the job, so that I now have resurrected at least three which will swim again!

Next are shown two RAPALA baits, the gold being slightly larger than the silver. Both sizes, 3 in and 2½ in, are popular, with gold again being the colour most favoured by salmon. Perch, however, are suicidal over the silver one, in smaller sizes especially.

There can be few baits with such a lifelike action, and even with the trolling speed reduced to a minimum they will retain plenty of action. A danger presents itself here, however, in that what suits one bait for speed may not suit another, and a happy medium will have to be struck somewhere with choice of baits related to boat speed. It is little use trolling dead slow to suit one bait whilst the other two suffer as a result, losing their intended action.

The Rapala is made of light balsa wood encased in plastic, and it is claimed that each bait has been tested for the correct action. Be that as it may, the makers warn against, and I can vouch for, their inadequacy should they tend to swim on their sides. A useful tip is to lower the bait into the water, with the boat moving slowly: if the correct wriggle is present and you have difficulty in seeing the gold sides of the bait, then it is swimming on an even keel; if it flutters, with either side of the flanks showing, there is an adjustment to be made. At the head of the bait is a small ring. It can be bent to the left to correct a bait swimming with its right side up, and vice versa. Only very slight adjustments are necessary. It is recommended that you should use fairly light nylon, about 8-10 lb, to preserve the bait action, lighter if your rod curve will suit. I favour adding the outpoint type of trebles and a fine swivel on the line, about 3 ft from the bait.

Next are a pair of DEVON MINNOWS, which are intended to swim on an even keel, spinning all the while. Brown and gold, or red and gold appear the most popular colours. Absolutely essential, as with the sprat, is at least one swivel (ball-bearing preferably), about 3-4 ft from the bait, and tied in with half blood knots. Be careful to moisten with the tongue before pulling up tight.

The angling world owes a debt of gratitude to the late Ian Kynoch (left), inventor of the much used Kynoch Killer. Seen here with the author

At the bottom of the plate are two KYNOCH KILLERS, salmon bait supreme for trolling or harling, with the treble hook, as supplied, between them. The one on the bottom right is the real article, the other a homemade effort, of which I have many, in a weird variety of colour schemes.

I knew the designer of this bait, Mr Ian Kynoch, and recall visiting him on his own beat, the River Tay, at his comfortable small hotel on the banks at Logierat. We talked much of his early days on Loch Lomond and, as regards his uniquely successful bait, he was a great believer in changing from one colour to another when response was poor. Since I adopt the same habit with my flies, I'm sure we would have made a great team!

Ian passed away some years ago but his "Killer" will remain with the angling breed for many years to come. The firm of Abu, a gigantic tackle concern, now supply the bait and I find it again fishes best for me on the "poker", as it darts about like a demented wee fish in the wake of the boat. I'm sure it annoys an otherwise tranquil fish into a raging fury, by its erratic, if somewhat natural, aquatic display. Another good centre bait is the ABU SALMO.

I have for some years experimented with a small paintbrush on Kynochs, evolving a variety of colour combinations: brown and gold, green and yellow, red and gold, and other common salmon preferences.

Invariably, I change the hook supplied for a finer, but just as strong, type of treble. Beware going up a size too many or else the treble will swing around, in reverse fashion, and foul itself either on the head of the bait or the line.

The Kynoch, or the "Lucky Lou" as it is often referred to in Canadian waters, seems to me to prove that, as has been suspected for some time, when the salmon really means to take, it comes at the bait from the side, not the rear. The treble hook dangles "amidships", and the open mouth usually, but not always, results in its lodgement in the corner area of the mouth, if not deeper in the same cavern. I remain convinced that the rise to the bait is similar to a "head and tail" to the fly, the fish streaking up and *across* the cast, then turning away just as sharply. The placing of the hook on this bait seems to endorse this point. An added bonus with the Kynoch is the floatability of the bait when a fish is hooked. When the fish is only a foot or so under the surface, the Kynoch should have slipped up the trace, stopping at the swivel. If the fish cannot be seen, the bait itself can and the frantic progress — or lack of it — can be followed by watching the bait closely, thus gaining an idea of the fish's intentions as it turns or dashes off in alarm. The bait will often hesitate, erratically, on the surface before another change of direction is attempted. Unlike the sprat, this bait remains usable after perhaps dozens of escapades, and it seems a minor price to pay to renew the hook if the slightest defect is found. It may explain my strong preference for this type of bait and the Toby, which awaits our comment, since it can become a distressing bore to have a carefully mounted sprat returned to you, much mangled by kelts and pike. Regrettably, there is much time lost in sorting out the mess, not to mention the heavy sprat losses. To this problem I have no ready-made answer, other than to suffer it and have a few mounted sprats, steeped, at the ready. I would merely add that Cafaro Brothers, the Glasgow dealers, have finally produced (or resurrected) a real sprat bait encased in plastic and many seasoned anglers will recall the durable qualities of the old "Nevison" sprat to which it is similar.

71

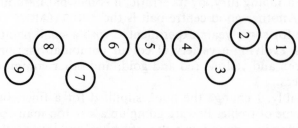

72

Loch Lures

1 Natural Golden Sprat
2 Normal Sprat Mount
3 Heavily Leaded Sprat Mount
4 Abu Killer
5 Rapala (Gold)
6 Rapala (Silver)
7 Black, Red and Gold Devon Minnow
8 Brown and Gold Devon Minnow
9 Home-made Kynoch Killer
10-15 A Selection of Toby Baits
16 Abu Droppens and Mepps
17 Kynoch Killer
18 Kynoch Treble

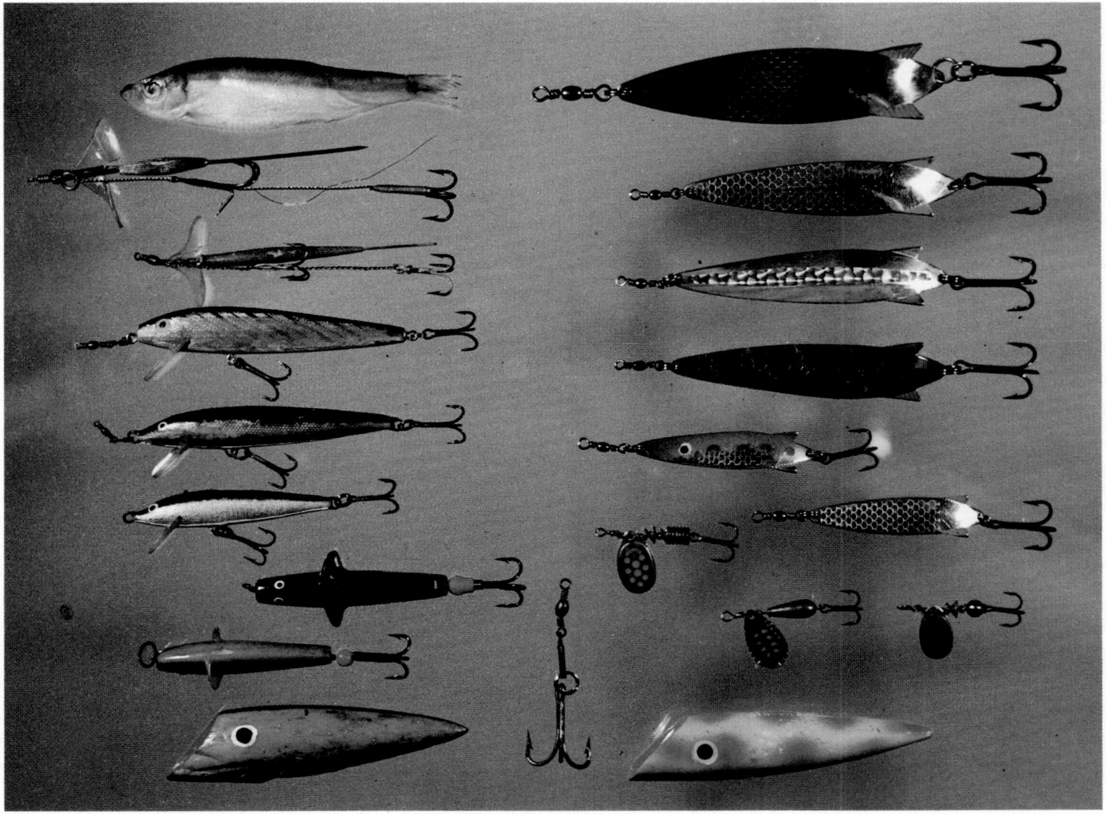

Plate 1   Loch Lures

Plate 2a   A 20 lb salmon taken off Darroch, between Inchfad and Ireland, the white marker post of which can just be seen below Ben Lomond. Note the large home-made net

Plate 2b   Balmaha Bay one June. Note the prevalence of haps

Plate 3 Dapping Flies

Many of these flies do not have individual names. They are, however, discussed in detail and identified on pages 137-8.

Plate 4 Wet Flies

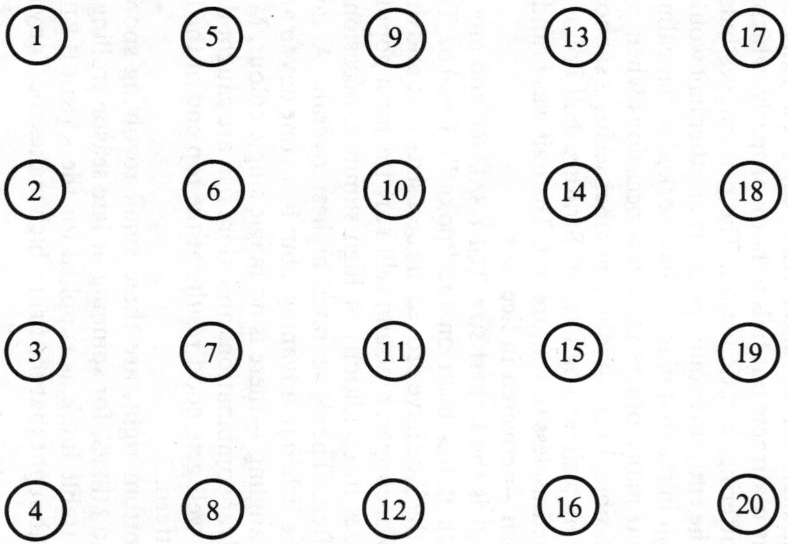

WET FLIES

1 Haslam
2 Silver Invicta
3 Turkey and Silver
4 Turkey and Gold
5 Butcher
6 Turkey and Mixed
7 Woodcock and Mixed
8 Burton
9 Invicta
10 Mallard and Red
11 Peter Ross
12 Bloody Butcher
13 Dark Mackerel
14 Mallard and Yellow
15 Claret and Blue
16 Blue Label
17 Orangeman
18 Turkey and Green
19 Turkey, Gold and Orange
20 Kingfisher Butcher

(17) (18) (19) (20)

(13) (14) (15) (16)

(9) (10) (11) (12)

(5) (6) (7) (8)

(1) (2) (3) (4)

The right-hand column contains a selection of TOBY BAITS, by the Abu company. As unique as the bait would be someone who hadn't heard of it! Renowned the world over, it appears to have caught practically all the species worth catching. I have landed cod to 30 lb on it and other species too numerous to mention, in the "briny", of course, and it has caught me salmon and sea trout in the Clyde estuary on many occasions.

I suppose that more fish are caught on the Toby than on anything else apart from the fly. It has a marvellous fluttering action, does not tend to kink the line, comes in a great variety of colours and is obtainable practically everywhere. Another bonus is that it can be fished fairly slow to quite fast. On the latter point I have been astounded, like most fellow anglers, to find it taken while accelerating across the deeps when, from time to time, it would leave the water in little leaps.

If it has one slight failing, and it really cannot be rated as such, it would be that it attracts but fails to hook properly, which could be due to its fluttering, erratic action. The percentages balance out, however, in the end, since quite possibly another bait wouldn't even attract the fish in the first place. It has worked in flat calms, having served me and many others on a few occasions when conditions seemed impossible. I can vividly remember seeing a salmon of 15 lb being caught on a silver 1 oz size, off Strathcashell Point, on a day when it seemed useless to venture out. The bait was brand new and so was the fish — covered in lice.

The top bait is the largest size, TOBY SALMO, and any success I have had with it has been on the "poker". The 1 oz Toby and, particularly, the ⅝ oz have proved the best sizes time and time again. Silver and gold, copper, blue and zebra are the most popular, down to smaller sizes in conditions of high summer, occasionally, and back-end, often. The ⅝ oz rates highest overall. A mixture of colours can be fished to advantage, but from one day to another — so typical in angling — there is no magic single colour. More seem to fish the silver combinations and more fish are caught thereby. A boat I know well gets good results at the top end of the loch with the zebra pattern.

Finally, bottom right, are three small revolving spoons, ABU, DROPPEN and MEPPS, for spinning or late season trolling. Bottom centre is the treble hook as supplied for the KYNOCH KILLER.

Recently I thought that the firm which makes the Toby had gone

one better. I landed the first two fish into Balmaha, a 9 lb sea trout and an 11 lb salmon, on the ABU ELLIPS, a new spoon bait, the largest size in silver. It was fished quite deep and more fish thereafter preferred the Toby but, since fly fishing was just beginning, there was no time to form conclusions.

Being frustrated from time to time by fish which have visited the bait without being hooked, I have resorted to much experimentation with the hooking arrangement. It is vital that the bait action is retained, however, and my current arrangement may only mislead me into thinking that I hook more fish, but I persevere with this slight change. Firstly, I remove the treble and split ring from the tail of the bait. To a treble of the same size, but slightly finer, I attach a piece of nylon of 20-30 lb strength, some 8 in long, by means of a half blood knot. The free end of the nylon is inserted through the split ring at the head of the bait and, by trial and error, the distance gauged so that the eye of the treble coincides with the drilled hole at the rear end of the bait. The second blood knot is then drawn up tight, and, if you have guessed correctly, the two holes at the rear will line up correctly so that a piece of thin fuse wire can be wound through the holes several times, and the ends twisted together, before snipping off with scissors. The basic idea is to retain the bait action but reduce the unusual positions which the free-flying treble, as supplied originally, can adopt. Although the bait still flutters attractively, the treble thus secured does not shift about so much, and breaks away when the fish is hooked. It does not pay to overdo the number of windings of thin fuse wire. The idea is to ensure that the hook breaks away cleanly, seconds after the fish has been hooked, similar to the result obtained with the Kynoch. If it seems like too much effort, with little justification, then so be it. It has become absolutely habitual for me to carry out this slight modification, but virtually hundreds don't bother and catch the fish, just the same. Very few of us knot our ties exactly the same way!

I would safely say that a selection of the baits shown will suffice for an entire season, on the troll. There are probably a good many others worth a try and on dour days there is often a rummaging through the tackle box for an oddity. Nine times out of ten, it doesn't stay on long enough to give it a chance!

Out comes the Toby once again!

* * *

To Spin?

The most popular type of rod, especially with the young, would appear to be a spinning type. There is little doubt that as an all-round instrument it can visit many waters with success and has very many good reasons to justify its use. On the river, fine, delicate casts can be made into areas where a cast of flies daren't enter. Likewise its versatility in both fresh and salt water use has been proven beyond all doubt. On the other hand, before methods become too instilled, I would at least urge that a light fly rod is presented to youngsters early in their loch fishing careers.

Having said that, I must admit to two things. My own son's deep-rooted preference is to spin, without much success admittedly, much as I have tried to persuade him to use the light fly rod from a drifting boat, on the loch. Secondly, in a lifetime of fishing, I have only possessed one orthodox spinning reel, and when it was lost there was not any great alarm or rush to replace it. I still have a "closed face" spinning reel which I use solely for sea fishing. I think it can be summed up by a close relative who observed that I am "the most right-handed person in the world", and my manipulations with everything the "wrong way round" are amazing to behold. However, a multiplying reel is almost second nature, and the position can be reversed when I see someone else, unfamiliar with this reel, attempt to sort out the overruns with a knife! I am entirely used to multipliers, and proceeds from the sale of a few salmon have been well spent on two very fast-retrieving reels of this nature. If one is fishing alone, they have a great advantage when it comes to reeling-in the two idle baits, rapidly, when a fish has taken the third.

I am often asked if spinning works, from a drifting boat on the loch, for salmon and sea trout. Some years ago I would have replied in the negative and advised fly fishing from the outset, or trolling, as superior methods. I have had little reason to change my mind, but must admit to having noticed a recent tendency for some boats to spin with light nylon, very small Mepps, or similar spoons, size 0 or 1, and enjoy fair success with sea trout at least. I did see a very coloured salmon of 11 lb or so take a spun Mepps on the Pilot Bank, only a few seasons ago, but I would rate it the exception.

One fairly regular boat has done well with the same two friends aboard, one fly fishing and the other spinning with fine gear.

Like the fly and the dap at work from the same boat, the combination can prove very useful. The spun bait, when it doesn't

76

catch fish, can still interest them enough to come up to the fly. Certainly, permutations of both age and methods are worth some thought.

There may be many catches which have escaped me, by anglers spinning from the shorelines of the loch. In general, the response is poor, and one reason I can put forward is the tendency for fish to prefer baits drawn from shallow to deep water. Fish might be attracted when the bait is cast from the shore and drawn into the shallows, but chances are they rightly suspect the behaviour of a bait behaving so, and veer away, rarely even being seen.

There is always the exception. On a Saturday evening some years ago, the Clachan Inn at Drymen was full of loch anglers bemoaning, as always, lack of catches and "rotten" conditions. Two perspiring and overjoyed bodies arrived and there was talk of "a salmon about 12 lb". No-one recognised them as boat anglers, which is no wonder, since they apparently did not need a means of floatation. They had caught the only fish of the day, spinning a Toby from the Bonnie Banks at Strathcashell Point. Before camps and bases are established there overnight, let me give dire warning that it will probably be another fifty years before the feat is accomplished again. How long can one wait?

Rods for Trolling

Rods for trolling can be a weird and wonderful mixture, comprising all sorts of lengths and materials including old greenheart, built cane, hollow and solid glass. I have not, as yet, seen anyone using carbon fibre! Use what you will; I will merely state my own preference for light, but strong, solid glass rods about 8 ft long, with a good through action. The tip section gives better hooking at long ranges, they are easy to stow and will take considerable abuse (even so, I normally carry a spare). Troll or not, I am still fussy that I get good control and action from the rod without any tendency to crude stiffness. The curve should be right for about 10-12 lb nylon.

Longer rods would *appear* to keep the baits further apart, as they spin through the water, and lessen the chance of them "mating", with messy results (you should always carry a spare spool or two of nylon); they certainly do when the trolls are short, but the longer the lines let out, the more chance there is of the baits merging, depending on their weight and type. On days when you have that good penetrating light and you feel daring enough to stand up at the rear of the boat, try watching the two outside baits as they go out

77

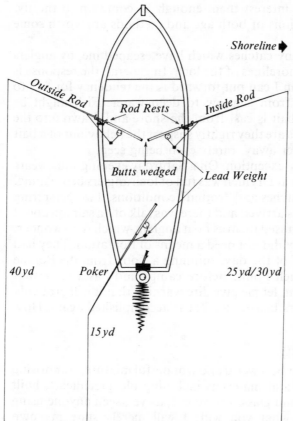

In the absence of proper rod rests, the rods can be rested against the rowlocks, care being taken that the butts are firmly wedged. There must be no "give" whatsoever or there will be a risk of the butt slipping when a fish is hooked. Between the reel and the bottom ring a loop of nylon should be laid on the floorboards and a flat, rounded lead weight placed upon it. When a fish is hooked the angler will have visual and/or audible warning as the lead is jerked free. This also enables the fish to complete its turn when taking the bait, which usually results in sound hooking. Whatever method is used, ensure that the line is free to run through the rings and that it does not cross any ragged edge. Test by pulling on the line when the rods are placed in their selected positions.

(you will need a pal) and you should see the pull of the wave and water bring the baits closer together.

Most boats troll with three rods on the loch, but I have seen one bristling with *five*. Even at that, I suspect I missed a wee one somewhere. For you and I, three will be plenty, unless you wish to sink in the knowledge that you had at least three fish "on" just before the fourth coil of nylon whipped suddenly around your neck!

Each of the three rods should have a different length of line out.

78

Improvised Trolling Rod Set-up

This is a very basic rig. The two outside rods can be placed opposite the lower rowlocks or spaced as in the sketch.

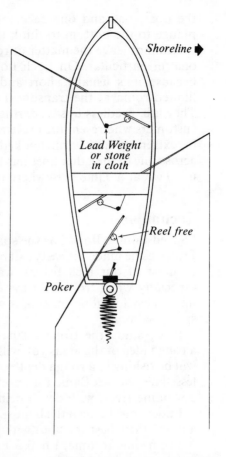

Shoreline ▶

Lead Weight or stone in cloth

Reel free

Poker

The inside rod, the one nearest the shore, can fish about 30 yd of line, the centre rod (the "poker") 20-25 yd and the outside rod deeper at 40 yd. There are no set rules on these distances and one good, experienced angler I know fishes much shorter lines.

Perhaps here I should relate a curious tale. On a dull, calm, clammy and overcast day, I once let out an enormous length of line, by way of experiment. No-one had a fish nor did it look likely. The bait was a Rapala and when a wee fish, a kelt I thought, took the bait I was busy lamenting the time it took to reel in the line and fish. It didn't show at all and came steadily in to meet its captor. When at last we met, I don't know which of us got the bigger surprise, but an extremely large salmon buckled the rod over sharply, as it realised its mistake! A tremendous fight followed, as I played the fish with great care, owing to the small and light hooks on the bait. At the final stages, a boat circled near me, shouting, "Hey, Jimmie, dae ye want a gaff...it's a big yin." With difficulty, I netted a fresh deep salmon of 28½lb.

Several more fish came to the Rapala that year, 1966, but it became more and more impractical to fish such a long line. One feature I have noticed about this bait is that bigger fish seem to be less aware of what has happened to them and seem bewildered by the jag and pull of the small fish they have mouthed. When they see the boat, one and one become two and, like all good fish, they plunge to the bottom to think the matter out!

I cannot leave the matter of rods without mentioning the centre one, in particular. On Loch Lomond it is known as the "poker" because it is usually short and stiff, for accommodating in the limited room at the transom. Fish caught on this rod are legion. They are, needless to say, daring and strike me as fresh-run, angry customers who resent the presence of the boat immensely. They can be extremely awkward, hooked at such short range, and a leap across one of the other lines has been described graphically, I hope, in "Two at a Time" elsewhere in this book.

Technique

"Speed Bonnie Boat", as the song goes, might well have suited the Prince as he made his hasty exit but "*Slow* Bonnie Boat", as applied to most of our loch fishing ways, seems a better tune to hum, especially when trolling in the early season. Slow and deep, that much heard angling maxim, is worth repeating when dealing with spring salmon.

First, study the trolling lanes marked on the maps and have a rough idea of the areas you will search. Most of the time, the boat will be fishing in a rough depth of 5-10 ft, sometimes a little more or less. The Endrick Bank, for example, can and should be treated like a winding river, with depth being the controlling factor.

Endeavour to keep the boat speed steady. The baits will get down and try their best for you, with their own built-in action.

From time to time, I make it a practice to reel-in and check for weed or debris, when either a rod tip acquires a slight bend or much vegetation is present from a spring flood. I could curse myself, too often, when the day is over and baits are reeled-in covered in green sludge or the like. The chances are they've been drawn, like limp rags, over keen fish, and I believe that even a small piece of foul matter is enough to take away the bait action and make the fish rightly wary. Would you eat bread with wee blue dots in it?

There can be little between success and failure, even with the correct tackle and the boat speed steady. The bottom of your boat will pass over many fish, all potential "customers", and yet you will constantly be amazed when another boat goes over the ground you have covered so well and *he* gets a result. When this happens you cannot wait to find out, later, what magical bait the other chap was

80

using. Don't be too surprised to find it is exactly, or near enough, the same as yours!

So why didn't you get the prize, and why is it more often than not the man in the boat approaching you who holds up one finger, or one fish? In the early days you will be tempted to put it down to their luck and your lack of it. To some extent you will be right. You can get everything correct and troll for literally weeks without success. But don't despair, there's one wee trick you can try. There's always a reason for success. Books have been written, in great technical detail, about how and why salmon will be in a taking mood at least once during the course of a day. Basically, it will be pointed out that a variety of conditions can bring them on the take, and I think it is mainly a *change* in conditions which awakens their interest. More so, on a day of constant, indifferent weather. On the loch, the one and only secret in catching fish is to be at that right spot, at the right time, when conditions change for the better — no matter how brief that period may be. It's hard to do.

I knew one angler who always had two reasons — and two only — for his success, no matter the conditions. I can hear him yet: "A wee blink of sun came oot" or "That dirty big cloud helped". Both *changes*.

Too many treat the troll with disdain, regarding it as an easy, almost pitiful way to catch a fish. Perhaps when you fly fish, later on, it will appear so, but I've always felt that to do it well requires something more than just trailing two or three baits through any old water. The qualities of perseverance, observance and alertness are as much required in trolling, as in any form of fishing, to get steady rewarding results.

Trolling for weeks on end can be a soul-destroying business, especially if the fish are not in the mood. If you have confidence in your baits and you are covering the most likely areas for the time of year, there is little else for it but to suffer the whole business gladly. Sooner or later persistence will be rewarded. It should be remembered that early season fish will not necessarily remain at recognised spots for long, but will disperse further afield. Twenty boats, for example, could round the Black Rocks dozens of times in the one day without even a run from a fish and yet, at the end of the day, a lone boat come along to catch a fish literally covered in lice, that had made the area one of many brief stops as it prepared to journey up the eastern shoreline. Luck, of course, plays its part, but persistence on the part of the angler is just as important.

There are many ways to attempt to relieve boredom when going through a bad spell. Some change their baits frequently and others, like myself, try to remain optimistic that the next fish is going to be *the* big one. Getting a fish or two fairly regularly is, of course, the best cure of all and it is not quite so difficult to remain alert and confident thereafter.

I could illustrate several occasions when boredom, in itself, has brought about some remarkable captures, but the following incident is the one which remains the most vivid.

After several outings in the early season, I had changed the "poker" bait several times, since fish had appeared to ignore the regular bait over a lengthy period. I finally put on a large silver and gold spoon and, hand holding the rod, kept twitching it, which caused the bait to dart, flutter and drop back in an erratic manner. I kept this up for some minutes before interest waned, whereupon I replaced the rod in its usual position. It had no sooner been put down when a 12lb salmon seized the bait solidly. Its interest *must* have been aroused by the unusual bait action and the event led me to wonder just how many fish must follow the trolled bait before losing interest. Perhaps, for the sake of vanity, it is best we never know the answer, and it certainly does not follow that baits must be made to behave this way as a general rule. The built-in action of the bait and the effect that the waves have on it is usually all that is required. In very fickle conditions, however, a result can often be provoked by a twitch of the rod, a turn of the boat or a change in its speed; provided, of course, that an essential witness is present — a fish, preferably one which is just as bored as you.

Even on the troll, stay as alert as you can and incidents like the one I am about to describe should never happen to you.

Some years ago, on a mid-April afternoon, I was passing Clairinch heading towards Balmaha, with the usual three trolls at work. I casually noticed what seemed to be a hire boat leaving the bay on a somewhat erratic course, with the Seagull engine going flat out. "Probably going to Clairinch", I thought. Gradually it dawned on me that his veering left-to-right navigation was calculated to bring him somewhere near my boat — if not in it!

Sure enough, he approached the bow and, no matter the business he had in his mind, I immediately stood up and shouted to draw his attention to my sunken trolls, jabbing with my finger and pointing it behind me. This was entirely the wrong thing to do because that's where he headed — right behind me — and still at high speed!

If you know that ghastly and utterly helpless feeling a motorist gets when the brakes fail, you'll sense my inward panic. While he and his engine wreaked havoc with my gear, I struggled with reels, releasing checks and tensions. After circling me *twice*, his outboard stopped dead, the propeller arrested by the three mangled baits, and his boat glided straight towards me, amidships, on the inevitable collision course. I fended off his boat by hand and, exasperated beyond words, got no opportunity to vent my feelings as he shouted "... Engine's jist conked out, Jimmie. Ah wis jist goin' tae ask ye where Inchmurrin wis again"!

Queer how you laugh in such a situation.

I mean you laugh *queer* in such a situation...

Day Out on the Troll

Secure, therefore, in the knowledge that your will has been properly attended to, and armed not only with rods and baits, but with a sense of humour, it is time to leave base, which we will assume is Balmaha.

There should be no rush to leave the bay because, as at Balloch, fishing begins the instant you pass the last of the boats on the outer moorings.

Having tackled-up in readiness for the start, there is one immediate decision to be made: left or right? If you are new to the loch, or unfamiliar with (or in a quandary over) the very vastness of it, I suggest a rough plan of where you are going should have been worked out beforehand after studying the trolling lanes indicated on the maps. The prevailing wind should be taken into account straight away, and if it appears calm down towards the area of the Endrick Bank it will be wiser to proceed past the pier and troll the shoreline from there to, say, Strathcashell Point or Sallochy.

As you pass the pier, be on the alert, because you will see elsewhere in this book frequent references to fish caught there. It happens all the time.

With the engine regulated to a steady speed, on the slow side, and the two or three baits fed out to the required distances, you can start to plough your way along the north-east shoreline. Just after the pier, you will swing out slightly, watching for the rocky shallows, and proceed through the first bay. It is called Manse Bay and has sometimes provided the first fish of the season. Leaving the sandy bay itself, the route outwards to the Black Rocks should be trolled on the deep side until the rocks themselves are reached. Most boats approach the Black Rocks and fish them very shallow, rounding the main rock and heading straight outwards to avoid a few nasty sunken boulders, the tips of some being easily seen.

The next bay is larger and many years ago was probably one of the best areas on the loch for salmon. It is called Millarochy Bay and there are boat moorings at the north-east corner, the Green Bank; otherwise it is fairly straight forward to fish, the shore being clean shingle throughout.

From the camping and caravan site at the end of the bay, there is a rocky shallow stretch with a Canoe Clubhouse and more moorings lying off it. At the small burn mouth in the centre of this shore is a good spot for a big fish, and the whole shore area is known as Critreoch. It ends in a small, fairly deep bay with a house standing very high above it.

The entire rocky shoreline is good fishable water, which will bring you to Strathcashell Point, one of the most famous points on the loch, holding both salmon and sea trout. As you round the point, the Sallochy shoreline sweeps ahead and should be fished quite shallow until the other caravan and camp site is reached. A shallow area at another burn mouth should be watched, both for a fish and for fouling the bottom.

The shore runs parallel to the road to Rowardennan then, and from the Blue Rocks to the great Carrick Rock is a good stretch, the rock itself nearly always holding a good fish or two. Beyond Carrick Rock lies Altevoulan Bay, which might well do as a limit north-eastwards, for the earlier part of the season. Returning to Balmaha through the same waters is straight forward and it may be that you have a fish to report.

The area just described and the one about to be covered are, in my opinion, the best of the spring lies.

Turning left, on leaving Balmaha Bay, you will be faced with the long, sandy stretch known as the Endrick Bank, where the actual river mouth can usually be spotted easily. Just off the boats at Balmaha, at the start of the bank, are the mudflats, a weedy sandy stretch which takes you to the hole at the mouth. Depth must be watched carefully all along the bank and, if done correctly, this will result in a somewhat winding route. There are several "holes" along the edge of the bank and large numbers of salmon can lie along its length from March onwards.

To some the Endrick Bank is a monotonous area, being half a mile of completely sandy bottom. Not so to me, since at any

The earliest grilse kelt netted by the author, in the first week of August one year. Taken off Inchcruin at the Rock, on the fly. Note the wounds

second along its entire length there is the expectation of a take. At the beginning of the season, unfortunately, a lot of these can be false alarms in the shape of kelts, spent and thin fish which are described in Chapter 7. Nuisance they may be, but they should be unhooked and returned to the water as unharmed as possible. Regrettably, many of them simply gorge the bait and it can be very hard to prevent bleeding when removing the hooks. Sea trout kelts have been more in evidence than salmon kelts over the past few years, but I still have a colour transparency of a huge salmon kelt which was weighed and photographed in the boat. It scaled 26 lb and must have been a beautiful specimen when in the pink of condition the season before.

A small percentage of our Atlantic salmon survive to spawn again. Some years ago, a survey was carried out under the supervision of Dr Peter Maitland, and anglers were requested to supply him with scales and the weight, measurement, etc, of fish caught in the Association waters. I recall three salmon which I caught in the River Endrick being confirmed as fish which had survived spawning once and returned safely again. It is fairly rare, but provides the best possible reason for handling each kelt, regardless of the species, with as much care as possible.

About mid-way along the bank, the boat will pass Aber Isle, deep off to the right, and from there on the area of the Net Bay is entered, just before the main rocky Claddich shore. Net Bay can be swept in a variety of ways, shallow and deep.

The rocky shoreline at Claddich ends in a small point, followed by a larger, sandy, weedy bay which terminates at a famous area known as the Stables. The old buildings can easily be seen on the shoreline, and behind them is the beautiful Ross Priory. The natural shoreline is a bit spoilt thereafter by the intrusion of the Power Station, but this water still fishes well. From there to Balloch would possibly be the extent of the early fishing, the entire route being reversed back to and beyond Balmaha.

Slightly later in the season, about late April or early May, apart from contemplating the possibility of starting with the fly, you can troll the islands, following the variety of routes shown on the maps. In guiding the boat along these interesting lanes, be sure to maintain a steady speed and exercise care in turning the boat. Movements at the tiller should be made in a series of short, steady strokes, so that the boat does not make too sharp a turn, fouling the lines in the process.

If I had a penny for all the fish which have taken just as the boat was turned, I'd know more about surtax. It appears that the bait sinks a little deeper or seems to be escaping into deeper water, but a magnetic attraction is present which has proved fatal to many a fish. Do not, however, attempt simply to go around in a series of wee circles. You will not cover much ground and I cannot imagine the reaction of other boats trying their best to guess your intentions.

There is a certain drill to be followed when a fish is hooked on the troll. Boats vary in their methods of checking the reels and setting them to a tension whereby a fish can take the bait and also line, becoming hooked in the process. Many boats use flat lead weights, placed upon the line on the floor or seat of the boat, between the reel and the first ring of the rod. When a fish takes, the lead weight is immediately hurled free, a momentary pause following which enables the fish to turn slightly with the bait before the reel sets the hooks. I do not use this method myself but have to admit to being in the minority. (I may have explained my reasons in the section entitled "Daymare", in Chapter 11!) I have, for many years, preferred to set my reels at predetermined tensions and, when a fish takes, hope that I'm alert enough to throttle up the engine *very slightly*, to complete the hooking, and then reel-in the two baits, as fast as possible. Neither method is completely foolproof. Fish can escape either way, and it's very much a matter for individual preference.

Once it seems sure that the fish is soundly hooked, as the reel screeches its merry message, it is time to be thinking about where to play it out — in deeper water. As a matter of fact, a very pleasant way of passing the time to advantage is to be thinking ahead and planning your actions for that lovely moment when you have a fish "on" and under control.

It may seem unbelievable, but many a time I have rounded a corner into a half gale, with nasty spumes of wave crashing over the bows, and prayed that I *didn't* hook a fish just there and then. It can happen. You are so busy tending to self-preservation, through spray-affected vision, that any added problem could result in unmentionable consequences. Thankfully, these situations are few and far between.

If, as you troll, there is a boat ahead of you going about the same kind of business and the occupant very suddenly stands up, faces backwards, grabbing rods with gusto, and then slowly alters the course of his very lucky boat out to deeper water, then you can almost be sure he has hooked a fish and is going through the normal drill. The type of fish is not so important, at the moment, but the actions are. Already stated is my own preference for a slight throttling up of the engine speed, not *too* sudden, but enough to keep firmly in touch with the fish. Presuming there is no-one else to help, the next tasks are to reel-in, as quickly as possible, the other two baits, taking the time to ensure their hooks are out of the way (that's another story), and edge the boat out into deeper water. You should have a rough idea of the size of the fish by then, and if he's big don't hesitate to take him out to an adequate depth. If you don't, then the entire procedure may have to be gone through again. Sometimes it's completely unavoidable, in restricted areas.

There is a trick which should be in every angler's repertoire, and it is usually learned on the river first. Even the heaviest of fish will succumb to it and you will find it indispensable in your armoury of angling short-cuts. It is called "walking the fish", and the word governing its entire success is *steadiness*.

As applied on the river, it is the best way to calm down a fish and walk it up the beach, where it will thrash slightly and strand itself. It is then a simple matter to lay down the rod and approach the fish, completing its capture by a further nudge, or lifting to a safer place.

On the loch, you will need to keep the fish under control whilst you seek the safety of deeper water. Every action must be performed smoothly and steadily, without any jerks whatsoever. The rod will be bent over, into the fish's dead weight, and the reel set so that any sudden jerk by the fish will give him line, but just a little. The constant strain is kept on the fish while you slowly engine out the boat.

If you have done it correctly, he will follow you like a little dog on a lead, until you are satisfied that the boat is far enough out. The engine can then be shut off and the fish reeled-in for closer inspection. Do not expect the behaviour of a small pup once he realises who is "walking" him. Usually all hell breaks loose as he admits his mistake, and the battle is on.

Throughout the entire trip, there should be no reeling-in, just a steady strain maintained, and line yielded only if necessary, in short amounts.

No two fish play the same way. A kelt will usually put up less of a struggle, due to its weakened state, but there's always the exception. When a kelt fish has recovered well and is putting back the weight lost in spawning, it is known as "well mended", and this fish can fool the best of us, putting up a display very similar to a fresh-run fish. Only when it's in the boat, shedding its scales *too* easily does its thinness become evident, and your disappointment will register. Sometimes you have to look at it for quite a wee while before giving the benefit of the doubt and sliding it back into the water. It may look like a bar of silver, but it will be a bright, "tinny" silver. When it is too late and you inadvertently kill one, it will remain flabby and soft when held up. A good clean fish should come complete with an approved *rigor mortis* and stiffen like a poker.

On the loch we often get sea trout known as "day trippers". They are really kelts who managed to get back to brackish or salt water and gorged themselves, then, for some unknown reason, returned to the loch to pose us a problem. I saw one killed in error, and it disgorged a mass of elvers (baby eels), whereupon its true thin state was revealed.

Kelts can be a nuisance, but they're also a good sign that much successful spawning has been carried out. The 2 lb sea trout kelt you return to the water may visit again next year, as a 5-pounder, so each one returned is an investment in the future.

However, in among the kelts we've hooked a fresh-run salmon or large sea trout. Pressure must be kept on him all the while, only giving line when necessary as he power dives in an attempt to gain his freedom. After the dive, reel into him again and keep up the relentless steady pressure. This is what weakens him, not the strength of the line. After each run, dive or leap, remain tight into him by means of your rod. That's what it's there for: to apply pressure and absorb shocks. Sooner or later, the fish will cease deep dives and long runs, and when you see it tending to surface and turn over on its side, it's about time to reach for the net which you have carefully placed at the ready.

There are many ways of bringing a fish back to life, but most of them happen at this stage! It's a time when I much prefer to keep a low profile and, over the years, have chosen to kneel at the gunwhale of the boat, low down, with the net sunk just under the surface and the fish drawn steadily over it. The net is then raised at the right time and the prize swung aboard.

When the fish lies on its side, close to the boat, since its eyes are different from ours — on the side of its head — it will have fair vision from the uppermost eye and is more likely to see you or your silhouette standing up. When you are kneeling down, I feel it has very much less chance of seeing you or your movements; but, before the loch fills up with potential "Quasimodos", let me state that this is purely a personal habit. It just depends on how many fish you've lost at the net!

Considering it's the first day out on the loch, we've done quite well. When your fish has been admired by all and sundry, the next problem is to debate its eventual fate. I have made it almost a religion that I keep the first two fish for the household, thereafter selling the others to local hotels or the like, but the section "After Capture" will further enlighten.

4
Fly Fishing

I HAVE never known for sure what aspect of loch fly fishing is the most attractive. Is it the solid, surprising thump of a good fish as it takes the fly, just under the surface, or the small deceiving "plop" which erupts into twelve pounds of thrashing silver spray? Could it be that moment of great tension when an 18-pounder — your neat little size 10 fixed into its jaw — glides across to the waiting net? Or is it the cunning aspect of the method, like deer-stalking, as the boat drifts silently, without outboard monotony, across the path of fish you have tried diligently to catch unawares and as clean as a whistle? Most likely, it is a combination of all these factors, plus a few more, which make me state there is *nothing* like fly fishing on a loch and the pleasure derived from the method.

It grieves me to hear claims that fish landed from the boat, on large Scottish salmon rivers, were caught on the *fly*. One reason for

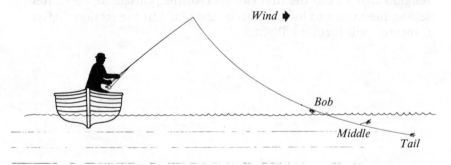

THE FLY

A 22 lb fresh run salmon taken on the bob fly (size 6 Turkey and Gold). Caught off Darroch early one May

my lack of respect for this type of claim was the entry and innocent acceptance of a large salmon in a fly fishing competition. Certainly, the fish took a fly, but it was trolled, or harled, from a boat and its size would have dwarfed many a natural bait. This pseudo-energetic method does not qualify as fly fishing as I understand it because, whatever the bait, the fish was caught in the process of trolling, with the engine for propulsion, and no casting involved whatsoever. I have more respect for those who catch fish on the orthodox troll, with bait or lure, than for those who deviously claim to catch them on the fly, although using the above method.

Casting on an open water from a slowly drifting boat, with engine noise absent, can be a temporary form of peace and tranquillity itself. An interruption, when it comes, is usually the welcome sound

91

of a hooked fish, thrashing on the surface, with the reel sounding its merry accompaniment as the battle begins. Unlike the troll, where the bait has the built-in action, you have to put in a bit more manual effort and work both yourself and the team of flies. All the action is in close-up, and many fish are seen to take, excitingly, only feet from the boat.

The weather will govern when to start with the fly, on the loch, and from year to year there can be a fair difference in the date of the first fish caught. As the weather warms, or should warm, around May, I usually start for short periods when conditions seem good and sometimes revert to the troll, sporadically, as they deteriorate to normal!

I have started very early, on mild years, with the loch a good level, fishing size 4s, slow and deep, and caught fish. When starting early, mid-April say, you don't expect to see the rise, yet quite often it's the bob fly that works, all against what you thought.

The maps show, roughly, the main fly drifts. Whereas, some years ago, it was generally accepted that the Endrick Bank would provide the first fly-caught fish of the year, quite often nowadays it's an island or rocky shore fish which starts the "game" off. But the bank will, more often than not, be holding the "springers".

In bygone days, the Endrick Bank was sacred to a dedicated group of fly fishers, and a beautiful sight to behold was that of expertly-rowed boats proceeding out from Balmaha, well spaced, and cheerful, chatty groups fishing the twisting lanes of the bank from shallow to deep, the whole affair being conducted in an orderly way. Catches then are now legend and the Regular Brigade have long ere broken up, apart from an odd few in the high summer.

It is most difficult to fish the bank when the wind blows straight into, or out from, the grassy shore — especially when out alone. Only a few I know, and one in particular, can make the best of it solo. A few slow pulls at one oar and then the other, keeping in the right depth and casting continually. It is a pleasure to watch, and the fish caught in the process are well earned indeed.

Since not so many enjoy, or choose, this method of fishing the bank, it is not altogether surprising, then, to find that the earliest and most of the fly-caught fish come from alternative drifts. The islands and shores are more easily drifted and two can fish from the boat at the same time.

* * *

92

Faithful Flies

It was not without a great deal of difficulty that I have reduced the "field" of loch flies to the twenty shown in colour Plate 4, opposite page 73. These have one essential feature in common: they have all caught fish. Thankfully, the majority can be readily obtained or, if you have started your angling career wisely, they can be tied with little difficulty at home.

If the flies shown are viewed from top to bottom, in rows, we will start with the left row with brief descriptions and notes of where I have found they fish best on the cast. I always fish three flies to the cast, equally spaced, with the bob fly — the uppermost nearest the surface — and the middle tied to the nylon on fairly short "droppers" about 3in long, secured by a half blood knot, well moistened before being pulled tight. The tail fly is secured by a turle knot, which is favourable in that the nylon extends in a straight line through the eye of the hook, the fly then not being prone to fishing upside down or on its side. At all times I try to tie in the top two flies so that they sit straight and do not come in, when being retrieved through the water, side on or back to front. How much it matters I'll never know, because I have been present when fish have been caught

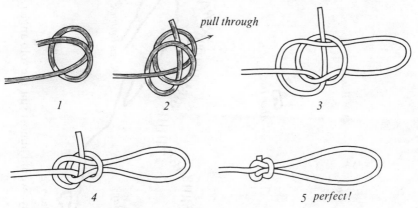

pull through

1   *2*   *3*

4   *5 perfect!*

THE PERFECTION LOOP

There are many good loop knots, but many suffer from slight imperfections inasmuch as they tend to form kinks and do not run in a straight line with the leader. The knot with least faults forms the aptly-named Perfection Loop. I have used it constantly, without disaster, and it is extremely quick and easy to tie.

93

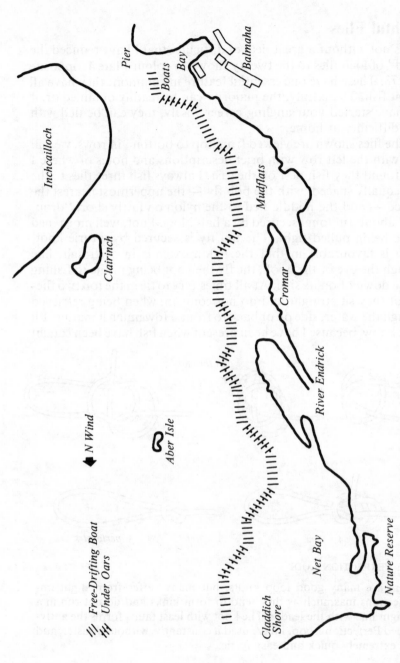

Comparatively easy: would almost suit the solo angler. The drift is the same when the wind is in the opposite direction.

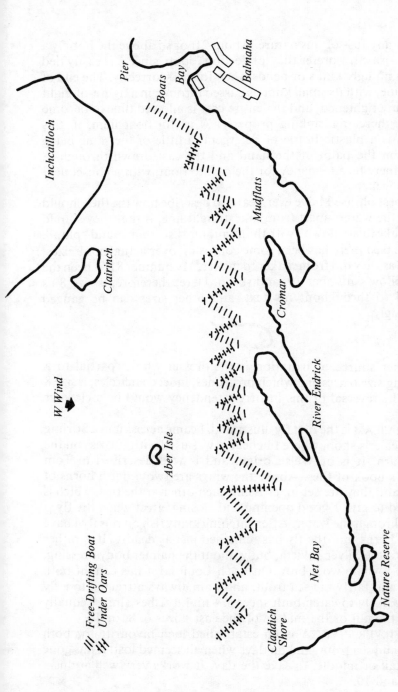

This is difficult when the wind is from the west (or east) and a number of short drifts have to be made. It is essential that one person works the oars while the other(s) do the fishing.

without any fuss of this nature. About 2 ft or so above the bob fly a loop is formed. I prefer the "perfection" loop, since it is easily tied and has no ugly kinks or bends when formed correctly. The end of the fly line, with its small knot, is passed through in a figure-of-eight knot, duly tightened, and the entire cast is allowed time to become soaked, thereafter sinking properly. A useful boat item, in this respect, is a plastic bottle of detergent, a little of the same being placed on the palm of the hand and the cast drawn through it, should there be a tendency for the cast to float, with a consequent tell-tale wake.

The best phrase I have ever heard to describe how the flies should land in the water, apart from in a straight line, is that they should "alight like thistledown" with the minimum disturbance and "plop".

In the past there has been some confusion over actual hook sizes, varying as they did from maker to maker. My number 8 has been the other fellow's number 10, and so on. Here, therefore, is size 8 as referred to throughout my text, and other sizes can be gauged accordingly.

Another source of irritation is the dresser who is partial to a straggling size 6 dressing which protrudes, indeed encircles, a size 8 hook. The reversal of this incorrect tendency would be a cleverer fault!

The HASLAM is the first fly illustrated. I came across it in a Stirling tackle dealer's shop, where I believe it was used with success on the River Earn. It is of Welsh origin and is well described in Tom Stewart's book of flies. Above the wings are two longish horns of macaw and they are set in, crossing each other at the tips, which is supposed to give a good opening and closing effect when the fly is drawn through the water. After catching many fish on this fly I have lost the horns, but the fly has remained just as deadly. It is rather similar to the Silver Invicta, but without the palmer body dressing, and has a white wool butt. On Loch Lomond it has caught both salmon and fairly big sea trout, and I am always attracted to a fly which is likely to catch both species. I find it fishes almost equally well on the tail or the middle of the cast. Sizes 6, 8, or 10.

The SILVER INVICTA is an established loch favourite for both salmon and sea trout, and on days when all seemed lost, it has gone on the tail or middle, to save the day. It works very well at dusk. Sizes 8 and 10.

TURKEY AND SILVER, another dual-purpose killer, can fish on any position on the cast, but I have a preference for the bob. The inventor and user supreme of turkey-winged flies was Mr Ian Wood, who had the gold-bodied version named after some of his fabulous catches on the loch. He stated a dislike for silver-bodied flies, feeling they were rather "cold" in appearance compared to gold. There may be days when this is so, but I find the difference nowadays negligible and am equally happy with gold or silver. I think, but cannot prove, that sea trout slightly prefer the silver. Sizes 8 and 10.

TURKEY AND GOLD, as stated above, is probably unique to Loch Lomond and I have shown it to anglers on other waters who have never heard of it. It is an extremely simple fly, which may be the basic secret of its success. The tail shown is a few tippets, but I prefer a few golden pheasant whisks. I like the type of ribbing on both the silver and gold bodies shown, being fairly broad, with nice effect. Sizes 6, 8 and 10.

Top of the second row comes the ever-popular BUTCHER, obtainable almost everywhere. I prefer it on the tail or bob. Always a good standby, it is a double duty performer on the loch. Sizes 8 and 10.

TURKEY AND MIXED is shown in the fully-dressed salmon version, size 6, but apart from early fishing on the bank, is more often fished in the smaller sizes of 8 and 10. For some reason, unlike some others, I find it best on the middle of the cast. This particular fly is nicely dressed within the hook, the proportions being neat and not straying beyond the hook bend. The most obvious projection is the hook itself, as it should be, making the fish mouth *it*, and not the dressing. With all turkey-winged flies, new ones can be split up with a pin or another fly hook, which opens up the wing fibres and gives better action in the still waters of a loch.

WOODCOCK AND MIXED to me is a grown-up trout fly, which I have found to my liking, and which has proved attractive to sea trout and to the odd salmon. I recall getting three sea trout on the trot with this fly, in the briefest of times, as if it was the only fly in the world. With 7lb nylon, in sizes 8 and 10, it is always very well seen.

Many fish go for a BURTON! Here is one of the very best and the dressing is exactly as I like it, but seldom see it. Dressed as shown, it has excellent entry. Note the streamlined effect of the wings, as they lie almost parallel to the body, and the piece of barred teal inserted between the cinnamon-coloured wings. I believe *these* to be the correct body colours, starting at the head: light blue, red and yellow. The hackle should be soft *hen*. Very definitely, with me, a tail fly. Due to its compact slim dressing, it sinks well, which must assist its success. On the tail, over the years, I have killed a great many salmon and sea trout, and in size 6 at that. I am especially fond of this great loch favourite, perhaps as it has caught me the biggest salmon of my lot and a few large sea trout too. Sizes 6, 8 and 10.

The INVICTA is extremely well-known and has met a lot of our loch fish, who were none too pleased at the method of introduction. On the tail for me, sometimes the middle. In the former position it caught me a 10¼ lb "Ballantine" sea trout, as described in Chapter 6, and I very much like the barred pheasant wing on the one shown. Some loch anglers, including myself, would feel almost naked without this palmer-bodied fly in the box. Sizes 6, 8 and 10.

MALLARD AND RED, on the middle or tail, has had some very good days for me, for some unknown reason with more success at the top end of the loch. Sparsely dressed, with the ribbing clearly showing through the seal's fur body, it possibly attracts more sea trout than salmon. Size 6 occasionally, 8 and 10 mostly.

PETER ROSS is one of the most useful flies ever. I had an elderly, but keen, angler out with me in 1977, and as we drifted Inchmurrin I noticed how much faster he drew his flies in, compared to my own. Too fast, I thought, and was unwisely about to say so when a faster 3 lb sea trout slashed at his Peter Ross, on the bob, and the pliers were needed to free the hook. I don't fish it a lot, but many boats do and it catches fish on the loch, which is the best reason for including it in my top twenty. Sizes 8 and 10.

The BLOODY BUTCHER was on the bob one morning, a few years ago, as the boat drifted over the north-west point of Inchfad. The sun shone relentlessly into *my* eyes, but *not the fish's*, for an 18-pounder sailed up and took the fly away beautifully. I fish it on the bob only and hesitate before saying in sunny conditions only. There were other days, not so sunny, when sea trout — very fresh at that — took it freely. I have plenty of other flies for the middle and tail. Sizes 8 and 10.

Not too well known is the DARK MACKEREL, so I introduce it with pleasure. It seems better known in the Edinburgh area, perhaps partly due to the fact that Messrs Dicksons, the tackle people, have a main branch there. The shop in Royal Exchange Square, Glasgow, has supplied me over the years and I, in turn, have supplied them with tales of success and frustration. I find it works best when retrieved almost "sink and draw", with its ample body hackling opening and closing. Many jaws have closed upon it, always sea trout, but to double figures. To some flies, on the bob or middle, fish rise almost gently or leisurely. When I have fished it, the rises have been almost shockingly savage. When it is good, it is very good, and I tend to use it most when bad light exists and it trails a nice wake on the dropper. Nevertheless, it seems to be urgently required just under the surface as well. Size 6 only occasionally, 8 and 10 mostly.

MALLARD AND YELLOW joins with the Turkey and Gold in popularity and I feel its greatest asset is that it is fairly easily seen in most light conditions. Like a few other flies, it can be either sparsely or heavily dressed, depending on the conditions. It is one fly with which I have caught fish on all three cast positions, fished fast or slow, but I would settle for the bob. Simple, and easy to dress, with yellow seal's fur body and furnace hackle.

I had never seen this CLARET AND BLUE in my life until I produced it, many seasons ago, from the depths of *my own fly box*. How it got there and where it came from entirely escapes me, but it has caught many fish, usually on the middle position on the cast, but occasionally on the tail. I think it is a very much simplified version of an Irish salmon fly, with the materials switched around a bit. It fishes well off our "Ireland" and district, and I have given many to friends who have likewise been pleased with it, on certain dour days. Sizes 8 and 10.

The "BLUE LABEL" — yes *blue*! I think I have stolen this simple pattern from the well-known Black Pennel and it must be good since I omit the black version in its favour. To date I have not hooked a salmon on it, but have risen a few. The reverse is the case with sea trout. Fished on the bob — nowhere else — I have had good success with it over the past few seasons. I used silk and wool for the early attempts but, like most flies, it seems better dressed with fairly light blue seal's fur, with broad silver ribbing. The generous spider hackle may be a "carry over" from my many dapping experiments but, no matter, I have found it extremely good when the light is bad and steel-blue. Sometimes 6, mostly 8; I have not tried 10.

Some years ago I handed what I call the ORANGEMAN to a fellow angler in the bay, who had immediate success with it. It is, of course, the Invicta, with an orange palmer body hackle. This is the fly which caused very odd behaviour in certain sea trout, when they left the water to take it on re-entry as it moved along in the middle of the cast. I accepted that it only caught sea trout until one night I came in with four fish, the biggest 8½ lb. "Sea Trout," I said to the late Alec MacFarlane. "Salmon," he replied. I can now say it catches sea trout most of the time, but has caught salmon once!

Another experiment is the TURKEY AND GREEN. The body is *pale* green with silver ribbing. Extremely simple to tie, with seal's fur body, it caught salmon and sea trout in 1978 and I am wondering, so good was the fishing, if it was merely a flash in the pan. Size 8 so far.

TURKEY AND GOLD OR SILVER WITH ORANGE HACKLE fishes well in bright conditions, something like the Dunkeld at the back-end. A flasher-type fly, like the one following, for the bob, it can be fished steady but fairly fast, attracting salmon and sea trout alike. The only problem I foresee concerns turkey-winged flies in general. The material is getting more and more expensive and the right type harder to obtain. I prefer, by far, the wings with a sheen to them and the white tips, in fact, grey. This may seem over fussy, but I must admit these fads get so deep-rooted that if I go against them my confidence ebbs to such a low level that my chin soon rests on my lap. All is lost . . . Sometimes, it's "to heck" with the fish, this is what *I* want them to have and up goes the confidence, so absolutely vital in this great game we play. Sizes 6, 8 and 10.

The KINGFISHER BUTCHER is a "steal" from our trout-fishing friends and, fished on the bob, gets similar results to the Turkey and Gold just described. Most certainly, if I were a trout angler most of the time, and had to reach the loch shores with only trout flies in my box, I would mount the following cast for Loch Lomond, preferably when sunny — bob: Kingfisher Butcher; middle: Woodcock and Mixed; tail: Peter Ross or Grouse and Claret. The inclusion of the last makes my list twenty-one, but the Mallard and Red is so similar I am not too concerned.

I know there will be clamourings over omissions from my Top Twenty and I will have to agree there are other flies well worthy of inclusion. But I have attempted to pick tried and tested killers with a contrast in the range. I reckon, so armed, Loch Lomond can be tackled with confidence in the knowledge that if the response is poor it's not the fault of the flies. It's the hundred and one other reasons!

One item I'm certain I'll have to purchase sooner or later is "Magnifly Specs", made by Dermot Wilson, Nether Wallop Mill, Stockbridge, Hants. I have tried them and find their benefits immense, especially when afloat and in times of crisis. They are half specs and purely magnifying, not being optically corrected. The eye of your size 8 or 10 fly becomes like an anchor ring and fine nylon looks like heavy hawser rope. The advantages are obvious. Regrettably, they are not cheap, but I reckon that to change or tie a fly with their assistance might just result in a 15 pounder, and the proceeds from this would more than justify the cost.

Fur and Feather: Tying your own

I would encourage anyone starting out on the great sport of angling to learn the art of fly tying. Attending classes under professional instruction can have enormous benefits: not only can one create one's own concoctions, or variants, but money and time can be well saved in the end by getting just what you want, and speedily into the bargain. (I have, in the past, tied a few very simple things when becalmed!)

Most tackle shops will be able to supply from the plates shown, but continual browsing through catalogues has revealed to me gigantic changes in wing and body materials now available. Synthetics, furs from funny wee animals from abroad and polythene all give added glow and effect if used properly. Certainly, I no longer curse our black labrador for casting his coat. I follow him — gladly!

Apart from dealers listed who have given really good service, I would like to make mention of two tiers who have excelled in their style and service.

Geoff Franks of Bromsgrove, Worcs., will copy any pattern or tie to specific requirements. He also has an excellent range of sea trout and salmon flies, neatly produced and reasonably priced.

Irish flies, like their loughs, have much in common with our own, and I have recently had much pleasure in dealing with Mr Robert McHaffie of Limavady, Co. Londonderry, who has a quite beautiful style of his own, especially I would say with shrimp-type river salmon flies. He is an artist with dyes and the effects he achieves are both efficient and attractive.

I hope to explore this vast subject at the greater length it deserves in a future book, but meantime learn the art, keep up to date with modern materials and substitutes and don't worry too much about the multiplicity of materials used by our predecessors. Even they would tell us that, in loch fishing anyway, they were better flies when almost chewed to death!

Rods and Casts

Recommending fly rods is risky. I am very often asked what the ideal rod is for fly fishing on Loch Lomond. In no way wishing to be evasive, I can only say it is very difficult to be specific. I might, for example, advise a rod of 14 ft, which seems light to me, only to find that someone has been inflicted with a weapon for which he will need an assistant, afloat. Not too handy. Likewise, a 10 ft lightweight wand may end up with a bionic he-man who will snap it with his first cast. Not too convenient.

How do I know who I am advising? We all have different tastes in most things, and rods are no exception. The guidelines I set down, therefore, apply to myself — a man of normal build, possessed of average strength, but with a strong dedication to the long rod. Compare, if you can, a 14ft greenheart (beautiful material) with a glass or carbon (!) tool of today's making. Weightwise, we've come a long way. I see women wielding rods of the latter type when it would have taken them all their time to carry the former to the boat.

Fly rods *don't* catch fish. What's on the end of them *does*. *Both* ends! The rod plays its vital part, of course, and a good one should blend into the user's ways. Like a sound marriage, the union of the angler with his rod should be a happy affair, each complementing the other to the full, and the partnership should bring about rewarding results.

The rod, then, should present the cast well and not leave the back nearly broken after the long sessions of casting it will have to cope with on Loch Lomond.

I don't (or hardly) notice the rods now, since they satisfy my requirements, physique and temperament. When others handle them they might be too stiff, too long, or too heavy. In turn, I often find the rods of others too short, too springy or too heavy. Sometimes, they can feel "dead". No matter the power of the rod, a feeling of life must flow through its joints, so that the same life doesn't flow out of yours!

Since, in loch fishing, there is no great length of line out beyond the top ring, the combination I find best includes lightness with power, and a tip section that doesn't tremble for minutes on end after a mere tweak. The first foot or so of the tip section gets the earliest message from the fish, and for years I have erred on the side of stiffness at the tip. There can be plenty of suppleness lower down, to give the old-fashioned pleasures of casting with only a fraction of the weight our predecessors enjoyed.

We are a lucky lot today, in that never have so many first-class rods abounded, to give us the widest possible choice. Choose well, and you will have a friend for life. Without implying disrespect to other makers of good rods, I would mention having witnessed, almost from the start, the steady development of advanced techniques by the firm Bruce & Walker. I am still using one of their earliest glass rods, which has suffered ample abuse aboard my bucking loch boat but remains willing to face yet more. When Mr James Bruce and Mr Walker visited Glasgow some years ago I spoke with them and became convinced that their patient research would benefit anglers to the full, resulting in the production of rods carefully suited to their task. There are several Glasgow tackle dealers who stock this range, and also other makes of cane, glass fibre and carbon rods.

As a "stop press" item here I might mention the recent introduction of Shakespeare's Ugly Stik fly rods. I am particularly impressed with the 14 ft rod, its most unusual (and desirable) feature being that the tip is made of about 6 in of solid glass incorporated into the carbon and fibreglass structure. "Ugly Stik" perhaps; personally I find it a most beautiful wand!

Fish are, of course, regularly caught on short fly rods, usually of enough power to subdue the average salmon, and you cannot argue with results. Many fish them standing up in the boat, which makes the rod "longer". For myself, I have always favoured a longer rod, no less than 11 ft.

When fibreglass first came on the scene, I was already in the queue to try out the longer rods on the loch, but found the early models much too springy in the tip section for sound short-range hooking. I reverted to my Sharpe's Spliced 12 ft, but soon found a few makers in glass who gave me the top section strength which I favour. As a result, I am happy with glass rods for the job now, but my Bank Manager is distressed to learn of my more-than-passing interest in carbon fibre. They *must* come down in price!

Being born lazy, I prefer a seated position in the boat, and usually only stand up to ease weary muscles or in the early part of playing a fish, and when netting. To complete the latter operation, I then kneel — as if praying — which is, in fact, what I'm doing.

Here I should like to slip in a wee remark about nets. They should be long-handled, strong, light and as big as possible. Try to avoid a bright orange mesh, as nothing will bring a "dead" fish back to life quicker than a mass of orange thrust at him from the side of the boat. Likewise, I don't think orange, anti-fouled boat bottoms are the best camouflage in the world, especially in fickle conditions.

Having got the rod right, the cast will have to suit its length. Netting a fish is easier with a short rod, unless your cast is too long and the knot between nylon and the main line has to pass within the top ring. A sudden dive by the fish will prove the point.

About 11 or 12 lb nylon should land any salmon you encounter

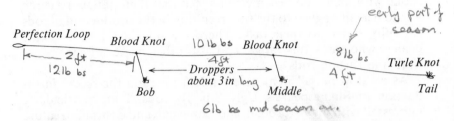

Perfection Loop   Blood Knot   10 lb bs   Blood Knot   8 lb bs   Turle Knot
2 ft   4 ft   early part of season
12 lb bs   ← Droppers → about 3 in long   4 ft.   Tail
Bob   Middle   Tail

6 lb bs mid season on.

Three-Fly loch cast: overall length is governed by the length of the rod; for a 12ft rod, say, a cast of 10ft would be about right. An average Loch Lomond cast would be about 10lb breaking strain nylon, although many prefer to taper from 12 (at loop to bob fly) to 10 (from bob to middle) to about 8 (from middle to tail). Blood knots should be well moistened before pulling tight. The average dropper length is 3-4 in. The stiffest nylon for making droppers stand out is "Tynex", available from Tom C. Saville, but this needs extra special care in knotting.

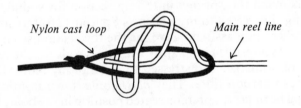

Nylon cast loop   Main reel line

There are many knots for securing the end of the fly line to the cast loop, but many disturb the "flow" at this junction by causing kinks and angular bends. I have used the above knot for years without disaster. The end of the fly line will lie parallel to the cast when tightened.

early on, but there seems to be a case for going down to, say, 7lb strength from mid-season onwards. Since our respective rod curves can vary so much, it will be up to you to pick the correct nylon to suit. I have gone through an entire season using 10lb nylon only, both for salmon and sea trout, but I now *know* there have been occasions when a change down would have hooked more fish on the tail. One example was when a tail fly I was using attracted the fish to the exclusion of the other two. It was size 6, so I changed to size 8 still in the same pattern, but a newer fly. No joy ensued and I then reduced the tail section of the cast to 7 lb nylon and put on the original size 6. Mismatching, you might think, but a 9¼ lb sea trout did not agree. I have tended to taper the cast at certain times when fish are fussy and much fished over.

I suppose if you tried really hard you could find a rank bad fly rod. Such is our good fortune nowadays, it should be harder to find than in days of yore. The main problem is to pick from amongst the multitude of extremely well made (and sometimes expensive) rods, one which will suit the job.

For Loch Lomond, and waters like it, the rod should be chosen with care, which is easier said than done. Anglers seem to suffer a similar dilemma to golfers, as they select or change their clubs. I well recall swinging many a club in a shop or showroom, feeling there and then that the magic formula had been found. Next day, with ever-changing muscular conditions, they would feel entirely wrong, either too light or too stiff or heavy. Like a golf club, the rod will be swung many times in the course of a day's sport. It should never swing you.

I personally have looked for the length and light weight first, keeping in mind that only a short line will be cast beyond the top ring, so that I take little heed of the line recommendations, which will disappoint makers no doubt, but I still buy the rod! It makes a great deal of sense, if one does not intend to fish lochs all season, to get advice on a single weapon which will suit both the river you will fish mostly, and the loch less often. In my own case, I'm so utterly fussy that the rod suits my loch ways that it will one day become a problem finding a river anywhere in the country where my cherished weapon can serve!

I tend to suit the rod more to the line I prefer for loch fishing (which is fairly light) rather than vice versa, and for many years used a light level line (too light for many), until the benefits of modern dressed lines came along.

With everything well balanced (or, as some would have it, entirely unbalanced) it is time to put the rod and reel to good use.

Reels

When I look at fly reels and their relatively simple mechanism, I often wonder at their cost. Compared to multiplying reels, their "works" are at once obvious, and yet one can often pay a lot more for the straightforward-looking fly reel. I have no axe to grind, however, and assume it is due to fine tolerances and the material used. A good fly reel should last a lifetime, though, and who would decline a gift of one of the best makes available? A good check is important, with a fair range of tensions, and it should be carefully set so that the average fish — if there is such a thing on Loch Lomond — can take line with slight restriction and not permit loops of line to flop out of the spool and cause an overrun. Having mentioned the word, I shall recall an incident which, due to certain acquaintances, I am seldom allowed to forget.

Three in a boat, we were attempting to fish, without wind, up the loch opposite Tarbet. We found this difficult. Much chatter and debating followed, but I finally persuaded the helmsman to head down the loch and we arrived at the Ross Point in as fine a little wind as you could wish for. Three rods were being fished, from time to time, but mostly two, as the middle angler corrected the boat with the oars. I hooked a brown trout of 1 lb almost at once and resumed casting as we drifted into the shallows of the inner Ross Isle.

I made what appeared to be one of the last casts, due to the shallow depth, and no sooner had the flies landed when I felt a tug and tightening. A salmon of easily 16 lb, and a bar of proverbial silver, crashed out of the water. When he re-entered, it was found that the other angler in the bow was attached to it also! The speed of the entire affair had caused his flies to delay in the water, when they are normally removed at once, and the frenzied fish hurtled itself, in three staggering leaps, away to the side of the boat. Rarely have I seen a fish act so quickly.

The cast which had hooked the fish remained on, but as the fish made one — I don't know which one — of its leaps, the other cast broke. Fair's fair!

Although I was still strongly into the "cratur", terrible damage had been done in a very short space of time. The combination of leaps and lines, with the slight hesitations, caused a belly of line to shoot out of my fly reel and, as it jammed, the rod buckled over too much for comfort.

"Start the engine", I yelled, "and follow him quick — everywhere!" There was a slight respite, but a quick look at the reel confirmed the worst. The line was seized solid, with several layers very tightly entwined. I again urged the helmsman to follow the beast everywhere he wanted to go, and for a time it worked, although the rod was taking some violent jolts.

What we did *not* need then suddenly appeared round the tip of the

Sea trout are fairly hard to hold up by the tail – hence the reversed grip. This 8³⁄₄lb trout took the fly and won three bottles of Ballantine's whisky. The Long Point, off Inchmoan

wee island, and headed over to our extremely busy bit of water — three youngsters, in a far too small rubber dingy!

Perhaps, in a way, it was a relief because all of us now had a reasonable chance to blame others. The engine of our boat stopped but the fish didn't and, pulling the rod over to its fullest extent, I awaited my first experience of a fish "breaking" me when there was nothing I could do about it. To free him thus was pathetic... but it was all the kids' fault!

A fair wind blew up and we towed them over to the shore, near Inverbeg, making sure en route that they didn't know too much about fishing and the catastrophe preceding their arrival.

I was left with the bob fly and the break was about a foot below it. The knots had held but the nylon was severed as if by scissors. The temptation was to blame reel tension being set too slack. Perhaps it was. Suffice it to say that I have fished with it ever since, without disaster, although for some odd reason I now appear to double check this point as soon as a fish arrives.

Remember, when fishing two in the boat, that you should remove your flies out of your partner's way just as soon as you realise he has hooked something. He, himself, may be unable to speak!

A good fly reel need not cost the earth. There are many splendid reels available today, some with the invaluable asset of "rim control" (a means of "braking" the outgoing line by finger pressure on an exposed, revolving flange. I still use a modestly priced Intrepid Rimfly for river fishing and it has performed faultlessly over many years.

A good loch reel should have an adequate "check" with a broad range of pressures. Good line and backing capacity is also vital (do not wait for a day of disaster to prove this!) Fly fishing the Pilot Bank one day, I hooked a $5\frac{1}{2}$ lb sea trout which sizzled off to Luss at a great rate of knots, taking the main line and 150 yd of backing with it. Luckily it stopped literally dead and was arrested for streaking, leaving me with only a few turns of backing on the spool and an aching wrist. Just a *few inches* of backing had saved the day!

The Speedex, Beaulite and Supercondex reels made by the Shakespeare Company are very popular, other good makes being Daiwa, Farlows, Mitchell, Berkley and the renowned Hardy series. Multiplying fly reels and the more expensive magnesium and carbon fibre reels (both extremely lightweight) are now available at most tackle shops for those who aspire to owning nothing but the best.

Basically, a narrow drum, lightweight reel, sound "check" and line capacity of no less than 200 yd, are ideal, rim control being an added bonus.

Technique

The beauty of fly fishing from a drifting loch boat is the extremely close contact you have with the hooked fish, both visually and physically.

There is no need to fish a long line and, if there were, a lot of the fun and excitement would be removed, as far as I am concerned. There is usually a time lag on the river with the line, or part of it, being sunk. Quite often a fish can hook itself and not be seen for a while. Granted, this *can* happen on a loch, but less frequently.

The fish which leaps clear of the water, the instant he is hooked, is the one to watch out for. He is more likely to leave you quickly than the fish which dives slowly and deep. Give me the fish which takes your fly and, when you tighten, is a bit puzzled. This momentary delay is enough for you to remain smoothly tight and usually all goes well.

When I started fishing, there seemed to be much advice given about what to do when a fish leapt. After too many years of practice I know what to do now — hope!

Authors would urge you to "lower the tip of the rod" when a fish leapt or "dip the rod at once" to avoid a break. It's all very well reading and writing this kind of advice but no-one has ever explained to me why it is necessary *all the time*. Had I carried out the instructions, as issued, I dare say I'd be out on the loch yet, bending up and down like an eternal puppet!

The object is not to give any more slack than is necessary. I agree that the rod should be dipped slightly when a fish runs and leaps *away* from you at high speed. But I think this is, or should be, an automatic function, and you might be better engaged having short, quick looks at the line on the reel to see that all remains well. When the fish leaps *towards* you, why should you dip the rod? He will have given you slack and this should be recovered at once, and the rod curve restored.

The art of hooking fish which do not intend to hook themselves cannot be dealt with by way of words alone. No, that would be too easy and we would catch every fish we interested. I'm afraid no matter what I write, the bitter pill of experience and many lost fish will teach you much more. Lose some, but learn in the process. Never will you do it all right and neither will the fish.

It's all very well reading books and all this and that about "strike quick" or "see the tail of the fish away". If you're learning and at all human, you'll react all wrong, but still manage a fish or two. I'm certain too much has been written about hooking techniques, to no avail, because the learner forgets the information the instant a fish rises. With no wish at all to depress anyone just starting — since they are possibly more likely to soundly hook a large salmon on the fly — I would say it takes a wee while and many misses to get a good percentage of the fish risen. More so, on the dap.

The more simple takes can be mastered early, such as when your cast rises slightly from the water surface, as a fish takes the middle or tail fly, without the angler feeling a thing. Tighten smoothly, but firmly, and usually you see the customer right away. *Keep* everything tight.

109

There is one word I cannot abide — and it's usually in capitals — STRIKE. Whispered, gasped or shrieked, this word has no place in my angling vocabulary. It is intended, I believe, to jolt the angler into action of some sort when a fish rises to his fly. It is usually uttered loudly by an envious boat crony or bored gillie and often brings about a result opposite to the one desired.

Since the fly rod will possibly be moving slowly backwards as the flies are retrieved, I believe that — most of the time — any word which brings about a jerk will not improve the hooking chances. The word "strike" assumes that the rod is still, whereas it is *moving*, and the quickest way to hook the fish would appear to be to continue the backward movement, at the same time pulling down line with the free hand and tightening into the fish. Everything then must remain firmly tight, only yielding to the first mad rush or leap from the fish. It should certainly be a fastish movement, but performed smoothly and firmly. After feeling the fish is well attached to the fly I personally carry out a swift visual check that all is well at the reel, with no loose coils about to cause a jam or an overrun.

A bit more excusable is the rarely seen technique of "striking down". I once shared a boat with a lover of the long rod, like myself, who had mastered this method to perfection. It calls for good nerve and much practice, and I am long ere resigned to the fact that my own method suits me best. When this angler felt a touch at his fly he flicked the tip of the rod downwards, *towards* the fish, with a slight but well controlled movement of the wrist only, thereby giving the fish freedom to turn away with the fly before he arched the rod back in a final tightening. It is most impressive to watch, but the real problem is where to practise!

A most awkward rise is one you don't see too often, but one day I had it three times. Had the rises been more spaced out, timewise, I'd probably have missed all three. As it was, I got two through lingering on my first failure enough to alert me to the answer. This rise is when a fish, usually a sea trout, completely leaves the water, at your cast, intending to take a fly mouth first on re-entering the water. It is very exciting and spectacular. The trick is to credit the fish with good aim and continue to slowly move the flies, without any jerk, and when he submerges and you feel him, tighten. The common mistake is to assume that the fish has nothing to do with you, jumping like that! What I have never heard explained too well is *why* the fish takes the fly the hard way. I often think it's because

110

he's frightened he'll miss it sub-surface and realises the fly will linger on the surface, hatching, when the odds are better he'll get it. One thing is for certain, he sure wants it!

Large fish can and do rise slowly, but not as slowly as we think. It is their very size that creates the illusion, but it pays to stay your hand and wait until you feel or see the nylon tighten. With this kind of rise, you have to steel yourself to err on the slow side when tightening.

I turn down many an offer to fish for trout — not because I don't like trout fishing, but, truth to tell, I'd be too afraid of my confused reactions to their very fast rises. I can get mixed up enough with our loch salmon and sea trout rises to the fly and the dap.

Generally, the smaller class of sea trout can come out of nowhere, at great speed, and often hook themselves, or only need a slight tightening to stop their ideas short.

Non-taking fish are a real nuisance. I'm referring to stale, dis-interested non-takers, not fish which could be caught by changing down the fly size or nylon strength. No, I mean the ones you can actually see, rising with closed mouths *near* your flies, or the big, slow and sluggish ring which appears on the surface as the fish drops back and sinks under the flies.

I recall two of us fishing above Ross Isles and I think there were three fish in the boat when we reached the north-east tip of Inchlonaig, late one August. I had the dap going, and my partner, the fly. We rose some *eighteen* fish or more, between us, over the sandy, weedy area which has a lone boulder on the shore. Not one of them took, nor intended to take. We raced across to the mainland to pick up a friend at 6 p.m., quickly collected him and sped back to the spot, filling his ears en route with the prospect of a mammoth catch, even yet. The friend caught a finnock of ¾ lb. The big fish had stopped playing!

I can promise you one thing. There is no magic fly which will ensure 100% success. I'm glad there isn't. Just think of all the people who would go out of business and how monotonous our fly boxes would look. There is, however, a small range of flies which seem to work well enough on Loch Lomond.

Fish are killed on some days on a big variety of flies. I once joined two boats ashore for a "drum-up", at the end of a great day's fishing. I was out alone, one boat had two anglers and a gillie and the other boat two anglers. We had all fished the fly, three each on the casts, giving a total of fifteen flies amongst us. They were all

111

A 12 lb salmon, taken with a spliced cane rod, held aloft by the author's son

different patterns, and I seemed to be fishing a bit bigger, but each of the fifteen flies had caught fish. They were very fresh fish and many conclusions can be drawn from this.

A turkey-winged. fly has always done well on the loch: good examples are Turkey and Gold or Silver, and Turkey and Mixed, and recently I had several fish, including salmon, on a Turkey and Green, size 8. The seal fur body was light green with fine silver ribbing.

It was a well-kent angler of yesteryear, the late Mr Ian Wood, who

112

imprinted the pattern of Turkey and Gold on envious anglers at the time. This fly was dressed for him in Glasgow and was named the *Ian Wood* in recognition of his fabulous catches on the loch: one day 7 salmon to 77½ lb, and a few days later 5 to 67 lb, in 1952, and many more of great merit.

I knew Ian slightly when I was a lot younger and worked in the *Scottish Daily Express* and he had a trusty life-long friend in Robert McLean, his boatman superb, at Balmaha. Ian "resigned" from the loch and was Editor of *Trout and Salmon* for many years, eventually retiring to a remote cottage in the Conon/Blackwater district, where he spent his last days. Sadly, the redoubtable Bobby McLean also died recently, shortly after returning to his beloved Balmaha.

Turkey-winged flies work well in the water but, funnily enough, hair-winged flies do not work at all — for me. Maybe I haven't tried them long enough.

Salmon and flies have changed a lot since the Ian Wood era. It seems to me that salmon are now fussier for smaller flies and finer casts. I have noticed some years pass by with hardly any free "head and tail" rises at all and yet 1978 seemed a lot better. Most of my fish were caught on the bob, and many were "head and tail".

In Chapter 5 I mention the importance of the light and the word opaque. Flies in this class could be the ordinary Invicta, Burton, Grouse and Claret or Green, Black Pennel, Dark Mackerel, Turkey and Mixed or Green, Woodcock and Mixed, Pheasant or Mallard and Yellow, Green Highlander and flies of a similar hue.

Flashier flies more easily "lost" in certain light conditions, but excellent in others, are Mallard and Silver, Silver Invicta, the Haslam, the Priest, Peter Ross and many more.

These days I can't find cast room for some of the flies I have accumulated, over many years, and often feel I should throw out many of them. I never do.

Apart from a very few patterns, beware the heavily dressed fly. In general, err on the side of finely-dressed, "skimpy" flies of neat proportions, although there *are* days when the wake of the more heavily dressed fly is needed, and will rise fish, especially when the light is bad.

With salmon patterns, or some good all-rounders, there is one wee thing which I am perhaps too fussy about, since I should know better. I like a tail on them, and have talked myself into such a state of mind that I throw away flies which are minus this small bit of flash which, to me, makes a difference. I have caught fish on tailless

113

flies and don't know where I picked up this eccentric habit. Even a few tippets, as long as the tail is there.

Another point I insist on is that my flies, no matter the pattern, are tied well within the hook, meaning that the foliage does not straggle out of proportion to the hook. Wings, hackle and tail should not extend more than is necessary. Fish are allowed a long look at your flies on the loch, and will pluck at such errors in the dressing without getting hooked.

Finally, a word on approaching good fly drifts. Give them a wide berth, on the deep side, before you join the queue. In a drift, there can be many depth corrections needed, and the quiet use of the oars will not disturb the water much. If you wish to leave a drift, row out and away from it, quietly, before starting the outboard.

The fly can be fished every year right on until the last day in October, and very often your last fish will be a fresh, late-runner. That's the ideal way to end a season and start looking forward to the next.

A Day's Fly Fishing

We have, in the previous chapter, been afforded a sample day out on the loch when the troll was the method. Imagination still at work, but guided as close to reality as possible, it seems only fair we should be allowed the same kind of outing, with flies as the bait. This time, although the trolls may still be in the boat, the cherished fly rod with its team of three flies will lie along the seats of the boat as you set out in what should be much milder weather.

For the first few weeks, I tend to use a mixture of flies, sizes 8 and 6, permutating them in no particular order. I find this tendency to mismatch sizes sometimes a benefit, but wisely — I hope — have left it to the fish to make their final choice.

As you leave Balmaha Bay, an immediate assessment of the wind should be taken, considering carefully the direction — or directions, as often happens — since this will largely determine the likelier drifts to visit first.

As can be seen from the maps, a good few of the larger islands are fairly long drifts and they are at their very best, especially when one is fishing alone, when the wind blows parallel to their shores. This makes for more straightforward drifting, with less need for corrections on the oars. Inchfad, Inchmurrin, Inchcruin and Inchlonaig come into this class.

Difficulties arise when the wind blows onshore, as it does on the

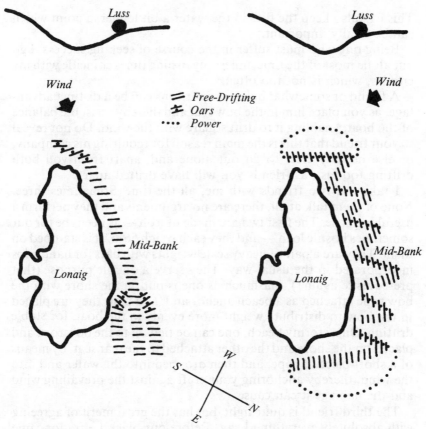

THE FLY

The easiest wind to suit the drifting boat would be the one which blows parallel to the shore in either direction. The first figure shows a wind blowing from a more or less westerly direction. Less correction is obviously required on the oars than when the wind blows onshore, as in the second figure, in which case the island has to be drifted in a series of irregular zig-zags, the boat being moved along like a crab. Because there is less disturbance, Lonaig will fish well over a longer period when the wind is from the west — although, of course, this will always depend on the number of boats in the vicinity, and their behaviour.

Endrick Bank, and it is then that a companion or gillie can greatly assist by fishing the boat in a crab-wise fashion, dropping and lowering you, as you cast, in a long series of "W"s, joined together.

115

This can also keep the flies in the water a bit longer, a point which can be vitally important.

Being one who must suffer in the course of seeking success, I go out alone most of the time, unless my fishing times coincide with my cronies, which is not too often.

A friend of somewhat bulky proportions can be a distinct advantage, as you place him in the bow seat and thereby assist the balance of the boat, enabling it to drift square with the wind. Do not reveal to your friend that this is the main reason for requiring his company, or else he may elect to go out alone and, apart from you both drifting too fast, as friends you will have drifted apart!

I take out two friends with me, all the time. Sometimes three. None of them talk at all, there are no arguments and they perform a useful purpose. The first two are made of iron — as needs be for our sometimes hostile loch — and they each weigh 56 lb. It is stamped on them. They are a pair of heavy scale weights with bars for handgrips incorporated in the usual way. They serve a double purpose (that prerequisite again!), inasmuch as one is put on the shore with the bow rope attached as a beach anchor and, as a pair, they are placed in the bow to distribute weight more evenly in the boat, for stable drifting. On a stormy beach, one can be tied on to the bow rope and placed on the shore and the other attached to the rear seat, by means of a short piece of rope, and then dropped into the water and into the wind, thereby anchoring your craft against the prevailing wind and the damage it can cause.

The third friend is quite light, but has the great merit of agreeing with absolutely everything I say! Before our black Labrador came into the world, my son had his name all ready as I fished the Pilot Bank one day. "If we get a dog, Dad, you should call it Pilot."

"Why?" I asked.

"You're a lucky dog here!" ... (Sometimes!)

We will direct the wind to blow from roughly the south-west today, to suit our solo status, and decide to fish some of the island drifts. It will perhaps be a little too early for Inchmurrin but, if the wind is suitable, we may venture across later on.

First call will be Darroch, the tiny islet off the south-west tip of Inchfad. It can be fished in a series of drifts, using the oars to correct the course of the drifting boat.

I seem to have amassed a multitude of angling mannerisms, some being easily explained, others remaining a mystery to their owner. The very mention of oars reminds me of how much I dislike fishing

116

The tiny outboard and side bracket referred to on page 118

with one oar dangling loosely in its rowlock from the side of the boat facing the casting area of water. When out three-in-a-boat, I still feel most uncomfortable casting when these blessed things disturb the water, no matter how quietly and efficiently it is done. That it bothers only me is very evident and no doubt fish are caught while the boat is being rowed. Friends of mine who fished the tap end of the loch used no other method and as one proudly pointed out the catch, would say, "All on the sidecast." Worst of all, I regard bright yellow or brand new oars a very real threat to your success. When fish are looking for wee size 10 flies, on fine casts, they may be fooled

117

into thinking your boat is but a drifting log. I use the oars on drifts, certainly, but when the depth correction has been made I ship the oar on the danger side. I prefer to fool myself that this is a good habit. Just show the fish your flies — not where they come from!

I carry aboard what many would consider a luxury, in the form of a tiny electric outboard. It is driven off a 6 or 12 V battery and it must be clearly stated that it was never intended for use as a main form of boat propulsion on the loch. Its main, invaluable, asset is SILENCE. A drift should be nursed carefully, yet many fish are disturbed by the thud of feet on floorboards as the angler moves to the oar seat. Noisy rowlocks and the carelss splash of an oar do the rest, and I'm sure it would do us all good if we could actually see the fish scatter in alarm at the strange noises from above.

I am certain that the use of this device has brought me a few extra fish from time to time, reason enough for enduring the incon- venience of both charging the rather heavy battery and then toting it about. To support it, I have a small bracket fashioned out of angle iron and wood bolts through the top side plank, where it is easily reached by the person at the tiller. It must be cautioned, however, that brackets of any sort mounted on the side of a boat should be designed for easy removal after use to obviate being smashed by craft lying alongside.

The tiny motor pivots through 360° and has three slow running speeds. Granted, there are days when big winds prevent much headway, but in fickle conditions I have blessed it often.

The next drift could be from the deeper water off Darroch directly to the tip of Inchfad, on the north-west side, expecting salmon and/or sea trout. The boat should drift across the corner point of Inchfad and the entire northern shore can be drifted to Mrs Leckie- Ewing's stone at the bottom of the island.

Upwind again, the boat can be placed so that the water all round Ireland can be covered. "Have we not strayed a bit?" you may ask. The little rock Ireland lies between Inchfad and Inchcruin and is a very dangerous rocky reef. Avoiding its obvious dangers, try to imperil the fish by fishing all round it.

To get a really long drift, with wind coming from the right direction, proceed some distance to the islet Inchgalbraith. Drift from there, covering the two main and well-known points, the Short and the Long, including every inch of the bays, until you reach the end of Inchcruin, where a very large boulder stands near the end of the shore. This is known as the Ladies Point but, unless it only contains hen fish, I would only be guessing at its derivation.

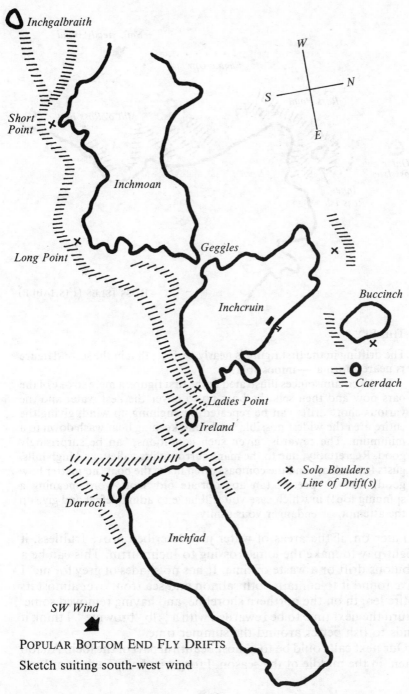

Inchgalbraith

W

S — N

E

Short
Point

Inchmoan

Geggles

Long Point

Buccinch

Inchcruin

Caerdach

Ladies Point

Ireland

✕ *Solo Boulders*
///// *Line of Drift(s)*

Darroch

Inchfad

SW Wind

POPULAR BOTTOM END FLY DRIFTS
Sketch suiting south-west wind

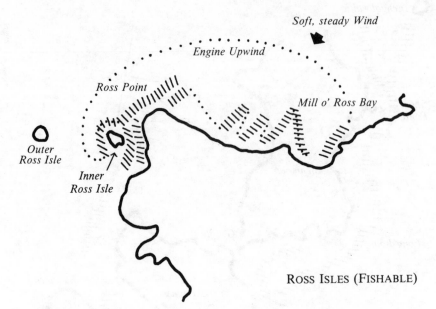

Soft, steady Wind

Engine Upwind

Ross Point

Mill o' Ross Bay

Outer
Ross Isle

Inner
Ross Isle

ROSS ISLES (FISHABLE)

THE FLY

The drifting in the first figure is nearly perfect; that in the second figure
is nearer normal — impossible!

In the circumstances illustrated in the first figure, a mere stroke of the
oars now and then sets the boat up to cover the best water and the
various short drifts can be repeated by engining up wind, giving the
entire area the widest possible berth, and keeping boat wash down to a
minimum. The rewards, given such conditions, can be surprisingly
good. Regrettably, due to the many surrounding valleys and high hills,
gusts from all around the compass often make the boat (no matter how
good) into a "peerie" (an appropriate old Scots word meaning a
spinning top!) in which case you will have to admit defeat and give up
the attempt, or endanger your sanity.

Later on, if the areas of water just described prove fruitless, it
might pay to make the long crossing to Inchmurrin. This can be a
fabulous drift or a waste of time. It has no shades of grey for me. I
have found it to contain both salmon and sea trout over almost its
entire length on the northern shoreline, and having removed some,
return the next time to be rewarded with a ½ lb "brownie". I think it
tends to fish better around the summer time.

Our next call could be to a most beautiful part of the loch. All too
often, in the middle of the season, I forget its halcyon days or have

120

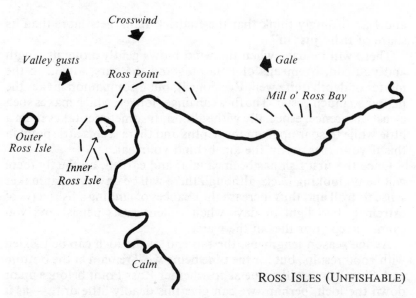

taken down the rod, and curse my thoughtlessness. There is no doubt many, many boats troll round its shore and point, but Strathcashell nearly always has the fish. I recall an incident there, witnessed by my friend in the boat. We had fished the Endrick Bank without result when I suggested Strathcashell. Off we sped and reached the rocky shoreline. On the first very short drift, I hooked a salmon almost up on the shore and the line fairly "sizzled" through the water. I thought the fish would never stop and, to reduce his gusto slightly, placed my right hand across the line, on the cork butt. There may be no smoke without fire but it was some weeks before the burn mark disappeared! The fish weighed exactly 12 lb and took a size 6 Thunder and Lightning on the tail, on the first week in June. A few moments later, at the end of the rocks, another fish took the tail fly, but he didn't return it. The cast was broken just above the knot, proof of my complete carelessness in failing to renew the knot. I seldom do, and admit it.

The entire Sallochy shoreline is fishable but, like the Endrick Bank, it will very rarely suit the angler out alone.

Inchlonaig lies north-west of Strathcashell, and its northern shore fishes something like Inchmurrin, almost the entire length. Again, like the "Murrin", I prefer it from mid-season onwards.

These then, are just a few of the island and shore drifts. I find that known stopping places, for big fish, tend to be the best bet early on

121

and I accordingly think that the Endrick Bank gets more than its share of fish "just in".

There will be days when the wind blows gently along its length and you can, by means of Polaroids and the oars, attend to the matter of depth quite well. I've done it, but a companion makes the matter so much easier. The flies can linger longer, which makes such a vast difference, especially with salmon. It sometimes takes them a little while to soar up from the depths and there seems little point in this if your flies are in the air, behind your hat.

Once the first fish has been caught, and earned, on the fly there will be no looking back, although there will be days when it makes sense to troll and thus increase the chances of landing a fish: days of extremely bad light or days when violent gusts persist and you cannot keep your flies in the water.

As the season lengthens, the tap end of the loch can be tackled with good results, but for the time being we'll remain at the bottom end. Since some will argue as to whether Ross Point belongs up or down the loch, perhaps we can give this deadly little drift — as it merits — quite special mention, to conclude this chapter. Short drifts are not necessarily the easiest, the Ross Isles being my pet example of a fly fisher's quandary, the wind tending to come from several different directions on certain days.

5
Weather Conditions

The Light (and seeing it!)

OF the many contributory factors to success in angling, I place the light highest in order of importance, especially when fly fishing, when it appears to govern my every move.

I have never been one to sit through an entire day, using the same cast of flies, if it is doing no business. I have lost count of the times when a change of well-tried flies, to suit the light, has paid dividends. There are days, you will have noticed, when what you know to be a good fly gets no response. I'm sure the reason is that it does not suit the prevailing light on — and *in* — the water. As a result it blends with, instead of standing out against, the surface film, and cannot easily be seen by the fish. Of course, by the same token, there are days when the light remains constant and your flies will be right, if you have picked them well, for the whole day.

At times when the light is extremely changeable, fish with your own favourite cast which has served you well and caught fish, and do not change it without reason because, if you are over fish, one or two of the flies will eventually suit the changing light and will be seen well.

How many times have you gone for hours with nothing happening, when suddenly two or three fish go for the same fly? Perhaps it simply stood out better by way of its colouring and/or density, or imitated fry present in large numbers. A well-sunk tail fly often does this same trick, because it can be nearer to the fish's depth and is slightly, only slightly, lower in the water.

One word which should be in our angling dictionary is "opaque", which means "not transmitting light, solid, not translucent". If you had to make the choice would you like to search a haystack for a

123

piece of straw or a red pencil? A field for a leaf of grass or a yellow pen? Treat the loch surface, therefore, as a haystack or a field and "lose" something in it which the fish will find for you easily — because they will *see* it. Like the fish, I hope you see my point.

It's all a matter of contrast, I suppose, and if you could look up from the depths of the loch (or river) you would soon realise how much glitter and refraction is present. It seems paramount to me that you have picked flies which are opaque and will contrast best with the surface.

The celebrated Mr Billy Connolly, who is a very keen angler, asked me one night, "What is your best tail fly for the loch?" I stated that there was no such thing. I could only reduce the field to six, adding, "Any one of these which will suit the light, the bottom and the overhead conditions better than the rest." I consequently change my flies quite a lot, sometimes rightly, sometimes wrongly, but at the very least it reduces wearying and often, on bad days, you feel as if you are starting all over again with more promise of success.

Of course, size is also important and 6s and 8s, and sometimes 10s, are the only sizes I manage with now on the loch. I rarely use smaller than 10s, but most certainly will not be dogmatic about it. A friend who has fished the same loch for years, with good catches, keeps showing me flies I can barely see, but the fish do! If err we must, I think nowadays it should be on the small side, 8s and 10s. To contradict this, I have an offering which works infinitely better in size 6.

If we could split flies into three tones, I would start with the darker ones such as Butcher, Black Pennel, Kate McLaren, Grouse and Claret, Connemara Black, etc. Middle-toned, say Turkey and Gold or Silver, Turkey and Mixed, Woodcock and Mixed, Invicta, Grouse and Orange, Grouse and Green, etc, and finally the brighter flies of the salmon type such as Bloody Butcher, Kingfisher Butcher, Dunkeld, etc. Thus we have broad groups of flies of different tones. They can be permutated to suit dull, changeable or bright conditions. It goes without saying that I have omitted many other good killing *patterns*, but I simply set out to separate the tones.

One thing is certain. From day to day your flies may not change, but the light will — often. Bad light always seems worse to me on the loch, as opposed to the river. There's always a certain amount of cover, on the smaller rivers at any rate, such as overhanging trees and bushes. Even the shadows of the river banks and bridges can be of some assistance. But for the sheer "third degree", a huge open expanse of water such as Loch Lomond, and a ball of fire setting in the west, can be the angler's nightmare extraordinary. We cast away like robots but, truth to tell, it's time for the camera to come out and the rod to be packed away.

Sometimes, when up the loch, you live in an eternal state of optimism, in the forlorn hope that the higher slopes will eventually blank out the dazzle. You guess it will take about an hour for the sun to disappear but, instead of that, some hidden hand keeps moving the hills away at the same rate of speed as the sun. Three hours later, having suffered enough, *you* eventually move away. When you do, you miss the last chance, slight as it is.

I have seen in the space of half an hour, when two-thirds of the sun has disappeared, a sudden burst of action from the fish as if they, too, can see again. Again, here is the old case for being at the right place at the right time.

My own tendency is to pick out the most concentrated lie available and idle the while away until the time is ripe. An area or point, less liable to the late-returning trolling boat, is the ideal, and can often justify the wait.

No two of us seem to see things exactly the same way, and the light can play its part. The River Endrick was dropping back to a nice fishing level one August night, but slight colouring was still present as I fished into the gloaming. The next morning the river was in good order but, if anything, had sunk to a rather surprisingly low level. I decided to make for the loch, but first had to have a look at the Oak Tree Pool. I carefully approached, in a crouched walk, along the bordering footpath. There, lying in echelon, were around thirty to forty fish, crammed into the smallest area imaginable, lying just out of the current, in well-drilled lines. Every now and then a white flash would appear as gills opened and closed, and occasionally a fish would disturb the pack for some reason or another, head upstream, then drop back to the end of the queue. They lay in positions of well-planned and extreme comfort. The initial and most obvious clue to their presence was a silver flash here and there as a fish wriggled its flanks. When you saw one, you saw them all. I had stopped counting at about thirty fish, a mixture of salmon, grilse and sea trout of various sizes.

My heart rate was a bit above normal as I kneeled in recognition of this river marvel. Above, on the bridge, several car doors banged shut which, curiously, did not disturb the fish in the slightest. I've seen a faint shadow do more damage, as it crossed a pool of already restless fish.

A lone angler appeared on the path, pipe in mouth and rod at the ready. He had started to shout a greeting when I signalled him to approach the spot with more caution. This he did, and enquiringly appeared at my side. "Look! Just look at that!" I said.

His eyes scanned the water at the wrong spot.

"No, not there — *there*." I said, pointing. "Look at the size of that one near us. I think it's a big sea trout."

He wasn't a spectacle wearer. He should have been. To this day, I cannot believe that he failed to see even *one* of the fish in that pool. Remarking something about wishful thinking, he departed up-stream, eventually to approach the "pool of no fish".

Two more anglers appeared and the outcome was interesting. One eventually saw most of the fish and the other saw even more than I did. He pointed out a solo fish, probably the biggest in the pool, separated from the pack a little downstream.

I thought there must be a hidden moral to this somewhere and there was! The fellow with the pipe caught a fish. I, in turn, was beginning to see the light. You don't have to *see* fish to catch them. What seemed a distinct advantage could, in fact, have resulted in over-stealth and much nervous casting. Probably not all the water would be given the most complete coverage, in anxiety to reach where the big head of fish lay. Wading down the river, you wouldn't see the fish anyway and *touch* would become the most important factor.

I often think that to see a fish streak up to your cast on the loch can be a slight disadvantage. Certainly it takes a lot of practice to get things right. Perhaps someday I'll mask my eyes or look the other way when I see a fish coming. Perhaps.

Comically, but with no rudeness intended, I fished with a chap on the loch who saw absolutely *everything* "out the corner of his eye"! A fish might have "slunged" to the back, or side, of his head and knowing he couldn't possibly have witnessed it, I would spon-taneously ask, "Did you see *that*?" Still facing ahead, he would invariably remark, "Saw it — just out the corner of my eye"!

My most vivid recollection of his ultra-keen vision was one day when we drifted off Inchlonaig and the *Maid of the Loch*, the famous paddle steamer, churned into our view. Sightseers were crammed aboard and, friendly fellow that he was, visual greetings were being exchanged, his in the form of head nodding in their direction. A fish rose to his flies and his line tightened suddenly. I saw the entire back of his head, still nodding away at the visitors, before it suddenly whipped round, too late to complete the job. "Blast!", he exploded. "Saw it out of the corner of my eye, too." Deep down below, a fish replied "nudge... nudge"!

An interesting point, worth more time than I have ever given it, occurs when you attempt to observe fish from a slowly rowed boat. I have noticed some salmon, put off by the boat, jerkily swim out and away from it to return very quickly to their lie. Rightly or wrongly, I always imagine that kind of behaviour to indicate a fresh fish not long in the loch. I could be wrong, but I have disturbed other fish towards the end of the season who have shied completely out of sight. Presumably they return to their spots, but in a much bigger circle. Herein probably lies the success of certain anglers who shorten or lengthen the distance of the trolled baits to suit.

Just before Strathcashell Point, opposite the cottage on the shore, there is a small cairn with bushes at the side. In certain water-level conditions, the boat can be taken between the cairn and the shore. I did this one day, on the oars, and clearly saw a salmon veer away, disturbed, but it very quickly returned into the wake of the boat and darted up to touch, but not take, the inside bait (a Rapala), which was on an already shortened line. I'm sure it must have seen the other two baits just as clearly, but quick circle completed, its interest vanished.

With two friends, I did see over twenty fish rise to, and *take*, the trolled bait! Before loud protests are heard, I will admit that I was at the Rhu Narrows, local *sea* water, and the fish were coalfish! Still quite exciting, but flavoured with suicidal tendencies.

Sadly, I saw too many fish for my liking, at the end of our first season, with "the disease" — ulcerated dermal necrosis. Below the floating autumn leaves in Mill o' Ross Bay, grey phantom fish swam around in lifeless circles, some nearly colliding with the boat, others working with their built-in radar systems only. They didn't see me, and I was mighty sorry to see them.

Old Sol

We don't have light without the sun and naturally, with the wind, it must be taken into account. We need the wind more than the sun, and even the merest ripple will do some days, as long as it is enough to drift the boat.

A mirror-like surface, with blue cloudless skies, would and should be considered hopeless, were it not that anglers do not know this word, and an occasional fish (mostly fresh-run or wounded) is caught, against all the odds. Energy should be saved on a day like this, the boat drawn up ashore and the section in this chapter entitled "Becalmed" re-read and its instructions carried out.

It was on a day such as this that I joined two friends ashore on the beach at the Geggles, around 10 a.m. one morning, and we all agreed we should have been there the previous day. I shoved off the boat, intending to head up the loch and chase the slender hope of a ripple. As I passed the west tip of Inchlonaig, I could see that my prospects were nil, and slowed down the engine. A $\frac{5}{8}$ oz silver Toby was fed out on a short line and such was my overwhelming enthusiasm that out came a copy of the daily newspaper. The surface was like polished glass and the sun beat down relentlessly.

Shrewdly, you will have guessed that I haven't gone this far without having something to report to you and, indeed, midway along the island and fairly deep off the mid-bank, along came a 14 lb salmon. Of the few I've played in calms, I could safely state that they have fought harder, deeper and longer than fish caught in a wind. Perhaps their vision is better and their energy less expended in stiller water. My! How that fish fought!

I duly sped back to my sunbathing friends and, after proper delay, opened the subject with, "Aye, hopeless. Imagine, only one fish, on a day like this too!" There were strong references to my parenthood...

Sometimes, then, all is not lost, but if I had a penny for every day I've spent chasing non-existent wind, I wouldn't be tying my own flies.

The worst set of conditions is when the bright sun is behind your back and you cast large shadows ahead of your boat as you drift. There is the problem of rod "flash" and the long moving shadow it causes well ahead of you.

Fish lie mostly with their heads into the wind and would thus be nearly completely blinded. More likely, they will have sought a more comfortable depth, unless you are lucky and a cruising fish arises. It's a pity God didn't give them eyelids and lashes!

It is then when the troll has a better chance than the fly, since the angle of the driven boat and bait can be constantly varied, with increased chances of interesting a fish. Apart from someone rowing for you and achieving the same result, there is only one thing left to consider if you are fishing the fly. Loch Lomond is BIG. There are many hills and valleys surrounding its shores and if, say, you are languishing in these poor conditions at the bottom end then you can cruise up the loch where wind might, and often does, come from an entirely different angle, coming in light steady gusts down the upper glens.

The reverse applies, of course, if you are up the loch, and since that area is so narrow it's more likely you will come down than go up. The ultimate frustration is when you arrive either up or down to find a grand wind rising in the spot many miles behind that you have just left! Cat and mouse.

But too many times to count I have fished off, say, Inchmoan in a south wind and ended up on the Pilot Bank in a north wind. So, petrol permitting, move around, and even binoculars or a small monocular can help you confirm a beautiful black line appearing nowhere, some miles away.

A friend of mine used to hate fly fishing into the bright sun and usually laid down his rod and had a breather. We had not fished a lot together and I personally don't mind fishing and facing the sun on a good drift. I hooked a few salmon, blessed my Polaroids, and his disinterest soon vanished.

Try this experiment, with the Polaroids on of course. You will be facing the sun and will find it fairly hard to see your flies in the water, as you retrieve them in the glare. Swing round in the seat, cast *into* the wind and you should now see your flies easily, without straining. This, also, will be more like the fish's view of them, so what may be a dreadful glare to you is not nearly so bad for them.

In such conditions, was the only time I have ever really been successful with a Blue Zulu on Loch Lomond — *on the dap*.

By and large, if Old Sol gleams brightly, hope for some cloud to appear and you will soon have a "broken" light which can, at once, make a very big difference.

Wind

As with most outdoor sports like golf, tennis and football, to name but a few, angling is greatly affected by the presence of wind. Whereas the aspiring participant in any of the other named sports may regret windy conditions, inasmuch as they may detrimentally affect his game, the angler welcomes them like a gift from heaven. They are vitally necessary to assist him "cheat" the fish into taking the trolled bait or nicely worked fly. With the dap as the method, a light breeze upwards is needed to get the lone fly out a respectable distance from the boat.

Given good wind, fish will often get a brief view of the bait or fly as it sails through wave troughs, and there is enough cover to conceal how the object of their attention is attached to the hunter above.

On a big loch there is no telling how long a fish may follow a bait or fly, and although fish will often rise in a flat calm their interest often wanes as they get too good a view of foreign objects suspiciously near the lure.

Wind, then, is the angler's main ally and lack of it has demented many an otherwise sane fellow into a sullen, morose being, quite unfit to converse with.

Some seasons have more than their share of flat calms, and I recall what must be nearly a world record in the sixties when anglers all over Scotland suffered the prolonged effects of major droughts and calms. An acquaintance of mine had much looked forward to a full month's holiday, with the fly and dap rods, on an Inverness-shire loch. He returned a shattered man, having suffered calms for every day of the entire month.

I often think we take wind too much for granted. It has a funny habit of disappearing just after a few liced fish have been caught and an obvious head of fresh-run fish has entered the loch, tantalising the angler as he languishes on a mirror-like surface.

Like most regular loch anglers, I have lost count of the many days when results have been unbelievably dour in spite of enjoying so-called perfect conditions of wind. The boat has drifted well, the flies or bait have worked to the manipulator's pleasure, but all to no avail. It would be completely pointless to attempt to give reasons for this kind of negative response, since we are only wiser after the event. We sail out knowing that as long as there is wind there is hope. We come in complaining that the fish are simply not there. But they usually are.

Nearly every season, again like most local anglers, I have caught fish when the book says you shouldn't. The most common occurrence is to fish hard for hours on end in a good wave and then, when the wind has almost died away (and one's hopes with it), up crashes a good fish to the bob fly to take with gusto. Chances are it will be played out in the ensuing calm.

The reverse, of course, often happens also. Before a wind has risen, you can set up the boat, and in making a few exploratory casts or simply wetting the nylon in a mere shimmering ripple with an eye on the approaching black line of wind, a fish can take you completely unawares and like the proverbial ton of bricks. Angling is full of the unexpected.

In between a wind rising and falling is usually the hardest part of the angler's day, yet very often the ceaseless casting effort goes completely unrewarded. I sometimes think fish wait until spirits are at their lowest before they make a move. Even then they can change their minds.

A Loch Lomond gale can be a living nightmare, something always to be alert for as it rises in all its sudden ferocity. The waves, unlike the sea, are viciously short and steep, giving little time for recovery. The last I saw of a built-cane rod was when the boat was hit by a mountainous wave from nowhere, accompanied by spray from everywhere. Gales, fierce and unwelcome as they are, can often bring about good catches after they subside. The whipped-up water is well oxygenated to the liking of fish and I have noticed their tendency to take well at the tail end of a big wind. Unlike the foolhardy angler, fish save their energy well, yet seem to pay the penalty during spells of *joie de vivre*.

We are extremely lucky on Lomond in that, unlike smaller lochs, our vast water can receive a variety of winds from different directions, at least one of them blowing on to good fish-holding water. Moving from the tap to the bottom end, as mentioned elsewhere, can remedy many a desperate situation and, of course, the reverse applies also.

By consulting the Angling Areas which are marked on the maps, therefore, and taking the prevailing wind (or winds) into account, you should be able to determine to a large extent where you should be on the day of your outing. For myself, I have long since ceased to pay any attention whatsoever to the pessimist who decries the east wind. Contrary to the opinion of many, I have had great days in easterly blows, even with its accompanying bitingly cold wind. It may be unpleasant, early in the season, but I have often suffered the Endrick Bank gladly during such conditions and taken part in good catches.

Finally, there is the real problem of becoming caught in the middle of several little, nasty winds, whereby the boat goes round in circles, with the flies performing impossible feats in an erratic airborne state. Fishless, after such a fiasco some years ago, I returned to the bay to learn where I had gone wrong. Five beautiful salmon were laid out, being admired by all and sundry, including myself. Caught on the troll, of course. How else?

A final warning — when trolling, you can keep a weather eye open; in fact, most of the time you will be preoccupied with the clouds and the wind. When fly fishing, if you are doing the job right, you will be concentrating on the patch of water ahead of the drifting boat, almost to the exclusion of everything else. What's happening over your shoulder or behind your back can come as a bit of a surprise. Like the fish, bad weather seems to wait until you're not looking before paying a sudden call. What strikes me most about Loch Lomond storms — and I'm sure it applies elsewhere — is that you are in the middle of one without noticing the start. I recall one of many really bad days when I was able to don only one leg of the waterproof trousers before giving first priority to the lee of an island shore. Needless to say, when safe and sound with the boat drawn up nicely on a calm beach, I tripped over the forgotten trouser leg. I laughed, which was something I hadn't been able to do just before.

Becalmed

The old song should have gone, "*Becalmed*, bothered and bewildered am I..."

You can always tell a dedicated angler. On days when the loch is an absolute picture — mirror-calm and shimmering in the sunlight — he will be the one who walks past and ignores your, "Lovely day, isn't it?" or replies, "It must be — for *something*." Neurotic as this may sound, there is little joy in travelling miles up the loch, in a good wind, to make your first cast in a flat calm.

Be not too dispirited, though: there's plenty to do, especially if you are new to the loch and its angling ways. You will seldom get a better chance to examine the bottom and shore depths and see for yourself why you have been told to fish certain spots. With luck, too, you may see fish if you steal quietly along, rowing from the bow seat and peering into the water ahead with the oars shipped.

One day, off Rossdhu shore, I stopped counting the numbers of large fish leisurely swimming out to the deep side of the boat — and they were all salmon. In a good wind, I was there again the next time out but, alas, the fish were not. These shoals may enter the loch together, near Balloch, but in a very short time disperse into smaller heads of fish and take different routes to seek out their eventual spawning area. Having found it, they are not guaranteed to stay long, due to conditions, and will break up again as they seek and

Becalmed: a good, roomy, clinker-built Orkney boat with a handy quarter deck to keep equipment and provisions dry

find more comfortable lies to accommodate their future months in the loch.

Although I have done it myself, there is little excuse for just sitting in the boat bemoaning the calm, and then, when a wind comes up and you start fishing, find your cast is all wrong, knots are poor, or something else in your tackle is lacking. Now is the time to check this and that, tie up spare casts leisurely and correctly, and seek out likely flies you will need if that wind does come along. If you own your own boat, there's always some odd job needing to be done. If you don't own your own boat, then tie up *more* casts or go ashore and explore.

Only then can I suggest that you take a nap. You have probably earned it. Be wakened only by the gentle lap of the loch wavelets, as the breeze you thought would never come grows into a deadly little ripple. Glide out by the oars if you are near a good rising spot, circle it quietly, on the deep side, and set up the boat. The adrenalin should start flowing. If it doesn't, go ashore again because you will lack what an angler needs most — enthusiasm and super-optimism. A rising wind can stir up the fish — just give it time.

Having mentioned comfort, perhaps I should add two points.

The floorboards of my boat have been the resting place of many fish. They seem to sleep well there, with a little assistance, and so do I — with none at all! I always carry a rolled "Kampamat", tied

133

under a seat, and find it a great insulator — especially if you creak a bit at the joints. It is sold mainly for campers — this being another most enjoyable local pursuit — and is of closed cell foam which will not absorb water. It can be bought at Black's Camping and Leisure or Nevisport, in Glasgow, and cut there and then to any size required.

The other point detracts from your comfort. Never try to have a nap on the floorboards when your boat sits becalmed in the middle of the loch. You may think that because there is absolutely no wind that you are safe enough for an hour or so of slumber. There may not be a boat in sight for miles. I tried it once and, at regular 10-minute intervals, could hear the approach of trolling boats, all assuming the same thing: "Maybe the blighter's deed!" — "Hey, Jimmie, are you OK?" You will grow weary of raising your head, in answer! They do the right thing, though, because in the past it has been known for no head to appear at all. In all innocence you have put these lads off their usual trolling routes and you can but hope it causes them to hook a fish as reward for their concern.

Finally, incessant heavy rain — the kind that makes holes in the loch — can kill the wind, and it is then I go ashore, draw up the boat and bless the hap as I rig it up for shelter and then wriggle head first into the bilges. Guess what I dream about!

Still somewhat becalmed, it occurs to me that very few angling books I have read exclude freak happenings, lost fish and other commonplace tragedies. There is one little event which I find still unique in my memories and, luckily, I had a friend aboard who witnessed the entire fiasco.

The wind had been lost and our bodies took on that droop which is peculiar to angling men who are frustrated by lack of action. Several hours of pottering about with casts, going ashore and reading newspapers left us debating whether or not to call it a day. Eventually, we persuaded ourselves that wind would come and, in the course of deciding when, I realised I was being slowly and luxuriously rowed around the deeps between Inchlonaig and the Ross Isles.

The only rods aboard were our respective fly rods and the lone dap pole. I did, however, have one wee *bait*, and it was rolled up in a hankie, in my oilskin pocket. It was a very small silver Rapala and as I dangled it before my far-from-puritanical partner, I got the response, "Might as well! I'm rowing anyway."

The problem was how to attach it. A spool of 7lb nylon was

produced and the fly cast removed from the main line, the rod then being laid down with part of the line trailing in the slight wake behind the boat. A few coils of nylon were unwound from the spool and the bait was tied on and admired, albeit no swivel was attached. Now for a clever wee trick. I punctured the paper disc in the centre of the nylon spool, so that it "freewheeled" between my thumb and forefinger. The minute bait was slipped into the water and it fluttered nicely, swimming backwards and taking line off very smoothly indeed.

You think that a fish suddenly saw the bait flowing out behind the boat and seized it, which would make the story interesting, at that stage, considering the method by which the bait was attached to the angler.

No! A fish was there all right but he didn't take. He waited.

About 20 yd of nylon had gone out. I stopped the spool revolving and twisted a turn or two of nylon around a finger, as a precaution, before biting off the end piece at the spool.

A fish could have taken now. It's almost overdue, you might think. But it didn't. It waited.

I curled the loops of nylon round the little finger of my left hand, then made a "perfection" loop. The idea was to slip-knot the fly line on to this loop. My partner had studied every move and I could almost hear him thinking: "What now?" As I reached for the fly rod, I had a problem: where to keep the loop while I used both hands to complete the attachment. Instinctively and safely, I placed it between my upper and lower teeth, where it lodged out of harm's way, as I reached for the tip of the fly line.

The fish was now ready. It took.

I must record that I found it a trifle awkward to notify my crony verbally of this sudden success. For once, I was speechless and remained so, but the alarm in my eyes prompted him to ask, "What's up?" Performing like a ventriloquist gone mad, I got the message over in a series of muffled, nasal grunts. Anxious hands reached out, a loop was whipped round my wrist and speech returned! I must censor the initial outburst, but it simmered down to "Strewth, I wonder if there's a chance?"

My extended right arm became the "rod", a one-piece affair and rather too short for good loch fishing. The "reel" was my left hand. I can't say that the reel "screamed" at any stage, but a slight cut was forming in the right forefinger — the top ring! The dives and runs were being reasonably controlled and finally a prime 3 lb fresh-run sea trout was triumphantly netted and laid, amidst fankled nylon, at my feet.

Incredible! But before tackle dealers proceed to close their shops for the last time, I would admit it's not quite the best way to fish for sea trout on Loch Lomond — or anywhere else.

A reflection on this odd affair, afterwards, resulted in a group of anglers, myself included, discussing how respective boat partners reacted when a fish was hooked. A census of opinion was that most said nothing, but emitted vastly differing types of frightened grunts! Try it sometimes and you will probably notice that it is quite some time before the angler actually *speaks*. It is only when he is the master and the fish is under control that words, much sweated over, reach your eager ear. Should the fish be lost you can be sure of an entire speech, but then, that kind of language can occur in the best of boats!

6
Dapping

The Dap Dopes: Flies

SHOWN on Plate 3 (between pages 72 and 73) are the dirty dozen dapping flies. Believe it or not, there *are* much worse-looking offerings available. One omission bothers me a little because it is probably the best known of all dapping flies: the Loch Ordie. To be without one on Loch Maree, say, would be like going out without your trousers on. A few resemble it but, although ginger in colour, lack the white throat hackle and small "flying" treble. Messrs Dickson in Royal Exchange Square, Glasgow, stock it, but I have done as well with others shown.

From top to bottom, starting at the left, there is a large black and dark ginger pattern which works as well in one or two sizes smaller. Next is the BLACK PENNEL of the upturned umbrella style, an established favourite with many, myself included. Bottom is a yellowish-grey pattern which had one or two good days.

The BLUE ZULU tops the second row. As a wet fly it remains an enigma to me. Off Inchmurrin one year I rose about ten fish to it on the bob. None of them took, nor, by the look of some well-observed rises, did they intend to. I more or less abandoned it, only to find it rearing its ugly head again in the form of this dapping fly. It works infinitely better on the dap, again on days of bad, steely light, and can be a successful last resort. Below it, is a dap fly of no particular name, but which has been most successful for me, on occasions, probably because it is "half and half". There is faint gold ribbing in the lower body section, only a few turns. Bottom is the BLACK PENNEL I like the best. I got this one from Michael Rogan, of Ballyshannon, Co. Donegal, whose staff tie all their flies, to this day, by hand. It dances about in great style, and I have found that many fish do not like its antics one bit!

137

Third row, top, is a very pale ginger palmer-styled fly which is either good or useless, but I cannot establish when, exactly, it should be good. The next two flies are smaller and tied on Waddington-type treble mounts. They were supplied to me by Messrs Dickson, again, who specialised in this type of mount and I believe they will, or did, supply it separately.

Later in this chapter, there is a graphic description of four fish, including a $6\frac{1}{2}$ lb grilse, which fell to the dap in a sudden frenzy, within about half an hour, and they took the smallish spider-type fly top right, as simple a dressing as they come. I tried it on the bob for a while but couldn't hook the rises, the same kind of thing that happens to me when I fish a Soldier Palmer on the bob. They were interested but not completely suicidal. In very fickle conditions this small fly can do well. There is no splash from a team of three wet flies, but just that wee nuisance skittering about on its own. When using it I often lengthen the nylon leader to about 4ft, simply in an effort to hide the light-coloured floss from view as much as possible.

The PRIEST comes next and, in common with most of the dapping flies, it is simple to dress. Simple, yes, but plenty of it! The priest in a slightly smaller size was fished by a crony of mine for several seasons on the bob and he did quite well with it, but not for salmon. It appears to be at its best, in dapping form, in not too big a size. Last is a bigger version of the fly just described, which damaged four prime fish and, in rough weather, this is a great favourite.

I think these twelve are more than enough for a season, only a variety in sizes being needed to complete a range. I have bigger umbrella-type Black Pennels, for heavy weather, and intend to try the Blue Label in dap form providing I get time to both tie it and justify its use on the dap.

Two little tips with the dap. The flies should be soaked overnight in dope (silicone type), and well dried out for use the next day. When a brown trout takes, the fly becomes almost useless thereafter, due to a slimy mucous which cancels out the floatant.

To restore dapping flies in general, boil a kettle of water and hold the fly over the steaming spout with artery forceps, or the like, and the dressing should balloon back into shape. They should be left to dry out naturally on sheets of newspaper, before once again applying floatant. Again, I would issue the warning to use care when handling dap flies, if you intend wet fly fishing also. Another good reason for carrying the inevitable bottle of detergent aboard.

* * *

The Method

Most people have heard of the *dry fly*, possibly because these two short words prompt a mental picture of sorts wherein a tiny fly tumbles down with the river current, high and dry, as the term suggests. Dapping is a very underrated style of angling which, although used quite extensively in northern Scottish waters and Ireland (the live daddy-long-legs!), is little used on Loch Lomond for reasons I can only guess. But more of this later. The dap is a form of dry-fly fishing but, unlike the river style, no casting or false casting is required. The extremely large dapping fly is carried out by the wind by means of a gossamer-light line which is known as floss or blowline. Usually of synthetic material, nowadays, it does to some extent resemble fine strands of candy floss, with its puffy and finely-textured characteristics. Frail as it looks at first sight, the breaking strain can be as much as 20 lb, a good deal less when wet, when it also becomes devilish stuff indeed as it adheres, almost like Sellotape, to the varnished rod surface. A brisk swish of the rod from side to side will normally restore the puffiness of the material, thus carrying the dap fly out to its most respectable distance.

Although floss comes in spools of approximately 50 yd, there is certainly no need to use this amount on the reel. Some 25 ft is all that is required, but this must be knotted every foot or so to reduce any tendency to fray and catch rod rings as it billows to the full.

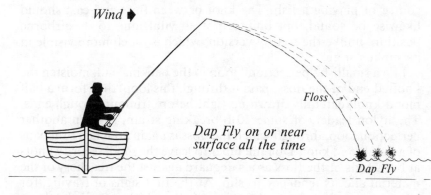

Wind ➤

Floss

Dap Fly on or near
surface all the time

Dap Fly

THE DAP

The diagram below shows how to load the reel with main line and terminal tackle.

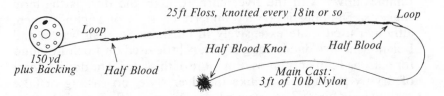

The backing should be a minimum of 150 yd of rotproof material, braided nylon or terylene, preferably, although many adopt the cheaper alternative of ordinary nylon. For myself, I find the latter material and floss have a fascination for each other on the spool, intertwining at exactly the wrong moment. A narrow drum reel, or multiplying fly reel, is ideal, providing normal angling practice is observed by using its full capacity; too much backing is always better than too little.

The knots joining the floss to the backing and main cast are similar. An important point, though, is to ensure that both ends of the floss are trimmed to a neat terminal knot which should remain after pulling up the knots tight. A neat union between backing and floss is needed, since this knot has to pass through the rings in the course of playing a fish. The knot between floss and cast should likewise be sound, but bulk is not so vital, due to its airborne position, unlike the wet fly version, which is much more visible in its sunken state.

I tie a smallish "perfection" loop in the backing end, moisten the knotted end of the floss, pass it through this loop, then form a half blood knot, carefully drawn up tight before trimming rough ends. The nylon leader, of some 10 lb breaking strain, is given another perfection loop, through which the floss is again attached by means of a half blood knot. Do remember to leave the small security knots at both ends of the floss as a safeguard against the treachery of the material and its tendency to slip. At the first signs of fraying, for whatever reason, renew the floss length, which is a fairly cheap price to pay for peace of mind.

Unlike trolling or fly fishing, this method makes more use of air than water. Simply put, the dapping flies are worked upon the *surface* of the water. At no time must they be allowed to become waterlogged and sink, since the art — if that be the word — is to dance them, tantalisingly, upon the surface film. I will not attempt, at this stage, to explain why fish will firmly accept the much smaller wet fly in a sunken state, but refuse the larger and bushier object below the surface. In the case of the dap, it is more what the fish do not see that matters. The nylon leader and floss line remain well above the surface, dangling above the fly but not too visible to the quarry. Only the rough outline of the dap fly and the disturbance it creates should be seen by the fish before it is goaded into action.

To some extent, the bob (or uppermost) fly, in the team of three wet flies, performs a similar function to the dapped fly, since as soon as the cast is retrieved through the surface film, it should trip through the wavelets in an attractive manner. Many fish — certainly a good percentage of mine — savagely seize the bob when it is so worked. A drawback, however (and this is where the dap scores) is that the bob fly can only remain on the surface for a shortish, set time, due to the speed and/or method of retrieving the wet flies. The

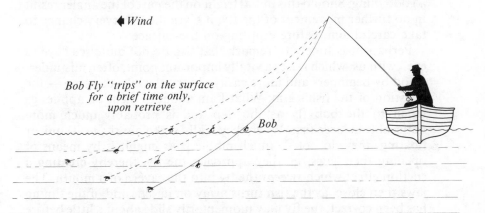

◀ *Wind*

*Bob Fly "trips" on the surface
for a brief time only,
upon retrieve*

Bob

THE BOB FLY AND THE DAP

Some days the fish have a distinct preference for a fly which is fished on the surface so that the dap, in dry fly fashion, has a slight advantage in that it remains on the surface, or near it, for practically as long as the angler has stamina to keep it there. The bob fly is also deadly when tripped through surface wavelets, although it can only remain there for a brief time as the cast is being steadily drawn to the boat.

The dap fly is on or near the surface *all* the time (see Fig. 16 on p. 139.

141

dap fly, on the other hand, can remain poised and raised and lowered over vast stretches of water. The time it remains on the surface depends upon the strength of the wind, of course, and the angler's staying power.

An important and fascinating aspect of dapping is that many fish can be seen to rise to, or encircle, the fly. They may be attracted, but undecided, and often a deft, sometimes erratic movement, which ends with the fly settling down on the water for a few moments, can make up the mind of the fish. Words cannot describe the sheer thrill of watching a mighty fin cut through the water, followed by the wide open jaws of the fish as it angrily attempts to engulf the hairy offering before crashing down in a tail-thrashing exit.

Only a big fish coming to the bob fly could equal the close-up sensations which the dap provokes. Quite often, the tension generated when a fish suddenly appears from nowhere, eyes almost afire with hatred, can raise the hair on the back of the angler's neck and paralyse his rod-waving actions almost at once. This, though, can be a good thing. Should this initial fright on the part of the angler result in no further movement of the fly, it gives the fish every chance to take careful aim, before erupting on the surface.

Perhaps it is timely to remark that fish do not quite see "eye to eye" with us, which raises a vitally important point, often misunderstood by beginners and more easily observed whilst dapping — the question of the fish's aim. What I am about to mention applies as much to the bob fly as the dap and is probably much more noticeable in large fish. When they really seek your fly, be it sunk or floating, they do not so much nibble it as engulf it by means of opening their jaws, as they approach the fly, thereby creating a suction effect which *sweeps* the fly into the cavern of a mouth. The jaws then close, as the fish turns away on its side and, if the timing has been correct, the fly may momentarily slide about a little before firmly lodging where it should be — in the corner of the jaw, the part aptly named the "scissors".

Due to the fact that the eyes of fish are located on the sides of their heads, in this engulfing scoop action they employ in taking the fly there occurs a blind spot — a few seconds wherein the fish acts from memory of where it last saw the fly. As it sweeps towards the fly, at almost the last second it has to turn slightly sideways, resulting in a fractional loss of vision. If its aim has been correct and *you* move the fly at this vital point, do not blame the fish. It has probably done everything absolutely right and, in spite of a sudden jerk imparted by you to the fly, it may return, more determinedly, if the fly is allowed to settle down back in its "window". A second lunge, apart from being the angler's good fortune, is often savage indeed and it is a time for a steady hand and nerves of steel.

I vividly remember a friend rising a good fish to the dap. As he told me, somewhat bad temperedly, how the fish had "missed", I noticed that in delivering the excuses his fly dangled about a foot from the surface. There was a fast "whoosh" as the sea trout left the water to snatch the airborne fly as clean as the proverbial whistle. My friend, disguising human frailty, had the indecency to utter, "That's better," as the reel began an erratic chatter, and the fish cursed its perfect eyesight!

Most of the foregoing applies to fairly large fish, which the dap undoubtedly attracts, and their more leisurely, but powerful approaches. Smaller fish can come at the floating fly at incredible speed, befitting their bantamweight build, and if we only told the acid truth, they virtually hook themselves in fast suicidal rises for which they deserve — and get — an eventual pat on the head!

One of dapping's most important, and often undetected, advantages is that on unresponsive wet fly days it can tell you where the fish are — particularly the big ones. Whether you catch them or not is a different matter, but at least you may find some new lies. Let me illustrate a few samples of days when it has paid off.

One August recently I drifted half the island of Inchlonaig, in reasonable wave and dull overhead conditions, without a rise. Next to me lay the dap rod, with a Black Pennel type fly well soaked with dope and dried the evening before. I have been fiddling about with a hollow glass fly rod to find a way of adding some 3ft to its length, without ruining the rod's appearane, and, with help from Lawrie Renfrew, a Glasgow tackle dealer, managed to rig up the extension piece. So there it lay and, with the lack of a rise, there was my excuse to try out the experiment.

Out swung the Pennel to sit nicely on the wave tops, and I began to adjust to the altered rod, feeling fairly pleased with the result. Pleasure was not to remain mine for long.

Quite the largest fish I have ever risen came out of nowhere and engulfed the fly, showing what I thought was its tail disappearing in the process. It was the dorsal fin — the tail appeared some seconds after! He was on. I cannot remember a fish of any sort not giving some jerks or tugs at some stage in the fight, but here was the exception. It simply started to swim round the boat with the rod

Referred to below, this 10¼lb sea trout was caught on the fly one August. Taken off Inchlonaig on a size 6 ordinary Invicta, this fish won the author three bottles of Ballantine's whisky

bent fully against its mighty pressure. I have a slight mental block about the next bit. (Always renew the floss or nylon, especially if it has been regularly saturated.) I will try to spare myself the memory of it all, but must record that like broken banjo wires the floss started to disintegrate at the top ring, bit by agonising bit. The fish just cruised on, round the boat, keeping the line distance constant throughout. If he had even dived and taken line I might have had a chance, but before any quick solution was found the rod sprung back, and it will always remain a haunting memory when I think of the floss landing so slowly, in a series of wrinkles on the surface. The great fish below sought further depth, the floss straightened·and went down with him.

I cannot blame the dap for the loss and, as I set out to explain, I had cause to thank it in the end. I engined upwind again, with no alternative but to revert to the wet fly and approached the danger area once more. Still wondering if I might see swimming floss about, I was taken under the surface with an almighty thud. Unlike its predecessor, this fish pulled out every trick in the book. I took an Invicta out of the corner of its mouth and it turned the scales at 10¼lb, for which Messrs Ballantine sent me three bottles of their lovely whisky! It was a sea trout, of course.

So, black mark for me for basic carelessness, but the dap gets credit for alerting me to the fact that at least one big fish lay in the area and the one captured came from the same spot. I doubt very much if I would have twice drifted the area were it not for lifting the dap rod and stirring up the interest.

Another big dapping moment came some years ago, after about four hours of negative fly fishing, off the Long Point, at Inchmoan. There were many boats out that day, but none of them — including myself — seemed very busy. Out went the dap! I had bought from Mr C. C. Mann, a Glasgow tackle dealer then and dapping authority, several medium-sized spider-type flies and they lay ready for action. Within a minute, a fresh black neb or finnock darted up and was duly landed. On went another fly and, in a lifetime of fishing, I have never witnessed such a spectacle. A fish of some 3 lb was hooked and its first leap carried it out of the water to thump the outer planks of the boat. It leapt again and landed fair and square on the floorboards at my feet! "No-one will believe it," I mused. "Who needs a net?"

Again the fly sailed out and was taken at once by a further sea trout, which had more sense, but not enough to ensure its safety. I looked around for interested parties, but none were behind me and ahead drifted six or seven boats still casting away, unaware of what they had drifted over.

Once more another fly was fed out and was taken with great speed, under the surface. This was a heavier fish and, as a trolling boat chugged into sight behind me from within the bay, I felt the backing slip through my fingers, and the fish surfaced some distance out. It was a beautifully-shaped grilse of $6\frac{1}{2}$ lb and liced.

The four fish were landed within about half an hour, on a day when the wet fly produced no results!

Indeed, many a good relationship has been ruptured when fishing two in a boat, one on the dap and one fly fishing, due to the fact that the "inferior" party has risen and caught fish to the dap — fish that were surely the fly fisher's in the first place!

The home of dapping is really Loch Maree and, for reasons I have never quite understood, Loch Lomond has gained no great reputation for the method. The obvious answer is that very few bother, since the loch has always yielded good numbers of salmon and sea trout to the wet fly.

I have heard it said that salmon are not caught on the dap on Loch Lomond. It is quite untrue. I have to date landed about a half dozen — not many, but for the limited time I do dap as

Four fish referred to on p. 145, all victims of the dap. The fish that landed in the boat is second from the bottom. The fly that caught them (also shown) is a fairly small one for the dap

opposed to fly fishing, it's not too bad. I know of at least two others who have had salmon thus, and there may be visitors who have come and gone without notifying their similar success.

For salmon, I alter the presentation a trifle by deliberately trying to create a wake on the surface water. Normally this isn't too desirable and with sea trout quite minor raising and lowering of the fly, settling it occasionally, provokes action. I say action, because all too often the rise is missed or the fish merely attempts to drown the fly with its body wake or tail. Often, very big fish will suck the fly under without showing and I can still hear the jaws of a monster clicking together as he "missed" off the Keeleymore Burn, in Mill o' Ross Bay. My boat crony was still saying, "For Pete's sake!" about two hours after the *crunch!*

Rods

The dapping rod should naturally be as long as you can handle without tiring, and after much experimenting I have reverted to a light fibreglass salmon rod which, again, has that stiffness in the tip section for close-range hooking. It is only 13ft 6in long, but I can extend this with a 3ft butt section. It is not *too* powerful and has a feeling of life in it, as opposed to some of the "poles" I have seen used. About 14ft to 16ft is the ideal length of rod and, since perseverance should ultimately bring about a visit from fair sized fish, it should have enough backbone to both drive the rather large dapping hook home and tire out the fish in a reasonable time. I am sure that the acme of rods for the job exists right now in the form of carbon fibre but, until I can solve the trivia of day to day economics which currently rule the domestic scene, I am not faced with the problem of smuggling such a dream weapon in and out of the house. I can explain away one such rod, but two might necessitate over-rapid excuses to bank managers and other interested parties who would, curiously, fail to see my point of view.

Telescopic dapping rods made a brief appearance, and I still have the remains of one. It was handy to stow in the boat, but whoever designed it had money in mind. He saved a great deal, by only providing five rings over its 16ft length. The floss formed into rainbow-type loops between the rings and made feeding it out a penance. There has since been some improvement. A friend of mine has a telescopic rod, made in Japan, which has two sliding rings per section, giving about fourteen rings in all.

Be careful when laying down the dap rod in the boat. The floss will catch *anything*, including my Labrador's collar, which once resulted in a mess so bad that it might have been simpler just to dap the dog for a while, to release the tangle!

A final warning: if you are mounting both the fly and dap rod, assemble the former first, complete with cast. Your fingers will touch the doped dapping fly first, otherwise, and you do not want floatability transmitted to your wet flies. The point has to be constantly watched if you switch methods while fishing.

Day Out on the Dap

We have already had sample days out on both the troll and fly, and it is now the turn of the dap. As stated earlier, the ideal is to have two in the boat, one on the dap and the other on the fly. I find the arrangements with three just a little bit cramped, since I do at times deliberately cast at an angle and this does not mix too well with the coils of billowing floss nearby.

Presuming that you cannot locate your one and only remaining friend — the one who hasn't dapped with you before — it remains to go out solo. There are distinct advantages. Language need not be too carefully controlled, and who is to know that you deliberately smashed the rod to bits, when you state you sat upon it?

Drifts for the dap are much the same as those for the fly, as shown on the maps. There are, however, one or two very small areas which can hold a single big fish and, being such short drifts, they tend to be by-passed by the fly fisher who seeks a lengthier spell of casting and a bigger area of water covered. Be that as it may, it's a fish that is required and sometimes it is worth a distinctly delicate approach to dap a few square yards of many square miles!

When I am out alone, fly fishing, and I reach the area of the Ladies Point, at Inchcruin, if the drift has yielded nothing I often decide to repeat the entire drift from Inchgalbraith back to the Ladies Point, and meet with success due to changed conditions of light or some such similar reason.

But today, perhaps the fly rod can be put down for a wee while and an interesting rock visited. Normally showing quite clearly at most water levels, it lies past the shingle bay whereupon stands a jetty and house, on Inchcruin, opposite Buccinch. The area can be a mixture of weed and rock, all round the stone.

Preferably, the rod nearest the big rock should be the one dapping, so wind direction and drift tendency should be taken into account before reaching the danger zone, close in. Time after time I have risen, hooked, lost and landed biggish fish there. After a good season of visits, it was something of a disappointment to find it had gone "off", but the reason gradually became apparent. A steady, suitable loch level had to be present to give this larger kind of fish the lie it required. So, perhaps today is the day.

The dap rod should have been mounted and the doped fly attached, say a Black Pennel. It is up to the person fly fishing, if there is one, to keep out of the way of the bouncing dap fly and floss. There are times when gusts of wind tend to make the Pennel "poach" the other chap's water, but to be on guard for this is the thing.

With *slight* movements of the rod tip, the dapping fly should be *placed* between troughs, then lifted and replaced. Such is the size of the fly, and its relative contrast, that it should be easily seen. From time to time it should simply be left, after these movements, or swung aside to broaden the water-searching pattern, and then settled on the surface again.

Should the fly disappear in the middle of a slight eruption, tighten

148

firmly and remember the size of hook you are using will need a fair amount of initial pressure to lodge home correctly.

I see that I already tend to fall into the trap of advising on how to hook every conceivable type of rise the dap will provoke. That there will be many rises, in a variety of forms, there will be no doubt. To hook them all is simply impossible. A lot of the time fish, including very big fish, will rise with no intention of mouthing the offering but merely to drown it with their body wake or lash out at it with their large tails. A normal fly would be drowned this way, so do not be surprised; *be alert for* the fish mouthing it the second time.

The tension in these circumstances can be high and the difficult bit is to remain with the fly and give the fish every chance of getting it the second time. If his body wake or tail doesn't succeed, as he planned, his mouth probably will.

Expect the fish to rise again. Do not, as one often does on the fly, turn aside and make comment at the fish "missing". He didn't really . . . and he will possibly attempt to take the fly with a vengeance the next time.

As with the fly, and slightly more so, a slow "head and tail" should be given time. It might seen an agonising wait until the nylon and/or floss stiffens but wait until it does, be it a large fish, and then tighten firmly and steadily to send the hook home. Many times will a fish do this for you, and in a great rush simply hook itself.

I find that certain areas which neither respond to the fly nor usually seem to hold fish can often give results. There is a sheer rock face some yards above the Ross Point, which appears a very unlikely lie for game fish, being sheer depth without shallows. Carrick Rock area is similar and both these examples have provided good-sized fish to the dap. I must assume that their proper lie, or resting area, is nearby and that they simply cruise around, as fish will do, until the dapping monstrosity comes along to disturb their peace of mind. Another theory is that above the rocks are heather clumps where bushier-type flies do actually reside, and they drop to the water's surface.

However, to my mind no theory explains the reaction of fish to the dap in open water. Then, again, the dap never does explain itself. It isn't meant to. It sometimes catches great fish, and that, after all, is what matters.

To me the method has great value in promoting rises when the fish are not really in the mood. I would not, in my weakest moment, confess to being the complete addict, preferring, when all is said and done, the fly. But the dap has a certain magic, it has provided many a fish and relieved spells of lengthy boredom. I owe it thanks and, when fly fishing from mid-season onwards, would feel a little bit "naked" without that troublesome long pole resting on the boat seats — but emphatically, as far away from the fly rod as possible!

Two seasons ago, a relatively new member of the Association joined a friend and me for a few hours' fishing. He boarded the boat with 3 ft of rod, which zoomed out to some 16 ft when extended. We sat him in the middle and my other partner laughed, in ridicule, as the "shaving brush" sailed out between our fly casts. "The day *that* catches anything... I've never seen a fish..." Bang! The fish arrived, to be duly seen disappearing with the dap fly in a completely suicidal rise. *We* caught nothing.

Another day I was leaving the bay, when a friend somewhat despairing of bailing out his boat when it wasn't raining (liquid plank and no hap!), joined me for a day's fishing. Although I can't speak for him, I always find it interesting to discover the actual interior of a boat you have only known from a distance, afloat. In my case, I usually find them surprisingly neat and tidy and I am at an entire loss, being used to gear and gadgets placed where only I can find them.

We reached the Long Point in good conditions. Quite perfect for the dap. We had only made a few casts when he said he had never seen "that dap thing" at work. I reeled-in the flies and he will readily admit that the dapping fly had only taken two bounces on the surface when a 3-pounder took it suddenly and firmly. The hook sprung free in the net, as it often does in dapping, and he said, "That was quick!" So it was. We were still discussing it only a moment or so later when a fish the same size took him on the tail fly, and a pair of identical twins lay side by side.

Typical of the dap, and for no reason I can explain, I reverted to the fly and caught another fish by the more "expert" method. The truth is, we were at the right place, at the right...

7
Facts about Fish

Kelts

PURELY for anyone new to angling are a few points which strike
me as worth the knowing. Instead of killing and then admiring
your first fish off the loch, have a good long look at it. The chances
are it will be a kelt. Not only are they *very* silver, but some of them
can look in the prime of condition. I fully sympathise with someone
new to fishing having difficulty in recognising a fish in this state. It
will, to many, be just a fish. The easily-recognised kelts have very
thin bodies related to their length and the head appears out of
proportion, too large for its length.

Look at the picture of the 4 lb "perfection" sea trout, which is
everything a good sea trout should be. Note the small head, very
large girth and the presence of sea lice, the small brown tadpole-like
creatures stuck on to its body. This is perfection; but there are other
"grades" of sea trout and they might be slightly slimmer or of a
darker colour, when they have been in the loch a while.

The scales of a good fish will generally be firmly affixed to its
body. The scales of a kelt will loosen readily and scatter all over the
net and boat. A kelt will gorge a bait, regrettably, due to its
undernourished state, and great care is required to unhook it
without bleeding.

To kill a kelt is an offence: but how do you know what a kelt is,
unless you have seen one alive? If you've seen one alive, then you'll
probably kill it. Later on, you will be told you have killed a kelt and
you may go on killing them, still committing offences, because you
won't know a kelt from a good fish. Once you've caught a good,
clean, fresh-run fish you'll soon know the difference and, at last,
know what a kelt is. You will then, I trust, kill no more.

151

A perfect 4lb sea trout. Note the tiny head, deep girth and sea lice

What Is It?

To the stranger on the shore, and often the complete novice to the game, the sight of a fish which is silver, dead and wrapped in polythene usually means a significant and worthy catch. After much admiration such as, "Oh, what a beauty...!" or, "Come and look at this, Gran..." there is a predictable pregnant pause followed by the sure-fire, "Yes, lovely... *What, actually, is it?*" You should have an answer, and it seems only right to impart a few basic facts to remove uncertainties and the red face which matches the unforgivable response, "I don't really know."

Without lingering on the subject of kelts much further, I would merely add that they will probably be the most glittering silver of any fish you will land in the early season. Beware, alas, the false "tinny" sheen and the free-flying scales. They suffer from what could fairly be described as a patch-up job at best, which disguises their underlying undernourished state.

At the start of the season, from March to May roughly, the fresh salmon entering the loch very often contain heavy sea trout in their ranks, proverbial bars of silver and, this time, the real McCoy. I have caught many a sea trout at this time of the year, from 7-11lb, say, and it should be early in an angling career that the difference between the large adult sea trout and the salmon is well and truly learned. Our problematic loch can set a further poser to the unenlightened when a genuine loch trout presents itself among the

152

sea trout but, for the time being, the Big Two should be dealt with.

I show below a sketch of a fish of the British *Salmonidae* family, which broadly covers our Atlantic salmon, sea trout, brown trout, char, etc.

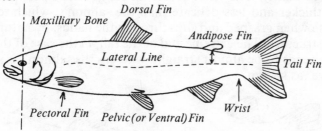

A FISH OF THE BRITISH *SALMONIDAE* FAMILY

An almost certain method of confirming the difference between adult salmon and the trout family is to count the scales between the back part of the andipose fin and the lateral line, as shown by the arrows. The scales run in a line, obliquely, towards the head of the fish. The salmon has between ten and thirteen (usually eleven to twelve), the trout family between thirteen and sixteen (usually fourteen).

SALMON   TROUT FAMILY

A second way to tell the difference is by study of the eye position, related to the maxillary bone close to the jaw junction at the mouth area, when the mouth is closed. As will be seen, if an imaginary line is vertically drawn through the eye, it will relate to the maxillary bone. In the case of adult salmon, the eye will appear almost in line with the bone, so that the mouth *seems* to be small. In the trout family, the same vertical line will pass through the eye pupil ahead of the junction bone, with the mouth *appearing* to be large. Although something of an optical illusion, it is a quick and easy method of confirming the initial difference between the species, albeit the more practice the better.

The trick is to be sure to catch *two* fish, one of each species, so that identification is made that much easier!

153

A final clue comes from the propulsion area at the rear of the fish. The tail of a salmon is slender at the wrist, thereby making it easier to grasp and carry, and the tail webbing itself is stiffer than that of the trout family. The wrist of the latter, in adults particularly, is much thicker and less delicate than the salmon's, which tends to collapse when grasped and slips through the hands, by nature of its softer structure. The extreme end of the tail, in the case of the trout family, tends to be almost straight, whereas the salmon's is slightly concave, as shown.

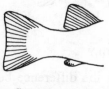 

SALMON   ADULT TROUT FAMILY

Many fish and much studying should bring about quicker identification until, as a seasoned veteran, you might almost be able to tell in the course of playing a fish to which family it belongs. However, sure as the Ben above, from time to time along will come a customer bent on baffling the best. Strange to relate, a "foreigner" in the shape of a true rainbow trout turned up where least expected — and never sought — in Loch Lomond. Such a rarity brought about lengthy investigation and a story to match, so that it appears best to confine our "identi-kit" interlude to species more commonly found in our sometimes surprising loch.

Before drawing the line on the subject, perhaps a closer look should be taken at the vital line which runs down the centre of the fish's flanks — the lateral line. It is doubtless the most sensory part of the fish, coupled with the skin surface, and it carries vibrant messages to the brain. Our Atlantic salmon were using this built-in radar system many moons before the man-made invention. The highly-developed lateral line nerves register vibrations in the water, direction and strength of current resistance, and pressure of water, thereby enabling the fish to avoid obstacles in its path. A miracle of nature indeed and, were I stranded in Greenland with an abundance of modern (and wonderful) homing aids to assist me set off for the shores of my birth, I'd swap the lot for the uncanny accuracy of the salmon's system. We may *know* where home is, but the fish *get there*. Without fail.

Losing the Head

Disregarding sea trout for the time being, there seems little doubt that salmon do *not* feed in fresh water and our flies and baits are not *food* to them — merely little nuisances who have dared to enter their domain.

Below is a picture of a fresh-run sea trout, and what was in its tummy seconds before it took my fly. Apropos, let's consider *Salar* and see if his actions might be compared to those of that suicidal sea trout.

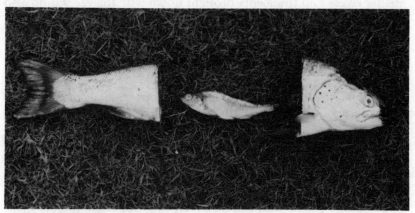

A 4 lb sea trout. The perch found in its stomach was probably swallowed more in anger than in hunger

The whole object of our angling loch exercise is to make the fish a bit annoyed or interested when *it is really indifferent*. We can also aim to catch them unawares at times when they relieve the boredom of what can sometimes be an unduly prolonged stay in the loch. Without the required rain, where can they go? Are they *ready* to go anywhere? The loch can fish very well for long periods when the fish are present and temporarily trapped. Even winter needn't stop the keen angler finding out a bit more about his prey, and many of us have watched the adult cock salmon, on the redds (see Loch Lingo), chasing away small fish in the vicinity of the hen. The male fish is angry at their intrusion.

How often in the course of fishing can we, the anglers, become *angry, excited, bored and suffering – or not really in the mood –* and yet still catch fish. The same emotional states, ironically, are usually

155

the main reasons for the fish's downfall. It is up to us to complete the picture, and ensure success, by being present, well-armed, when any of these moods are on the fish.

When fresh fish enter the loch, for the first few hours, perhaps days, they feel a natural excitement, or *joie de vivre*, at having reached the area of their eventual spawning ground, be it the region of a river or burn mouth. Conditions might change and cause them to move from the comfort of their lies, and again they will become disturbed and excited and as they settle will take very well indeed. Rising rivers and the scents brought down with the vegetation also thrill them and they will move around, perhaps away from the colourful region, but still remain most "takeable". They can sense their eventual terminus.

If we could keep a tame salmon in a tank at home, I'm sure we could throw away the barometer. The fish has a built-in one and will have forecast rain long before the first drops make us reach out for the waterproofs. You should have some (if not plenty of) fish *before* that rain and — despite what I've often read — *during it*. Especially the first rains. I have lost count of the number of times I've come in like a drowned rat, with fish in the boat, all caught in the rain. But rain is not always the same and certain kinds of rainy conditions deserve a book in their own right.

To return to the salmon, however, the four basic factors mentioned, and a few others, excite fish and this is when to be amongst them with the correctly-presented fly or bait.

None of us would like to be locked up, for long, in a spartan room when our favourite surroundings are not too far away. Anxiety and boredom would set in and we would take more than a passing interest in anything which would relieve our feelings — even something to which we would normally be indifferent. Dangle this kind of carrot before the fish and the response should be automatic.

We are never at our best when ill, or suffering any of the multitude of ailments which can easily come our way. We snap at our loved ones, behave badly to strangers and get annoyed very easily at any intrusion upon our recovery. Pity, then, the poor fish which is being eaten alive by a lamprey or is still recovering from a seal bite or scars caused by escaping the nets. The fish's ill humour is completely excusable and, again, here is the chance to visit his domain and administer your own form of surgery!

The two prime fish shown on the cover of this book, a 16lb salmon and 5lb sea trout, were both liced when caught (one is still

156

showing on the flanks of the sea trout), yet a closer study will reveal injuries not perhaps evident at first glance. The salmon has a badly grazed anal fin and light scarring on and below the pelvic fin on the belly zone. The sea trout has a fresh wound also — a small, neat chunk of its gill cover having been removed. These are trifling injuries compared to many I have seen, yet enough to put a fish into an irritable "taking" state and the captor into a deliriously ecstatic one.

Due to stored-up body fats from rich feeding in the sea, the salmon does not suffer from hunger in fresh water. It is simply its state of mind, and not its famine, which prompts it to take. These moody factors, present in the fish, and your timely arrival, combine to ensure success. Out there, somewhere, are many willing "clients". Finding them will often be hard but, if you are really lucky, you may meet up with a group of individuals who are bored, angry and hurt. They may get too excited. Arrest them at once!

Loch Trout

Over ten years ago, in the first week of October, I thought I had drifted too shallow in Mill o' Ross Bay, and made a hurried, and careless, last cast. The nylon landed in an untidy bundle, with all three flies plopping into the clear shallow water much too close to each other. A large brown shape broke the surface, in the middle of this mess, and shot away just under the boat, ripping off line at a steady pace.

The rod had to be held at an awkward angle to let the running fish clear the sunken outboard propellor, and I thought, "Anything can happen here." The boat started to grind against the rocky shore and there was hectic panic before a final push with an oar floated her again. Line was still going out and out, but eventually I was able to start the outboard — not without trouble — and guide the boat out slowly at an angle away from the fish and also a stony cairn in the bay. All the while line was still going out with the fish.

When everything seemed under control, I stopped the engine in deeper water, to start and play out the fish properly. But it wasn't there any more. The line went slack. The horrible, vacant feeling when you lose a good fish is only understood by fellow sufferers and there's *never* another boat about to weep with you.

I was still reeling-in when, suddenly, a large dark fish leapt out of the water, off the bow, and "stood on his tail". The rod buckled. I was re-connected! Again the boat had to be engined out and the fish fought so hard that the whole process had to be repeated before the tiring fish, and angler, met at close range. It appeared to be a ripe, coloured sea trout, but weren't the spots *red*? It weighed 12½ lb, and was confirmed later to be one of our loch trout. The proportions were beautiful, the head small and no noticeably large jagged teeth. Very unlike the *Ferox* of Assynt and Veyatie, whose appearance could verily scare you to death.

I'd caught a good number of loch trout before and have managed a few since. They all fight well, giving the impression of well-rested fish with strong fin and muscle. But the main quality I now associate with them is a crafty, foxy cunning which seems to improve with old age. I do hope I develop these qualities likewise, which will enable me to spend less time engaged in what seem ridiculous contests.

A year later, in August, I was fly fishing on the south side of Inchfad, near Darroch, and noticed what seemed to be a boat in some difficulty or other, out in the deeps to the north-west of Darroch. There were three aboard and the bodies of two kept permutating, while the other rowed, tiredly but steadily, towards the area of my own boat.

It was some time before I realised they were "into a fish". Sensing their difficulty, I flipped in my flies and rowed towards them. It was a Balmaha hire boat and the three young men in it looked rather ashen and upset, especially the one standing (or half kneeling, as he was) on the stern seat. His rod, a short one, was bent completely over and the end ring kept submerging below the surface.

I shouted over, asking if they needed help. Back came a reply to the effect that they couldn't get the fish to come in. I could deduce a fairly obvious reason for that: apart from the rod appearing too light and whippy, they were keeping the fish alive and well by rowing it along, without really tiring it out at all.

"Stop rowing!" I yelled, and with reluctance they did. "Give it some stick now," I urged, getting the obvious reply, "I'm giving it the lot." "We've no net," yelled another. Bit by bit, the plot was unwinding.

I got as close as I could and safely "flopped" my net into their boat and, with steady pumping, up came the fish, which was fairly well netted and swung aboard. There followed delighted shouting and handshaking and I hurried back to them to collect my share and see their catch. Amid gleeful faces and backslapping youth, lay quite the most ugly cock fish I have ever seen in my life! Its head was gigantic, the eyes bulged and the body was as lean as a rake. It was a loch trout of only 5½ lb. I hadn't the heart not to join in their merriment at this, their first fish on the fly. "Where did you hook it?" I asked. They pointed to Inchgalbraith, an islet about a staggering *mile* away from the netting spot! "We've rowed it from there." "Strewth!" I thought, "and the fly old brute *swam* all the way!"

After Capture

My great joy in angling, nowadays, lies in the pursuit of the loch's salmon and sea trout, with the fly as method. The feeling of satisfaction is immense. Struggling to be at the right place, using the fly best suited to the all-round conditions, and timing the tightening to match the entirely different types of rises one encounters: all combine to create an instantaneous feeling of a successful "stalk". The 10-pounder lying at your feet has succumbed to your tactics and, somehow, it appears more of a prize than a fish caught on the troll.

Whatever the method, there is always the pleasant problem of what to do with the fish. Fresh salmon from the fishmonger's slab fetch a handsome price per pound, though, throughout the year, there is of course price fluctuation and, even locally, there can be inexplicable differences between prices in one hotel or restaurant and another.

It pains me to admit it, but this side of angling is the one I like least. A tired angler venturing into bargaining basements seems to detract from the sport and, certainly, never presents a true picture of what went beforehand. As I hand over a fish, the picture of the rise is still present and the moment shared only by fish and angler seems to be degraded, if that is the word, when it simply becomes another fish.

Like it or not, however, expenses are always present and the sale of a fish can help us last out and maybe even sneak in another quick visit to the loch!

I have mentioned the use of a well-soaked sack in which to keep the fish. This can be rinsed and then the fish transferred to a polythene bag for transporting to the place of sale or disposal. Speaking for myself, friends often mention their needs in advance, which is nice to know, but hardly helps in bringing about the correct size of downfall!

It surely would be a pity if, for some reason, the angler could not eat his own catch and yet I know of many who have stated their preference for "the stuff in the tin". I have no problems at all in that respect and relish poached salmon or sea trout, or a finnoch fried in butter . . . fit for a King!

It has almost been a ritual for me to keep the first two good-sized fish of the season for the deep freeze. These are usually eaten within two months and, in spite of reading that salmon and sea trout will freeze for much longer, I find a distinct flavour loss, possibly more so with the salmon which has a stronger appeal when eaten just after being caught.

Of all the fish to gut and clean, our game fish are by far the cleanest and simplest. Unlike the well-filled cod's tummy, there is little present to remove and, personally, I find the distinctive aroma of the salmon's visit to the sea quite pleasant.

There are many knives today specially designed with serrated double-edged blades which will cut through the spinal column with great ease. I have lately acquired an electric knife which, although the makers do not advise its use on bone, seems little troubled by it providing undue force is not used. The steaks, particularly the flesh, are a revelation in their perfection of cut.

I give each steak only a light rinse before individually packeting in polythene bags, pressing as much air out as possible, then packing tightly into a polythene box which bears an important date label. At the top of the rib cage of each steak is a thick black layer of matter which many remove, arduously, under a running tap, but I prefer to have it remain until defrosting when it virtually drops out, with little trouble.

Poaching salmon and sea trout is simple and quick. The salted water, to which I add a tablespoon of vinegar, is brought to the boil, the steaks entered and brought back to the boil for no more than 5-8 minutes. To retain firmness and flavour, the steaks should be allowed to cool in the same water, from which any scum can be removed beforehand. Cookery books provide many alternatives.

Were it not for the multitude of small, dagger-like bones, I would place perch high on my list of favourite foods. For this reason, only good-sized perch should be chosen and baked in buttered foil. Many find pike a tasty offering, baked, but my recipes here would lack authority. To anyone owning the luxury of a microwave oven, the permutations are endless, plus the great advantage in defrosting. My experience with these machines is that fish suit them very well. They can be defrosted, seasoned and then cooked, all on the one

160

plate, with great results. I have not found the need to fillet many fish, but simply place them in, gutted, but otherwise whole. When cooked the spinal column and other unwelcome matter is easily parted from the steaming flesh by careful use of a knife.

8

Problems Small and Large

Two at a Time — or Keep our lochs tidy

YOU all know the old saying, "Just take one thing at a time". In fishing you can observe the saying closely and so, too, can the fish. A slight complication arises, however, when two different fish each take one fly, or bait, at a time when you are fishing three flies on the one cast or three trolls from the one boat. We now have a very interesting situation in which the saying has to be altered to, "Just take two things at a time"!

The original saying is usually delivered in mellow, soothing tones and is meant immediately to calm down a distressed or upset person. Its effect on an angler out solo, with two fish on at the same time, I would dearly love to witness! Imagine, on the troll, one and then two reels screeching away with two rods bent beyond words into a brace of salmon, tearing about with gusto all over the loch.

It's not very tidy!

As to many others, such a fate has come my way, and I think I now know what Izaak Walton meant by the "compleat angler"! Any fool can catch one fish. It takes two to tangle...

Now for the cure. Since it has happened more than once to me, after prolonged thought I have come up with a speedy answer to the problem. I'm sure you'll see the sense in it. *Throw one rod overboard at once*. You will now have one fish on at a time and, with luck, you will boat it and already be making mental arrangements with your unfortunate insurance company!

The alternative needs extremely nimble feet (in a lurching boat), sharp eyes and hands that move quicker than a card cheat's. Since you have presumably three baits in the water, it is obvious that one is idle. Such will be your panic that you will feel you should have a fish on *it* too. Pick it up to be sure, reel-in, and if you do have

162

another fish on, then it's up to you. I've never heard of *three* and my advice strictly ends at *two*.

So things are OK so far, albeit you have only seconds to think, "Which one do I play first?" The fish are already tossing up for ends, and you will pick the wrong one. He will fight you like a fury, leaping and diving, and his aim will be accurate enough to carry him, in a sudden jump, straight across your other line and this, in turn, will get a response from the other fish. He will leap straight back across the first line. Some people, at this stage, think such a situation quite good. They reason that they can virtually treat the two fish as one, since the lines are now united, and proceed to place both rods and reels together, in the one hand, and carry on from there. I suppose it *could* work, even if one reel is a multiplier which must sit uppermost on the rod and the other an orthodox reel which hangs below the rod.

But, *to be serious*, fish rarely do exactly what you want them to do when hooked. You must, in the main, stay alert to their every change of pull and movement through the water, without any slack line whatsoever. Most of the anglers I know, with great experience, have learned what to expect at various stages of the fight but, rest assured, they have all had the acrobatic, uncontrollable brute who brings out the sweat by the gallon.

If you are out alone, it is well-nigh impossible to ensure that one of two fish on doesn't get slack. On the odd occasion you may get lucky, as I was, off Carrick Rock, when a pair *were* landed. One was an 11 lb salmon, which got most of my attention, and the other a 6 lb sea trout. Throughout my playing of the salmon, the other reel merely gave short squeaks rather than frenzied pulls and, from time to time, as the salmon *swam* rather steadily, I did have a chance to check that the other fish was still there. You do get a little help in the respect that the "idle" fish is keeping off the bottom, wondering what is happening, but sometime or other you will have to sort out the two lines as they try to foul each other.

The salmon *had* to be killed at once because the net would again be needed. I had to bite through the nylon and shake off the hooks, leaving the sprat mount fouled in the mesh. Small matter and it could have been worse. The sea trout came to more urgent life and, when safely aboard, I found the treble was right down the gullet. No chance!

I have seen it happen, several times, to others on the loch. Passing the pier at Balmaha, two cronies from the bay had just sat down

163

Two 7 lb salmon and a 4½ lb sea trout, taken on the fly one July on the Pilot Bank. The centre fish was one of two hooked at the same time. See *p. 165*

when they had to stand up — quickly! One landed a salmon on the Toby, and his friend another on the sprat. I am told onlookers thought it was some kind of Highland Jig aboard, with each party ducking under the other's "sword" from time to time.

It also happens on the fly fairly often. I was just about to net a 2 lb sea trout on the Pilot Bank some seasons ago and, since I always kneel and crouch when netting, it was perhaps easier to see a silver flash below the dangling 2-pounder. The wee fish must have wondered where the blazes he was going *again*, as a 6-pounder took off with the tail fly! They both stayed on and, for the record, the bob fly was a Pheasant and Yellow and the tail a Burton, size 8.

Many times two fish will rise to the one cast, sometimes both taking, sometimes one breaking. Off Mill o' Ross Bay I once saw, as clear as crystal through Polaroids, two salmon rise to my cast in different directions, across the cast. They were speedy fish but, as sometimes happens, there was a time lag caused by the sudden surprise, a good thing with salmon. Both fish took. I realised later that the tail fly, a Woodcock and Mixed, is now rusting in a kelt's jaw somewhere, but the 7 lb salmon on the bob came in nicely and I prised out a Turkey and Green. Guess what fly I put back on the tail?

Finally, on the subject of braces, there is a rather sad note to relate. Years ago now, our lochs and rivers were hit by the dreadful UDN (ulcerated dermal necrosis). On a very bright day late in May, before we had heard too much of the disease, a friend and I shared a drifting boat across the Ladies Point, at Inchcruin, both of us fishing the fly in a good fresh wind. I vividly remember noticing a change in the light through the Polaroids; I could now see my sunken tail fly, a Claret and Blue, very clearly indeed. I took off the glasses next cast but could barely pick it out. My friend was fishing without glasses and said he couldn't see his tail fly at all. I think the Polaroids, in addition to enabling you to see into water, must also train your eyes to see the flies for the next cast or two after you have taken them off.

What happened next, I will not forget for the rest of my angling life and I hope I never see the like again. From very deep below my flies appeared two white circles about the size of tennis balls. One ball headed straight up to the bob and the other crossed up to the tail fly. "I've been fishing in the sun too long," thought I. Then suddenly all was revealed as the balls disappeared, as if a conjurer were present, and became the broad silver flanks of two salmon, no less than 12 lb each. The white balls were snow-white, round patches of the new disease on the crowns of the fish's heads. It took a while to figure it out. My friend heard and saw the bob-fly fish crash the surface water but did not, from the bow seat, see its mate at the tail. It's the only time I have ever been glad not to have hooked fish.

A sight which can still distress me, when I stand ready with the net, assisting a fellow angler on the river land a grilse or the like, is seeing its mate swimming alongside, following every twist and turn of the hooked fish in sympathy.

Large Fish

Everyone hears of a really big fish, whether it comes from the loch or elsewhere.

To start off a fishing career, I often think it would be a mistake to catch a 20-pounder. If your next fish is a mere 8 lb and fresh-run, then you may be in for a surprise. The smaller fish, be it a salmon, will be less predictable and will generally lead you a merrier dance.

The first sight of a big salmon, as it surfaces in the open loch, gives the hopeful captor a great thrill indeed. Maybe too great, on reflection, since he will be so impressed with the size that he will concentrate on, and become mesmerised by, the fish, instead of thinking out landing arrangements in advance. In general, the throb of sheer power being transmitted up the line is something never forgotten, and the ultimate netting is a very tense affair indeed. When you cannot physically lift a netted fish aboard, using both hands and all your strength, you've nearly got an OBE coming (Order of Biggest Ever)!

But my original point is this: it is rarely that the sheer size of the fish automatically guarantees its fighting qualities. When you think of it, being oversize can sometimes be a problem, and I feel this is so with very large fish. With nearly every big salmon or sea trout I have caught, there seems to have been more time to predict the fish's next move and, although powerful, the runs are more "readable" and many leaps less likely.

The initial and most memorable thrill is when you see the line stretch deep into the water without seeing the creature when it is near your boat. The hair on the back of your neck should be the sudden cause of temporary blindness, as the skip of your cap slides over your eyes!

Perhaps seasoned anglers would agree with my assessment of large sea trout behaviour, as I've often found it. The hen plays much harder, faster, and gamer, which sometimes reminds me of real life! I have lost count of heavy cock sea trout which, apart from an initial skirmish, are dully content to swim round the boat slowly, then suddenly give up. This certainly would apply mostly when the species is ripened and far from silver. The fight seems to leave the male a lot easier and earlier.

Most cock fish weight a pound or two less than you guess, unlike the hen, which should have a build-up of heavy roe at the back end of the season, and can give your over-oiled scales a shock.

166

The best sport, on the fly of course, comes to me from the 4-7lb class fish, whose mobility can be astonishing. Grilse are marvelous and, for their size, fresh finnock take a bit of beating. Much has been my surprise many times when the 4-pounder I played arrives aboard at $1\frac{1}{2}$lb.

Talking of fight, or the lack of it, a salmon of 16lb did a most surprising thing, when hooked off Darroch. It came straight to the side of the boat and turned over at once. I had to repeat twice to my mate, "Net it! Go on, net it!" But, "Why wake it up?" thought I. Without the slightest fuss it arrived at our feet. It seemed quite unbelievable, and many might have given the fish a prod or two to make sure the imagination wasn't playing tricks. It was a most beautiful salmon and was complete with sea lice slingers (lice with the long tail sacs still attached), showing it was straight out of the salt water. He had made his first stop, probably, and taken up his lie at Darroch, as the King of Fishes does, and chased away the first wee nuisance of a fish that had the cheek to linger. The "wee fish" was mine, and was attached to the rod by a line! The salmon was almost entirely exhausted by his fast journey into the loch and I felt a certain guilt at being there to welcome him. It didn't last long!

You can go out on the loch for a wee while, in a wee boat, fishing a wee rod and wee flies — then get a wee tug. It should weigh, on average, about 12 wee pounds! It could be that, since you have been diligent enough to keep practically everything "wee", in respect to your quarry, that you will then say, "Pass me the wee net." This will be your first, and *last*, mistake of the day! It's all very well to say, "We'll catch the fish first and worry about the size second." Prepare for a 30-pounder, and be not embarrassed by the size of your net to suit.

On three different occasions I have seen or heard about fellow anglers having to board a captor's boat in order to assist him to remove, or lose, a very big fish.

Even with a large and strong net, catastrophes can happen, and such a fate befell a Balmaha angler in the late stages of landing a very large salmon. It happened on the Claddich shore, opposite where the power station now stands. The fish had fought like a fury and appeared spent as the net was slipped under its body. The technical details escape me, but the fish disappeared, complete with net, to a fate we can only ponder.

It's amazing how a fish can dislodge a foreign object. I remember standing on the bridge at Ballochruin, over the River Endrick, to see what I thought was a small fish fluttering and disappearing, always at the same spot. Curiosity being what it is, I slipped down to water level and was astonished to find that the wee fish was a rather large silver Mepps spoon, attached to the head region of a fair-sized fish. It appeared to be standing on its tail, rubbing against a rock, in a continuous effort to dislodge the hooks.

Another rather odd sight, concerning large fish, was a near 20 lb fresh salmon floating upside down in the Net Bay. When I circled the boat to approach it closer, the fish righted itself and disappeared slowly. I subsequently heard that, on the same day, from near enough the same spot, a salmon had been removed from the loch, suffering from the effects of a ·22 bullet. Acting as my own censor, I refrain from further comment.

As mentioned under boat gear, I always carry a tailer in the boat as well as a net, and have had to use it several times. With large salmon and their slower movements when ready (if they ever are) to leave the water, it is a tense but fairly foolproof method of landing fish. As with the net, there are no unsightly marks left on the fish, but one or two precautions are necessary to avoid disaster.

Firstly, the fish should be virtually "dead" or only moving slightly with the wave. Allowance must be made for distorted images of both fish and tailer, as water can play tricks on us; the same sort of thing happens when you drop something in the shallows and what appears a simple retrieving task is complicated by your misjudgement of depth and position. The loop formed by the tailer should encircle the tail of the fish and continue about one third of the way up the body, avoiding any contact with the flesh — which is the difficult bit.

The next step should be carried out with authority. It is a two-stage step, performed in almost one movement. The loop should be released and a firm, smooth upward pull exerted. Done correctly, the tailer loop will contact the fish's body and slip down as it tightens into the wrist of the tail. If it is a salmon, all should be well and the grip should be maintained firmly as you swing the fish aboard; this usually involves releasing the rod and reel so that both hands are free to complete the landing. If it is a sea trout, you will have been extremely lucky! The tail of this fish tends to collapse under pressure, quite unlike the firm, angled wrist of the salmon.

In states of emergency, I have removed a fish by the gills. However, this procedure should be unnecessary if you carry a large net.

If the net is large enough, I prefer to slide the fish, or glide it slowly across the net, and make the upward thrust when the fish appears centrally placed. The part of the fish requiring immobility is the tail and I find the centre part collapses in a curve, reducing the danger from both head and tail.

There are situations which call for different methods, more so when the fish is hooked on one of your three flies. Beware the other two! Much better that the tail fly is the "hooker", and you can see the other two. Watch them just the same.

A big net is a boon and eases many a headache, and prevents untold excuses being uttered to a (sometimes) unsympathetic audience.

To lose a fish during the course of playing it out can be a bitter pill to swallow, but after years of losing the odd one here and there I have become inured to the fact that nothing can be gained by dwelling on early departures. In fact, if I am to lose a fish nowadays, the quicker the better, thus averting the biggest tragedy of all: for a "dead" fish to come unstuck at the final tricky stage when the net is presented to it. To have been in intimate contact with a good fish for some ten or fifteen minutes, and to have played it with consummate skill, only to witness it sink almost within touching distance, at the rim of the net, is probably the biggest angling catastrophe of all. An empty net and an empty feeling... It happens to all anglers at some time or another and, speaking for myself, there is only one old Scots word to describe how one feels about the entire experience: *scunnered*.

I must admit to one huge depression when it comes to large salmon. There are times, it seems, when we have done entirely the wrong thing by catching them. I still feel, when I am allowed the privilege, total and deep-seated aggravation to be told by a hotelier, say, that "It's far too big. We want them about the 10 lb mark." It is at that moment that I feel an overwhelming desire to cut a 20-pounder in half, in front of their blood-spattered trousers, to compensate for my original sin! I jest, of course, but reluctantly accept a reduction when an increase seems more fair. Big might be beautiful, but...

In its way, therefore, this does reverse the earlier reasoning to "We'll think about the weight first, and worry about catching it later!"

* * *

169

Some Bad Habits

The following list of angling crimes relate to Lomond only because I committed them there at some time or another. Fishing foreign waters tends to make one more careful about basic preparations, but perhaps over-familiarity with Lomond may have led to the development of a few bad habits, all too easily acquired. Some can be comical but most invite disaster. They are certainly bad angling habits *anywhere*.

It is a small point, but probably the most important part of your tackle: the POINT of your hook. Be it a treble or fly hook, if you cannot make a scratch with it on your nail, either sharpen it with a small honing stone or throw it away. Some rascals give them away, then wait for the sad stories!

There is little excuse for using blunt weapons, since it will take longer to relate tales of misfortune than to put the matter right at the start. From the instant contact is made with a fish, a lot depends on the keenness of the hook point. The first few jerks of the fish need give only slight penetration, which will rapidly improve, but a dulled point will slide off the bony jaw. Thankfully, but not without much searching for good irons, dressing your own flies helps in more ways than one. You deal with the hook *first*.

SMOKING is bad for your health. It can also be bad for your tackle: so much so that every spool of nylon or floss should carry another Government warning. I am ashamed to admit that too casual an approach to fly casting one day, with cigarette held in the first two fingers of the right hand, caused the cast and a good 5 yd of main line to shoot freely into the loch. It is infinitely easier and speedier to part company with floss, using the above method, the merest touch of ash being enough to set free the only fish of the day.

WADERS can be folded down to knee level, once safely aboard the boat, to cool the thighs. It is a much cooler experience to forget you have done this on returning to base in 3 ft of muddy water! Always fasten the rubber loops (I haven't met a good pair yet) at the top of your waders around your belt before un-happing your boat, otherwise you may fail to notice the entry of a trickle of the loch into the upper part of the waders. Sitting down contentedly at the tiller you will be surprised at the steady rush of cooling fluid to the private parts.

Still wading, beware the end of the day as you converse with a fellow angler when happing up. As you continue some minor point of argument, you linger at the transom cleat end, in soft mud. Task completed, you step away, noticing a bootless foot appear at the surface. It is *yours*, and pondering where to put it can be a sudden and perilous decision. Even worse, both feet have been known not to move at all!

CAMERAS are delicate and should be kept dry and insulated from shocks received in travelling through rough water. It does not pay to keep the camera *too* long in what you think is a dry polythene bag. Dampness can be present and the repairs which may result tend to be expensive. My biggest tragedy was, when carrying tins of powdered milk in my rucksack, the lid of one came off. Of course it was also raining hard. The bill came to £20.

I don't do it all the time, but I must *try*. FLIES should be taken in, at the end of a drift, and the cast hitched around the reel via the tail hook and secured in a lower rod ring or fixed into the cork handle. This applies particularly to owners of outboards with reverse gear, which I think is self-explanatory. The flies *should* be cast out astern if you intend to row off a drift in a circular route. This is a good habit and is in the wrong chapter. Do not be too surprised at the number of fish which find your flies more attractive fished this way. It would need confirmation, but I seem to recall a 9lb sea trout being captured thus off Inchlonaig, some years ago. I hope it doesn't happen too often or we will be unable to enjoy normal drifting for boats going round in wee circles

If you hire or own the rather noisy, but completely reliable SEAGULL engine, make allowance for the fact that you will converse too loudly with your pal in the bow, so you should remember to whisper confidential messages, or pass a note over by hand.

Better two small FLASKS than one big one, unless it is made of stainless steel like my own. Nothing is more disheartening than to pull ashore for a cuppa consisting of cold water laced with finely ground glass. Better an old Primus aboard with much blackened kettle to match. Nothing is much good without MATCHES, so hide plenty in sealed plastic bags.

If you must POACH, stick to eggs. It is a cardinal sin to share a boat on the loch and whip your flies into the other fellow's rightful half-share in the water, especially when he's tying on the dud fly you have just given him. It would serve you right if he caught a 30-pounder on it by a retaliatory cast zipped into your area as you linger too long on the back cast.

Because you have finished with a DRIFT, don't finish it completely for others coming behind. Either drift into what may be fairly considered "dead" water before starting the outboard or row off gently. If you don't, expect the same treatment. The drastic outcome, when many boats are out, has been experienced all too often. The fish won't have it, and *nobody* will have them.

Being too lazy to shorten a DROPPER which is maybe only an inch or so too long, causing it to persistently twist round the main cast, deserves no sympathy. It takes up very little time and spares your companion much bad language. Constantly changing the tail fly, as I often do, can result in too short a space between the middle and point fly, easily cured by renewing the end length of nylon to normal distance.

Baits and flies should always be checked for WEED which usually clings to trolled lures. Do this regularly on the troll or discover it too late.

Knowing your CAST is floating and dragging an undesirable wake is rarely cured by simply hoping it will soon sink. Oiled cotton jackets or dapping fly floatants often contaminate the fingers so that a quick rinse in detergent will soon cure the problem.

Sticking to the same cast of three flies when a change of only one, perhaps, can bring about a difference, is more fully covered under fly fishing, but I still tend to consider this a fault. Which one to change, admittedly, is often a problem.

Not PLANNING how to best set up the boat for a short drift, or a series of short drifts, can disturb your peace of mind and the *one* fish which might be willing to give your flies a chance.

NYLON is used by anglers to help catch fish, *not* birds and precious wildlife. I know it has been said before, but do cut into small pieces (or burn) discarded nylon, rather than come across the distress of some strangulated little creature. Makers strive to create near invisibility in this material but its lethal properties when entwined round a little innocent being are pathetic in the extreme.

It is easy to cultivate any of the foregoing slipshod ways, but, in concluding this minor list, I still find it a sad business to meet someone who has practically no bad angling habits at all. Often he will come in puritanically "clean", all because he cannot lay down an absolutely sloppy, unenticing cast. His dapping is usually too perfect as well, minus the crazy antics and errors that can drive the most serene of fish into a suicidal frenzy. He does not occasionally stray into ultra-shallow water when trolling, in case the baits are impaired, preferring to remain well out into the deeps where he can safely watch the wayward play out their fish! He never looks away from his flies when casting, thereby reacting too quickly to hook the salmon that others would allow more time as they turn and wave to the *Maid of the Loch* with one hand. His boat is usually immaculate, not the scale-covered, blood-ridden, nylon-strewn and beer-can littered mess it might be. He always delays to be safe until the wind goes down a bit or goes ashore at once when rain threatens. He's a good bloke really, though, leaving the fish to the daft ones who don't even know that it's raining.

The trouble with bad habits lies in acquiring all the wrong ones for use at the right time and, speaking for myself entirely, I would not at all mind exhibiting a few on days when you apparently do everything right and yet come in with results that are all too obviously *wrong!*

9

Of Coarse

Pike

WHEN I think of the little footbridge in Balmaha Bay, I tend to suffer from a kind of double image. I can picture it easily enough during the busy summertime, when literally thousands of tourist feet trample to and fro across its tiny planks. However, the other picture portrays it more as an interesting spectator's platform, around dawn, when little else stirs but the irrepressible angler. It was at that otherwise gently revealing time of day that I witnessed, in a most vivid and unforgettable manner, the skulking, crafty qualities built into our largest coarse fish on Loch Lomond. At close range I watched the lethal and ultra-swift dart of the pike as it struck down a wayward morsel.

A mallard duck was swimming with her chicks close to the jetty end and, whilst musing over their cuteness, I noticed a dark projection right below my feet, under the footbridge. Whatever it was appeared harmless until one little chick cruised away from the brood, hell-bent on adventure. Suddenly the inert shape vanished and, in a split second, the chick was sucked under to lodge in razor-sharp molars reminiscent of those of *Jaws*. *Esox Lucius*, typically, had struck again.

Apart from being a base for game fishing, the Balmaha district abounds in coarse fish, including pike, perch, powan, roach and eels. Both the pike and perch favour the shallow, weedy areas in the district, particularly in the summer time, and it is not unknown for pike to bask in the sunny shallows, as still as the menacing crocodile.

When setting out in the morning after the loch's salmon and sea trout, the boat often scatters huge shoals of small perch, which swim around the hull in an almost tame way to regroup their forces. Quite often these well-camouflaged shoals are harried by small jack pike,

The author's largest pike, 28½ lb, caught on a Golden Sprat. In its stomach were two freshly taken fish – a brown trout and a finnock, both 1½ lb

which relish their taste and suffer little from the perch's plentiful small bones. Roach and powan are high on the pike's list of favourite mouthfuls, thus explaining why many coarse anglers consider the gift of small perch, powan or roach, dead or alive, as a bait sent from heaven. The pike is used to feeding on these species and is therefore less wary of them, one reason for their deadliness as bait.

It is little wonder that each year sees a great increase in the number of visiting coarse-fishing anglers, many in search of the great specimens the loch can produce, others well content to spin or fish worm and maggot for the perch.

Unlike the streamlined game fish, pike could never be called pretty, with beady eyes set atop an iron-hard skull and a fixed stare which must almost hypnotise smaller fish into submission. They certainly mesmerise me, being the only fish which can look a human straight in the eye, due to the placement of the binocular-type eyeballs. I don't like this feature one little bit, since I feel the angry stare intends some kind of explanation for *my* behaviour! The main purpose of the eye positioning is to enable the fish to look upwards, for prey, and it is not endowed with the all-round vision which most other species possess. The jaws impressively complete this ferocious-looking customer's appearance and, seen at close range for the first time, it is not easily forgotten. The mouth simply bristles with jagged teeth, the front ones designed to grip and hold the prey rather than chew it. Even the roof of the mouth has smaller teeth which are cleverly designed to flex and collapse under the pressure of the meal

175

it attempts to swallow. To simplify the latter task, the pike invariably seizes a small fish sideways, then turns it to be swallowed head first, a point worth much consideration when it comes to baiting up for them, later on.

You are not meant to *see* camouflage clothing, quite the opposite. The pike is well dressed to blend with its often weedy surroundings. The overall colour of the fish is a limey, mottled green dotted with dark spots, with a belly of paler colour.

Speaking for myself, I rarely welcome them aboard, for reasons of safety afloat. Great capture they might be, but the skin surface is covered in a slimy, mucous-like, protective substance which I have always found a complete menace when deposited on the floorboards. I find it all too easy to slip whilst afloat without any help from this gel-like substance and, again, here is reason enough to justify the old sacks I recommend you have aboard. Even they will require rinsing beyond belief.

For many years the pike has been referred to as "the poor man's salmon", and there is little doubt that, considering their size and the moderate amount it costs to fish for them on the loch, they give hundreds of anglers pleasure aplenty, summer and winter. They are designed to do a job and, although I firmly refuse to be drawn into the never-ending debate about what damage they do or don't do, I must in all honesty state that I admire the ways of Nature too much to join the ranks of pike haters.

When all is said and done, it is we, the anglers, who interfere with the ways of the fish rather than the reverse. The poor pike who takes the angler's salmon bait often suffers to the full, this being the angry reaction of one disappointed that his catch was not the one sought. Hardly the pike's fault, and the basic truth is that if our baits did not range so freely through the waters of the loch, containing such varied species, these problems would never arise. Much as I am steeped in the sport of angling, I still have to admit that *we* are the interlopers and I'm sure Nature could manage without *us* very well. The fish were here first!

Before outlining some of the modern methods of tackling Loch Lomond pike, I am reminded of quite the most furious angling argument I have ever heard. Languishing in the Inchmurrin Hotel on a windless day, a group of idle game fishers momentarily ran out of debating points, which, knowing the breed, is a rare occurrence. There was a pause before someone fired the unforgettable question to the nodding gallery. "*What*", roared the voice, "is the fastest fish in fresh water?" I left as sleeves were being rolled up. It was salmon and sea trout versus pike — again! My own involvement came at the late dramatic stages, when challenged as one of the "Don't knows". It was no time for a smug reply and I risked, "It depends what you mean. Over what distance?" I still prefer to answer this question with a question, in spite of the fact that every penny I have would go on the pike, *over a short distance*. The point was proved in a recent TV programme in which it took ultra-slow motion to show clearly how fast a small baitfish vanished from the scene as it swam several feet away from a lurking pike. Whereas pike have few challengers over a short distance I would not care to wait on one returning from the stamina-sapping trip from Greenland to the Endrick mouth. Give me the salmon's tail every time!

In the course of trolling for game fish over the years, many fish have been landed and a good proportion lost, but invariably the mounted Golden Sprat has at least been returned — admittedly often mangled by the gyrations of the frenzied fish. Frequently, due to carelessness in the use of weak or old nylon, a break can occur, which is entirely the fault of the angler. Likewise, knots have a strange way of coming adrift when they have been tied in haste or with not enough care. But, on the troll, there are times when an unseen fish breaks away and, when the trace is recovered, there are strange frayed ends in the nylon some inches above where the bait once was. The answer is often pike.

A careful look at their jaw armoury should impress the would-be captor with one obvious fact: the fish is armed with a pair of scissors for jaws. He should tackle up accordingly.

Although pike will sometimes play around with a bait before finally swallowing it, the resting place of the hooks is often far back in the mouth, leaving some inches of nylon to float about under tension, across the efficient and plentiful teeth. This state of affairs is bad and, although it happens perchance to the game angler, the fish will never be given the same chance of escape by the expert fishing for pike. He has rightly considered his quarry and eliminated, or reduced, the chances of parting company with his hard-sought fish. I tend to disbelieve that salmon really mean to swallow the trolled bait, in spite of the odd few which are hooked far back in the mouth after an engulfing take, and am inclined to think that, were there no hooks on the bait the salmon would eject it after its damaging attack; but the pike has a more straightforward and natural object: to gulp it down into the depths of its tummy where the acid juices will soon do the rest. It really makes a meal of it.

There are several distinct bonuses enjoyed by the pike angler which the game fisher on Loch Lomond often views with envy. The pike are residents in the loch all year round, whereas the game fish enter it early in the year, linger until autumn, then fulfil their sole aim in the spawning act during winter. Pike, of course, spawn similarly, but at different times, and when the game fisher reluctantly packs up for the season at the end of October, pike fishing continues all through the winter, albeit at the mercy of the weather.

When the water warms around mid-May, I am never too surprised nowadays to land pike either on the troll or the fly. It is no coincidence that around that time our smolts (young salmon and sea trout) are donning their silvery coats for the first time, preparatory to entering the sea. First, though, they have to suffer the hazards of dropping down rivers like the Endrick and entering the loch via the river mouth, before making their exit from fresh water down the River Leven to the sea.

All along their migrating routes, especially around the sandy area where the Endrick meets the loch, lie log-like objects casting beady eyes at the darting shoals. The pike knows a tasty mouthful when it sees it.

One year I was making my first casts with the fly in late May when I must have disturbed a small shoal of resting smolts of Darroch. I had returned two or three (very carefully) when I was taken in quick succession by two different pike of around 4 and 6lb. They had fancied my rather large silver-bodied fly, since it was the same colour as the small fish they sought. Both pike carried the marks of what appears to be customary battling amongst themselves. One appeared to have only just resisted being swallowed alive by a bigger brother, evident by twin curved teeth marks across both flanks of its body, high up near the gills. Although they invariably seize their prey sideways, it appears they have to be extra crafty when it comes to sneaking up on fellow members of their own species!

Apart from small fish, pike will feed on practically any small live thing which they can swallow, such as rats, mice and waterfowl. But they are a fish of many moods, often not taking a thing unless it is presented right in front of them, yet, on other days, feeding as if it was the last day of their lives. After frenzied feeding bursts, they can go "off" and lie dormant for days, although some of the species favour more regular, if smaller, daily intakes.

Such is the bounty in Loch Lomond and other large lochs that pike can live to a fair old age, perhaps thirty years or more. Small pike are known as jacks and weigh about 4 lb and under, and adult male pike are usually much smaller than the females.

It would be difficult to lay down hard and fast rules for the best weather conditions for pike but, in the course of game fishing, I must make mention of a regularly observed set of conditions when the game fish are completely "off" and the pike very definitely "on". These are the sultry days of a low ceiling, when pike (if not all fish) are alleged to become sluggish. On the contrary, I landed seven large pike off the Mudflats of Balmaha in these very conditions. They took in shallow water, smashing at both a largish Rapala and Gold Sprat as they trolled by their noses. For what it is worth, there have been many such days on the loch when *Salar* went absent and along came *Esox Lucius*. Unlike the game fish, the take of a pike on the troll is a slowish affair, almost sluggish, as the rod bends back and stays back, without the tremendous yanks and tugs of the salmon. Again, this is probably due to the way pike seize a bait and hold on until ready to swallow. They are members of the same club, though, when their mistake is realised!

Generally, however, since most fishing for pike will be afloat, light wind and fresh conditions are to be preferred. Conditions of extreme cold are bad and make the fish sluggish. An ever-present threat are the bitter northerly winds, which can make a short trip, from Balmaha to the Endrick mouth, say, a hazardous affair indeed. Hardly a season passes without the loch being "closed for the day" as far as hire boats are concerned. "No boats goin' oot the day," is sad news, but it is sensible never to ignore this advice or the sound reasons behind it. I have all too often seen the torment of genuinely concerned hirers when dusk comes and about ten boats and twenty lives are overdue. Although the bodies often *walk* back to base, beaten by atrocious conditions, the hire craft remain drawn up in some of the most inaccessible places. The rounding up is not at all funny.

Just before dealing with recognised "hot spots" for pike, it seems worthwhile passing on a tip which has recently benefited the pike man. There are some delightful, if strange-sounding, angling short-cuts, which could only exist in a topsy-turvy sport such as ours. Here is one (the moral follows later): do not hesitate to speak to any of the local game-fishing trolling fraternity who roam almost the entire loch's area, year in, year out, from March until October. They seek salmon and sea trout. Illogical as it must sound, they are the people (admittedly not the experts) who will advise you on pike, sometimes in a curiously unsympathetic and angry way. It would pay to ignore the rantings and carefully note the variety of spots where they have regularly, and recently, met up with *Esox*. I am guilty, myself, of familiarising two English coarse fishermen with a new spot or two, now shown on the map in this chapter, where I hear they have met with some success.

Mile upon aquatic mile is covered by the Loch Lomond troller, and practically every nook and cranny is explored by the hard-working trolled baits. It is inevitable that pike are encountered in spots many miles apart and unlikely to be sought out by the pike angler fishing, as needs be, in a more static fashion.

Regardless of the species we each seek, *they are pursued on the same loch*. The moral should be clear. As anglers, we have much to learn from each other and it still seems incredible to me that, when conversing with pike men one year I asked if they had ever discussed their particular prey with game anglers and was told, "Not likely, mate . . . don't seem to fancy us." I'm sure they were wrong, or had been disastrously unlucky with their choice of boat and crew.

By the same token, the game angler can often gain by swapping "tails". Not for the first time has a salmon or sea trout rise been pointed out to willing rods by the coarse angler fishing to anchor.

To complete a somewhat general Pike Report, before the specifics of tackling-up, it appears safe to say that many of the visiting pike experts rate our Lomond pike very highly indeed, some stating that pound for pound they are beyond comparison with the same species caught elsewhere. A tremendous sight can be that of a frenzied pike "walking on its tail", something like a miniature version of the great tarpon leap in big game waters. When caught in the best of condition they really are fit, and better shaped than those caught elsewhere, explained by the abundance of small perch, powan and roach to be found in their choice feeding places. Our pike are truly wild.

It also appears unanimous that, if a pike *must* be lost, it should be on Loch Lomond, where the splendour of the surroundings helps minimise the suffering. There is no shoulder-to-shoulder state of affairs in fishing for them and I know of many who state, without reservation, that fishing on Loch Lomond for its pike and coarse fish has been the highlight of their angling careers. As a Scot and dedicated "Lomondite", it is cheering indeed to hear of so many visiting anglers from the south, and abroad, being rewarded for their long journeys and careful preparation.

I used to think that no one could equal the Lomond man in his preparations for catching the game fish. It now seems minimal compared to the painstaking effort expended by the coarse angler. I cannot, however, resist being thankful that — so far — I have not heard of a game fisher transporting his bait live to the shores in carefully monitored tanks of water!

Where to Catch Pike

I still have somewhere in my archives a picture of a Lomond pike's skull, which I believe was found on the banks. That southern all-round expert angler, Dick Walker, estimated it to be over 60 lb, perhaps nearer 70! Loch Lomond is still top of the list when it comes to the specimen hunter and record-breaker, and I have little doubt that there are headlines still to be made.

For those who want to fish from the shore, the well-known stretch of bankside at Balmaha called the Cromar is a good pike lie. For those in boats, there are two major "hot spots" on the loch which can be singled out for special attention. One is near the much-mentioned base of Balmaha, south of the Mudflats to the Endrick Mouth and Bank area, and the other at East Portnellen, on the Boturich shoreline at the south-east side. The latter spot, by coincidence, is almost equidistant from the two major bases of Balmaha and Balloch, which conveniently gives the angler a choice of base for the hire of boats. This can be a decided advantage on days when the loch rears its uglier head, when the safest beat for home can be weighed up beforehand. If anything, the Balmaha boat has possibly quicker and easier access to a greater variety of pike lies but, as ever, the weather should be watched.

These two spots have one thing in common, although Balmaha easily has the better share: *a busy traffic practically all year round in small fish*. Summer and winter, the mouth of the Endrick, as it enters the loch, could well have a traffic warden to direct the flow going in and out, up and down. *Esox* sees to it that there is no loitering, and traffic jams are speedily broken up!

Smaller prey fish entering and leaving the loch via the River Leven tend to hug the south-east shoreline but, something like crazy paving, the Portnellen area requires careful navigation on the part of the wee chaps. There is a diversity of routes across this pike blockade but, in searching out a safe crossing, many perish.

At the original Long Point, as the shore sweeps out from the present-day power station, there stands a tufty islet so small that it

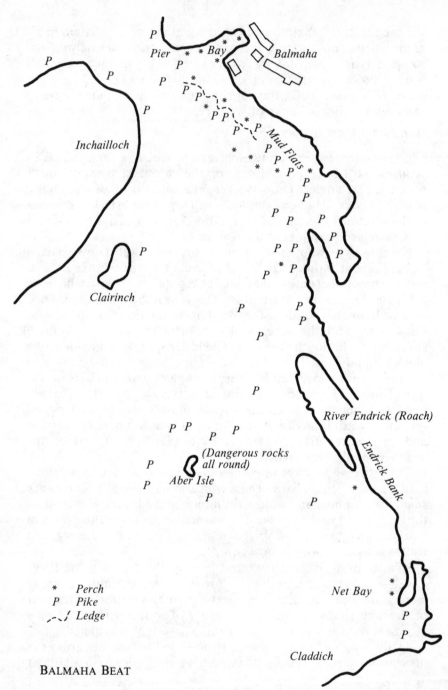

Balmaha Beat

Inchailloch

Clairinch

River Endrick (Roach)

Endrick Bank

(Dangerous rocks all round)
Aber Isle

Net Bay

Claddich

Pier   Bay   Balmaha

Mud Flats

*   Perch
P   Pike
ᘓᔓ   Ledge

barely qualifies for the title. The regular troller knows to pass it very deep, but a wise pike man might give it a go (fairly shallow) before starting a series of drops over the wider area of Portnellen. My boat and I nearly called it a day to the west of this little tuft when, three times, pike of over 15 lb took hold and the wind was blowing dangerously onshore. I tend to think that the shallow crossing round the islet must be a favourite route of small fish. So does the pike. Portnellen also has 5-star accommodation for pike of heavier stature and a good deal of comfortable privacy is afforded, with a choice of menu!

There have been many expeditions to Portnellen, headed by some big names from the south, and I'm sure that, under continued assault, either of the two popular zones mentioned will one day give up a massive fish.

You will see that there are a few pike spots marked on the map where I have seldom seen boats at work. They are shown because I, and others, have taken pike off them more than once. The tiny bay and ridge marked at Inchcailloch, for example, may yield a blank and yet I both saw and caught pike there, five in one day, the biggest being 14 lb. Above the small weedy bay, very close inshore, is a shelving ridge. In near calm conditions, I was rowing down the shoreline with two trolls at work in the rear. Through the Polaroids, I was carefully watching the depth from time to time and, as the blackish deep water gave way to lighter slate-coloured shallows, there lay several varying sizes of what I took to be salmon. They didn't move an inch, however, as salmon normally do, sweeping out from the lie to return after the boat has passed and often taking the trolled bait in annoyance at being so disturbed. The oars were shipped, and almost as soon as the engine was started a rod with a small gold Rapala buckled over into a "salmon". It was green, and so were the other four.

As users of the deadly little Rapala bait know, it is made of light balsa wood and floats to the surface when momentum is lost. Under the pull of the boat and wave it dives and wiggles (sometimes I think it *is* a fish), and the depth can be controlled, within reason, by the amount of line let out.

I later thought of how many times a fish (especially a salmon or sea trout) will seize a bait viciously when it does something totally unexpected, like the small Rapala rising to the surface when I ceased rowing, and then taking a violent nose-dive when the engine started to pull. Pike, apparently, seem drawn to odd behaviour too, especially the sight of a small fish trying to escape.

Another area where I have known pike abound (the majority small jacks), is off the east end of Inchfad, a mixture of weed and shingle, and to the centre of the short shoreline between the large rocks at the north-east tip and the houses on the shore. Inchfad, which is being farmed and where the private jetty is in constant use, should be respected accordingly.

Round the same island, at almost the exact centre of the main shoreline on the northern side, there is an old fence running into the loch, with a dense weedy patch lying just above it. In the summer there is little difficulty finding the weed, which sprouts to the surface and bends over like the weeping willow. Pike are frequently caught there, more in the summer, or when the black nebs and small trout are about.

Considered to be still within the Balmaha precinct is Aber Isle, where good-sized pike lurk from time to time. I cannot emphasise strongly enough that you should approach the islet with extreme care. It is almost entirely surrounded by jagged rocks, especially off the western shore. It may be difficult to fish, but Aber has pike.

Recently I was discussing pike with two visiting anglers, who mentioned how likely a spot looked on the south-western shore, Rossdhu Bay, with its dense weedy straits and sunken logs. I had to tell them that most who have fished it have returned in disappointment. I will merely add that on each side of the *entrance*, especially on a short stretch of shoreline opposite Rossdhu House itself, I have encountered pike.

Whereas most pike fishing carried out at the bottom end is from a boat (the Cromar being a slight exception), good results can be had from the shoreline if the longish trip to Ardlui, at the northern end, is undertaken. As spawning approaches, pike are known to frequent a few shallow bays near where the tumbling little river Falloch empties into the loch and there can be good sport, justifying the somewhat arduous roadside journey and, at the same time, avoiding boat hiring costs and fuel into the bargain.

PIKE FISHING METHODS

Pike can be caught trolling with engine or oars, spinning from both the shoreline (*viz* the Cromar area at Balmaha and at Ardlui) or a boat, dead and livebaiting, ledgering mid-water or on the bottom. To go below about 10 or 12 lb nylon while spinning or trolling is inviting disaster.

In fact, in practically all fishing from the boat, a short wire trace is used, generally not more than 2 ft, say. The reason for the short trace is that pike have a similar habit to eels inasmuch as they can roll round and round on the surface, cutting through nylon like butter.

Baits I have found good for trolling are big Rapalas, largish mounted sprats, gold or silver, Abu Hi-Lo and the jointed type of plug like a wounded baitfish, favouring perch-like colouring or a tendency to silver, like the roach and powan they imitate. Tackle dealers have a large variety and few of them are on the small side. The "Big S" of the Shakespeare company is winning friends and this bait even rattles inwardly when retrieved. Perhaps some day baits will be made to scream as they must do when *Esox* is spotted! Plug baits in general get good results when trolled or spun and I often see baits of the Heddon company sprouting from well-filled bait boxes.

As stated, pike *can* be caught by spinning from the shoreline at a lot of the areas marked, but by far the most popular and successful method is from the boat, using live or deadbait. Supreme are small to medium-sized perch, powan and roach, so that time spent in Balmaha Bay or nearby spinning for perch (or worming) is not wasted. Roach and powan are not quite so easily caught for bait. In fact, terrific as they are in this respect, more is made of them as a quarry in themselves as they take on the shy characteristics of harbour mullet. Roach shoals are pretty hard to locate on the loch, but easier to find on the lower reaches of the Endrick, in very large numbers, where I have seen the deadly hempseed at work. Their stomachs were bloated with the stuff. I have over the years caught the odd roach and powan while fly fishing (size 10s), but the poor wee things come in like a wet handkerchief. Twice powan have taken a small Peacock Spider in the mouth, which is fairly rare, and I would not care to be sentenced to fish for them for life!

Light spinning gear and the boy's rod, with small Mepps 00, 01 or similar size of Abu Droppen, will do the trick with the perch of the bay and district. Should you wish to try for perch by trolling then I would heartily recommend the smallest Rapala, silver just having the edge over the gold. Much to my son's delight and my own impatience I have been given the task of removing this deadly little bait from the mouths of dozens of perch by trolling the very shallow areas between Inchmoan and Inchcruin, known as the Geggles.

Should trolling be favoured as a method, certain dangers arise in the form of mixed interests. The Loch Lomond Association man seeking the game fish and the coarse angler after pike or perch would appear to be inviting harsh moments (and hard times) if their boats criss-cross within limited areas. Anger afloat on our lovely loch is completely out of place. That pike do not disturb salmon is well recognised. Indeed I have known them occupy lies only feet apart, each bent upon their own task and respecting their contrary ways of life in fresh water. Surely fishermen should find it not too difficult to follow their example.

TACKLE AND BAITS FOR PIKE FISHING

It is important to carry some sort of anchor or grapnel hook, with enough rope to grip securely in a maximum of about 30 ft of water, although the depth most of the time will be a lot less. If the boat tends to swirl to the bow rope, then it is often a good idea to lay out a stern line, with weight attached, so that the angling platform remains as stable as possible. As I have mentioned in the game fishing text, my two constant "pals" are made of iron, in the form of two 56 lb weights. They have endless uses, and here again one can be laid out, at the stern, but take care when hoisting back aboard, especially if you are more tired than you think!

A generally accepted length of rod for Loch Lomond pike is around 11 ft for ledgering with float, and there are a great many kits on the market which can be made up to near enough this length. As with game fishing, I have a distinct preference for a firm tip section, with good through action in which the rod forms a strong, but even, curve.

Even whilst ledgering for pike, it is a good plan to carry a spinning rod for casting plug baits, say, into water well away from your floats. Two in a boat, therefore, would mean about four rods aboard, but lest you think that's a lot, I have actually seen a pike crew disembark at Millarochy campsite with ten rods, plus two echo sounders, aboard!

Youngsters usually start with a light spinning rod, and I've yet to meet the seasoned angler who can resist using the boy's rod at the slightest provocation. It is a useful tool ashore and afloat.

At one time spinning reels of a fairly high line capacity were the tools of the trade and although they have not vanished from the scene, the multiplying reel—much used in beach-casting and sea fishing—seems more to the fore these days with experienced pike addicts. There are many reasons for their popularity, amongst which are excellent line capacity (using 12-18 lb breaking strain), an intimacy of contact with the bait and fish with none of the vagueness which a fixed spool reel can impart. Easily the most popular

186

BASIC HOME-MADE TRACE

Basic deadbait traces will be much used, so several made up in lengths of between 2 and 4 ft should be neatly coiled in the tackle box. Crimping kits comprising a pair of pliers and a variety of sleeve sizes are nowadays available at tackle shops. Two good types of wire are Seastrand and blue anodised from the Midland Cord Company. The basic trace is shown below:

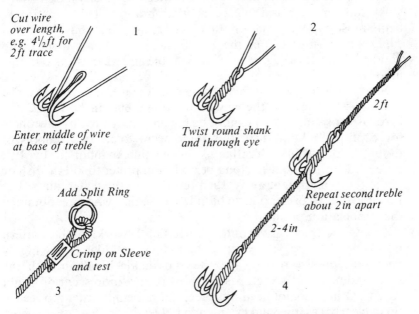

Cut wire over length, e.g. 4½ ft for 2 ft trace

1

Enter middle of wire at base of treble

2

Twist round shank and through eye

2 ft

Repeat second treble about 2 in apart

2–4 in

Add Split Ring

Crimp on Sleeve and test

3

4

To get maximum sport and yet return the fish alive, there is a trend these days to file down the barbs on two of the hook points of the treble, inserting the remaining barbed point into the flesh of the bait. Both sets of trebles are so treated. Quick tightening and skilful playing of the fish will ensure easy hook removal.

comes from the giant house of Abu, in the form of their Series 6000 multipliers. Without trace of a blush, I can here state that I would wish for nothing better than their 6500C reel, which has the advantage of very fast retrieval of line. Over the past few seasons, some of the proceeds I have gained by the sale of *Salar* have gone back into tackle for catching more. The 6500C is a boon when fishing solo and trolled baits need to be whipped out of the water before finally engaging with the one rod and reel. A good salmon spinning rod

187

with one such reel will help quell *Esox* and restore contact with him very quickly after a stuttering "tail walk" on the surface.

Nylon line should not be under about 10 lb breaking strain, and in seeking *the* specimen the sensible man will be using between 15 and 18 lb strain. Coils of multi-strand wire and crimping pliers won't be far away either. Early in a pike-fishing career, familiarity should be sought in the use of modern wire for traces. Most city tackle shops stock this for fresh and salt water use, a brand called "Seastrand" being most popular. I have noticed lately many pike rods fitted with superb Fuji rings—from the Far East again. Apart from being good-looking, the leg guides are very stable and wear rate is very low indeed.

Should this book achieve nothing else, I would hope to see more sensible-sized nets on the general angling scene on Lomond. For pike, as for salmon, they cannot be big enough. Many use keepnets for captured pike and on this there seem to be two schools of thought. Some think it a rather useless pastime to retain the live fish at the side of the boat for long periods and prefer to kill the fish or photograph it straight away, then return it to the water, alive. The L.L.A.I.A. now prefer pike to be killed by anglers who have obtained the Association permit.

Floats and traces are kept to a fairly simple workmanlike pattern on the loch. One successful angler does not like floats highly coloured, preferring to have the end tackle blend in with the surroundings, and so scrapes off most of the fluorescent or bright colour. Others do not heed this precaution, being content to see the float clearly, as the maker intended. Deadbait floats vary from about 4-8 in long, by about ½ in round, with one end painted to choice (orange, white or black) over the last inch or so. The other end will have a small wire loop and the entire float will be well varnished. Many are the permutations, but this basically simple rig serves well.

The best deadbait, in order of preference, would be powan, roach, small pike themselves, herring or mackerel fillets and small perch. The last two, especially herring, are least popular with the angler since eels fancy them better and nibble the soft, often mushy, deep-frozen flesh to bits.

Hooks are always a vital part of the end tackle and though I wouldn't announce it in a tackle shop, I am glad to think I would pay twice the asking price for the right kind of trebles. Only now am I managing to rebuild a stock of my favourites — the Outpoint.

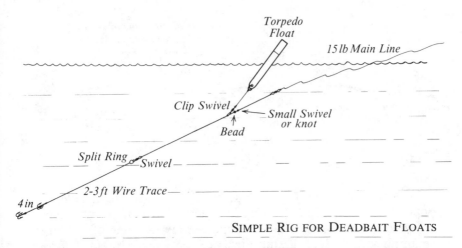

SIMPLE RIG FOR DEADBAIT FLOATS

Messrs Dickson in Glasgow always carried good stocks of this hook (Martins Outpoint), made by Messrs Sealey, I believe, but like other dealers they have found the right sizes scarce. I hope the position will soon change, but the hooks of Partridge rank about equal and are more easily obtained. Sizes 2, 4 and 6 are the most popular sizes, the last being the popular choice of size in trebles. Do not, with hooks, settle for second best or that's what you'll get nearly everywhere. The more we anglers cry out for our needs the better, and I for one could often weep when I think of the passing of several items of tackle. We surely didn't know a good thing when we saw it.

Rod rests are very handy aboard. I would doubt if any two game fishing boats use the same type for trolling rods, and there has been some ingenious thinking before the evolvement of weird and wonderful contraptions. The relief they afford the pike angler is inestimable, if he is fishing more than two rods, when using deadbait. An ideal combination is when two anglers use both methods at the same time, live and deadbaiting, so that rests of some sort are a *must*.

Deadbaits are not mounted just any old way. The trebles should be entered near the tail region so that they are not buried too far forward, near the head of the bait, where hooks can embed in harder flesh and be less exposed to the cavernous mouth awaited. A simple and popular method is shown below. Remember to puncture the bait's swim bladder to ensure good sinking. Baits should be fresh if possible, but that is not to say that baits on the stale side will not interest fish. Some large pike have freely accepted baits so "off" that the angler can hardly bear the mounting procedure.

189

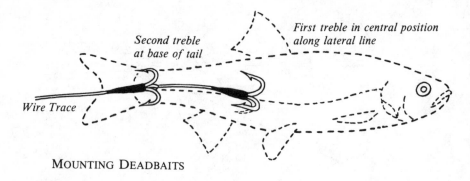

Second treble
at base of tail

First treble in central position
along lateral line

Wire Trace

MOUNTING DEADBAITS

Whereas I urge my fellow fly fisher to err on the small side, the opposite applies to pike fishing in general. Nothing seems too big for them at times, as is evident upon study of some of the large spinning baits such as the Jim Vincent Spoon, made by Hardy Bros. Knowing a big fish's predilection for a mouthful, a herring or the like of about 1 lb would not be turned down. Pike are used to, and seek out, good-sized prey, of which there is plenty in Loch Lomond.

Most good-sized pike, contrary to popular belief, are not caught whilst skulking near weedy ground. Most often they are taken in open water as they harry small shoals of baitfish. They will spend all day patrolling the Endrick Bank or Mouth areas on a savage scouring mission before retiring to where they are often *seen*, the denser and weedier zones. Smaller pike may be lured from such hidey-holes, but first-hand experience tells me that bigger fish will be caught whilst they roam with abandon in comparatively shallow and clear water. As with most angling matters, it is fatal to generalise, but I would stand by these remarks.

Pike spawn in the shallow waters of the loch and possibly the lower Endrick during the spring and they will mate in pairs, often when the winter loch is very high, in grassy or reedy areas. I recall walking near the Cromar, one winter, when there was an eruption almost on the grassy shoreline. It was a head of mating pike scurrying out to the safety of deeper water. At this time, the females' eggs are eagerly sought by waterfowl, eels and the like.

Little wonder that, when spawning is over, a livebait properly presented will be smashed at, with relish.

The large shoals of roach which frequent the lower Endrick do not tend to move around a lot in the colder winter water, and craftily easing its rather lethargic way into their privacy is old *Esox*. The pike, practically throughout the season, will not be far away from

190

small shoals of baitfish. Find the latter and problems are greatly eased. Not so easy to do, in practice.

Livebaits about 5-10 in should be impaled by means of two trebles spaced approx 4 in apart, thus:

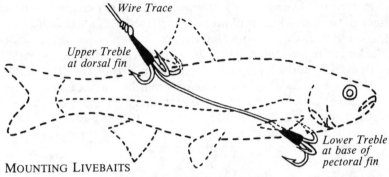

MOUNTING LIVEBAITS

A simple livebait float of some 2-3 in round is required and can be clear, red, black or white in colour, to suit the surface light and the user's eyesight. During the summer there would seem to be a preference for livebaiting and an hour or so in the Balmaha district with the light spin rod and Mepps 00 or 01, with 4 lb line, say, should provide the easiest living prey — perch. The poor wee things, having sought the sanctum of the bay — away from fly old *Esox* — are then transported to water they have no wish to visit, and guess who's waiting?

Livebaits can be left suspended in the water for periods of 20 minutes or so before being re-cast into either deeper or shallower water. Deadbaits can be left a little longer and, if ledgered on the bottom with little response, the rod tip can be moved to flutter the bait on and off the bottom from time to time. It is fairly common practice to start off with the livebait fishing on or near the bottom, but again, if response is poor, it can be raised to fish a foot or so off the bottom.

Being highly principled about the misuse of the word *strike*, I will refrain from using it in connection with game fishing — but here I would admit that pike can sometimes be tightened into rather fast without the same risks attached to doing so with the game fish. In the hope that you will catch many pike and become familiar with them, it is policy to prevent the sets of trebles from lodging in the lower gut of the pike. Our fish means business, and it is easier by far to remove the hooks from the jaw or mouth zone than delving into

191

the pits of its stomach, past the razor-sharp teeth. An item called a gag can be used to jam open the pike's jaw but, perhaps because they have been known to collapse or are thought to injure the fish, I do not see this device used often nowadays.

Put forward very often as a reason for the superb condition and fight of the Loch Lomond pike is the presence of game fish entering the same loch throughout the season. Perhaps *Esox* will harry our black nebs more than a little, but there the reasoning ends. Pike are crafty devils and I haven't met, seen or heard of even the odd daft one who would dare disturb *Salar* when he's at home.

So study the letters "P" on the map. There may, inevitably be some missing, so the need to roam — like the baitfish — should always be remembered. Other days the pike will come to you and it won't seem such a big, bad loch after all!

Perch, Powan, Roach and Others

On an early summer evening some seasons ago, I hooked a fish on the troll, along the Sallochy shore. It surfaced once and, with little resistance, came to the side of the boat. A perch of 5 lb was landed, weighed and returned. They are extremely plentiful in mid-season and Balmaha Bay sports millions of their fry. Young and adult fish alike will take a variety of spun baits and youngsters land them freely from the jetty. My own son finds them "not so boring, Dad" as the salmon family. He's the one to write on how to catch them, but you can be assured that a small Rapala, Mepps, Abu Droppen or the like will do the trick. I do it the hard way, catching the odd one on an Invicta, heavily dressed, on the tail! Incidentally, beware when handling perch — they have a habit of raising a sharp pronged dorsal fin, in self defence. A good-sized one, baked, provides a delicious meal, but watch out for their wee bones. They fight to the last!

Perhaps some will consider that our roach and powan have been given scant mention. I would thus reiterate that chances of really worthwhile catches of roach are to be made in the lower reaches of the River Endrick, a little outside the scope of a book primarily dealing with loch-located species. Certainly roach are liable to pop up when least expected in varying areas of Loch Lomond. It would take close and expert study to locate these smaller shoals when, as some anglers reason, the more abundant pike and perch are more easily found and ready to do battle. I have found them, like powan, while fly fishing at spots miles apart on the loch, and the few landed

This perch, the author's biggest at nearly 4½lb, took a trolled 2in Silver Rapala

have been partial to a heavily dressed Invicta. However, for those who actually set out to catch them, sweetcorn from tins has been recommended as an excellent bait, likewise the eternal maggot or hempseed. Frugal amounts on tiny hooks, paired with the lightest nylon, will bring good results.

Powan, our unique "fresh water herring" are only to be found in Loch Lomond and a loch in Ireland. They are supposed to give off a certain smell, similar to the sea fish, and I have a soft spot for these gentle little fish. Their numbers are vast in the loch and seldom are the nets drawn near Balmaha or Rowardennan without scores of them being beached, without going to waste I might add. Too may coarse anglers know their worth as bait.

The powan is not unlike the grayling in looks, with the same type of down-turned, bottom-feeding mouth. They feed mostly on plankton which doesn't make them any easier to catch. I had several on the fly, by accident, but only three hooked properly in the mouth, twice with a size 10 Black and Peacock spider, the third on an Invicta. Many more have been foul-hooked and returned. They cruise the loch all summer long and many a newcomer has returned to the bay full of tales of astounding rises of trout: "Hundreds of them! And we didn't hook one!" Little wonder. The "trout" were our wee friends the powan. They will "dimple" all round the boat, even in flat calms, and for some reason, I am usually entirely unhappy about their presence. It may be imagined, but I rarely appear to find what I'm looking for — salmon or sea trout — when these little fish appear to have the freedom of the loch's surface.

Not too many years ago, a disease struck them in the spring, and by early summer thousands lay decomposing on the loch and island shores. Old-fashioned wooden clothes pegs nearly made a comeback as boat occupants considered ways of avoiding the unforgettable stench.

We are proud of our little powan and I hear no protests from old *Esox*, either, who gets the last word as usual. By sheer coincidence the heaviest pike I have caught in the loch, was exactly the same weight as my heaviest salmon — 28½ lb. It was caught in the shallows off the bay, between the Short and Long Points on Inchmoan island, as the Loch Lomond Association bailiff's boat encircled me, in the act of playing *Salar* (as I thought). It was taken into the garage at Balmaha and inside its gut were two fish of about one pound each. One was a brown trout, the other a finnock, or black neb as we call them. How on earth could such a crafty old fish have mistaken my large Golden Sprat for another easy mouthful?

The loch has a plentiful supply of eels, averaging about a pound or so. They were once professionally caught, in eel cage traps, sited at the mouth of the River Endrick. I recall my utter astonishment on seeing into the carefully guarded tanks in which they were transported. I would still be counting their numbers yet! Little fished for, they are a nuisance to the coarse angler when deadbaiting on the bottom. Soft baits like herring fillets are devoured rapidly.

My son disputes their average weight. Baiting up with sea trout guts, his trace was broken three times when he tried to lure the slippery customers one summer night off the small jetty at Rowardennan. Like most promising anglers, he guessed at a weight, then trebled it, which enhances most angling tragedies and diverts attention from more likely shortcomings in the tackle — like newfangled granny knots!

In leaving our coarse fish, for the time being, mention should be made of a strange visitor to the lower reaches of the River Leven — grey mullet. They have appeared over the last few seasons and, whereas we would welcome with relish all new species to our waters, they would have to be, *of course*, one of the hardest fish to catch.

194

10

The Early Bird – Boatpacking

THE word "backpacking" has been established for quite some time now and suitably summarises the idea that the "packer" carries all his worldly wealth, and his home for the night, on his back. For Loch Lomond it seemed to me that we needed a new word to describe the increasingly popular pastime of camping on the loch (with proper permission) and using the boat instead of our backs to transport the lightweight load. I fell for *boatpacking* and, although a few might assume it means that we Lomondites travel cross-country like the ancient Vikings with our craft perched skywards on our backs, the majority will see the real meaning of the word, dismissing our capacity for such effort at once.

Camping Equipment

My first taste of the Great Outdoors was being allowed to stay out of the house an hour or so before bedtime, "camping" in the most rugged fashion, with an old linen bedsheet straddling the clothes rope in the back garden. No-one, parents included, dared enter without permission, which was not easily granted!

Many tents and a lot of fresh air later, I still faintly retain the romantic boyhood idea that he who can camp alone need fear no-one and that this way of life is a little closer to what our Maker intended. Camping, therefore, has become a habit I will un-ashamedly admit I have not outgrown, especially when combined with angling exercises on Loch Lomond.

To be honest, the effort expended in camping by boat does not bear comparison with the willing undertakings of youth, when the entire gear was carried on the then supple back, or adequate cycle panniers.

In the past few years, there have been tremendous improvements, especially in the field of lightweight tents and allied gear. It has all become less of a burden and the equipment is much lighter and more efficient, with the required accessories as compact as could be. Today, a two-man tent, with its minimum of lightweight alloy poles, can pack away into less space than the sleeping bag, which is the reverse of how it used to be. It can weigh a mere 4 or 5 lb, lighter if single-skinned. Erection is simplicity itself, limited only by the nature of the terrain and, due to the nature of modern materials, drying out does not present the problems of yore. We have much to thank our backpacking cousins for in this field, since it has primarily been their dogged insistence on keeping weight to a minimum, without any loss of efficiency, which has provided us with such advanced and improved gear. Manufacturers early cottoned on (so to speak) to the manifold benefits of lightweight, polyurethane-coated flysheets, and groundsheets are now sewn on to the base of the inner tent walls.

Light and efficient tents are supplied by many makers today, the best known possibly being Messrs Blacks of Greenock. Their perennial favourite, the "Good Companions" model, can now be had in either conventional canvas or a modern nylon version. In 1978 the firm revived another old favourite, in a modern nylon and cotton mixture, the "Itisa". The great advantage of both these designs is the centre head room.

At the time of writing, many of the leading makers have their own version of the backpacker's ideal tent, small nylon "A" pole models in streamlined wind-cheating designs which can be erected speedily. Ultimate, Saunders, and Field and Trek, to name but three firms, now produce such tents and I have only recently tried out the two-man Field and Trek "Trailmaker". Suffice it to say that I could not imagine the severest gale budging either the occupants or the well conceived pegging points. For single overnight stays, these designs have much to commend them. For longer periods, more headroom would be my choice and, going by this year's catalogues, most of the leading makers have some revolutionary ideas up their sleeves.

Of course, there is an even lighter way to camp (if that is the correct word): by carefully planning the best use for the boat "hap", or cover, which should be present, methinks, on all good loch boats. It can be a damp, lonely and claustrophobic existence, sleeping

196

aboard, though, when much water is present both above *and* below the occupant!

There are a great many lightweight tents to suit the solo sleeper, but those suitable for two or three are not quite so numerous. As one manufacturer rightly points out, today's camper would like his tent to weigh nothing and cost little, so that a small ultra-light ridge tent, accommodating three in comfort and at a reasonable price, is always an interesting discovery.

In a conventional tight-fitting small ridge design, there has always been a tendency for the user to brush his head against the inner when rising suddenly (which, I freely admit, does not happen too often in my case). A design which makes an extremely functional room of the inner, with only a slight increase in volume, has been achieved by a designer who has obviously devoted a lot of his time to the Great Outdoors. Funnily enough, this is also the name of the British Firm which markets the tents from Leeds. This range of "Caravan Iglu" tents will I am sure satisfy the boatpacker in all respects. Their welcome paperweight feel disguises the fact that they are made from mighty strong material. It is quite amazing how much extra comfort is derived from an offset ridge in a transverse design, giving the user the impression that he is in a much larger room altogether.

The two-man Saunders "Dalomite" lightweight tent. Quick to erect and fast-drying

Certainly, we have come a long way from bed sheets draped over the clothes rope!

I personally find the Saunders "Dalomite" a little palace for two, especially for overnight stops. Missing the last ferry to a remote little Scottish island once, it came to our rescue in great style, enabling us to be first in the queue the following morning. It is a two-skin tent, having an outer flysheet which enshrouds a matching inner tent, this being suspended in the simplest way by rubber loops and clips which attach to the outer roof from the inside. The flysheet can be erected in no time at all, and on days of torrential rain it can be used as a beach shelter. Within the tent's welcome sanctum, hands can at last be properly dried, thus avoiding soggy rolls and drunk-looking damp cigarettes.

A thin foil space blanket, as mentioned elsewhere, which rolls up to the size of a cigarette packet, makes an agreeable temporary groundsheet. It can also make a useful windbreak if you attach short pieces of nylon fishing line to the corner eyelets and fix them to trees or bushes.

Pillows are carried on the angler in the form of pullovers, fishing jackets, trousers and the like, but heads should never rest upon them until you have first checked that your faithful craft, beached nearby, will not receive a totally undeserved pounding during the night. The evening may be calm when you retire, but it is a far from funny experience to be wakened by the sounds of a hull crunching on stony shingle in a fast rising wind. The sudden shock of having to re-enter cold, damp waders and venture out into the gusty rainswept darkness, first to find and then to make fast the boat, can destroy the "Great Outdoor" feeling for quite a long time!

Cooking need be no great problem since always aboard is the old Primus, complete with professional-looking soot-blackened kettle and pre-non-stick frying pan!

Browsing through catalogues during the winter has for long been a weakness of mine, resulting in the acquisition of odd bits of gear (*some* of them useful). For people who do not much care for the flavour of Loch Lomond water, Field and Trek make "The Water Bag". Seldom have I come across a more compact, ingenious carrier of liquids. It costs but a few pounds, and you can put in it any liquid of your choice. Should you use the loch as your drinking water, you can always blow into the bag and use it as a pillow.

The same firm has recently imported from the United States the most ingenious little stove. Fuel problems (availability mainly) seem solved for ever. It will burn any grade of petrol, petroil mixture (God bless the designer), paraffin, diesel, turpentine or, if you have it, peanut oil! The MSR stove packs into two main parts: the small burner unit and the fuel container, which is, conveniently, the original SIGG bottle, available from any good camping shop. A spare bottle filled with any of the above liquids would seem to answer almost any emergency.

A compact little tool, made by AB Optimus Ltd, is their "Kamp Kit", which is really four tools in one: shovel, axe, hammer and saw, with bottle opener and nail remover included as bonuses. Packed in a neat nylon belt sack, it is a mighty useful little item.

A useful aid to modern camping has been the introduction of a material known as Closed Cell Foam (CCF), which makes an excellent insulating mat. It has solved, for me, many an angling as well as camping problem. I shall mention but a few, but am certain that fellow users will find other uses just as beneficial.

It can be obtained from most good camping shops (such as Blacks and Nevisport), and is sold in sheet form in various colours and thicknesses. One common trade name for it is "Kampamat". Placed *under* the inner tent groundsheet it prevents puncturing the same on rough ground, and also forms an almost impenetrable barrier through which dampness cannot pass. It is non-absorbent and never feels cold to the touch.

A problem I had previously never quite cured was the eternal hardness of the boat seat! Until this material arrived, it was the same old polythene bag round-a-cushion story. Loch Lomond water may be little different from any other, but I somehow feel it can find the slightest pin-hole available and enter through it by the gallon! It may *wet* CCF, but only on the surface, and will not penetrate. A few strips of this material placed together can be taped on to the thwarts and a little of the suffering taken out of our many, many wet days.

With CCF cast-aside fly boxes can have their linings restored, or new boxes may be designed and made-up from scratch, with inner *and* lid panels fitted to shape. I take the matter a stage further by adding a panel to the *outside* lid of both fly and dap box so that there is always somewhere obvious to store and change flies, which I do all too often in the course of a day. I particularly like this idea, being guilty of not opening the fly box enough to remind myself of its contents. A limited set of flies can be stuck into this outer lid which, if nothing else, keeps the mind turning over the importance of a

199

change of fly. The same applies to pre-doped dap flies, and a few of similar pattern but different size can lie exposed to view and at the ready.

Needless to say, the hooks of lures can be dangerous if spread about the boat, and a few pads of CCF here and there solves this problem too. I have previously mentioned the material as a first-rate deck mattress for a cat-nap aboard, and it also makes an ideal lounging pad for the beach. To me, it has endless possibilities, and I have gone as far as to cut out insoles from it to fit my leaking waders!

Pests

The manufacture of camping aids has become so sophisticated that it seems to me the only remaining gigantic fortune to be made will be by the genius who can eliminate *at birth* the huge population of midges which plague the loch shores and its users beyond the limit of human endurance! For some considerable time now there has been much lamenting about lenient sentences meted out to present-day delinquents. A night forcibly spent ashore, with only our special special loch brand of midges for company, would cure the wrong-doers for all time!

The most successful advance in dealing with these mind-destroying parasites just had to come from Japan — where else? To suit the larger frame tent, or caravan, they have provided the answer, which will easily be found in any good camping shop: mosquito coils. They come in boxes of ten or so and resemble an asbestos-like material which, when lit at one end, smoulders — harmlessly to us but fatally to the menace. It gives off a pleasant Eastern aroma and appears to have partially, if not completely, cured the problem. However, it is some time before the beneficiary can cease from slapping his or her face — so long has the pest been endured.

Sometimes extreme measures are needed and, watching the little devils scatter away from the wafting puffs of mosquito coil smoke gave me quite a useful idea. If you break a coil into pieces of some three to four inches in length and wrap the ends of each in silver cigarette paper or the like, and stick the little weapons into part of your headgear, the puffs of smoke will stay adjacent to the head area no matter how and where you move it, giving great relief to the victim's face. Naturally, a check should be made from time to time that smoke issues only from the coils and not the headgear!

In living with Lomond, one must endure another variety of pest. The poor game fish has to contend with the lamprey and we humans are demented by the midge, but there is another nasty little parasite which infests sheep, cattle and dogs: the tick.

My own black Labrador had his first visit from one on a recent loch camping jaunt and was completely unaware of its presence in spite of the fact that he was already, unwittingly, a blood donor.

If you stroke your best friend's coat and feel a small bulbous lump, open up the hair fibres and you will find a tiny object like a miniature balloon of about $\frac{1}{4}$ in diameter. This is the expanded blood sac of the pest, and many make the mistake of bursting it in an attempt to cure the problem. This does not help as the small burrowing head, furnished with a pair of little probing horns, will remain embedded and either turn the area septic or continue to feed.

It calls for manual dexterity and good eyesight, but the insect's head must be removed. I could not relate here the many delicate surgical attempts I have either heard of or witnessed on the loch, but outstanding in my memory is a drastic affair involving two anglers, a tick lodged in a posterior, and a "scalpel", which was an artfully wielded razor blade. It is preferable either to carry a small amount of meths to dab on the tick's head, making dislodgement easier, or to buy one of the modern tick and flea collars from the pet shop — for the dog, of course.

Lest the reader is unattracted to Loch Lomond for fear of these pests, let me assure you that they exist all over Britain, and it is usually our dogs which pick them up whilst meandering through fern and scrub. It is good advice, therefore, to be alert to the little horrors' preference for ferns and to carry out ablutions in the vicinity of good clean shingle... midges permitting.

One of the sheer delights of a camping holiday on the loch, can be a late night feast with the blackened frying pan and fresh-caught sea trout to size. Thus fed, a contented sleep awaits the deserving, but only if arrangements about the disposal of the guts, etc, have been carefully plotted before retiring. Seagulls will have spotted your entire operation from start to finish and they won't appear to be quite the same bird when seen at daybreak through bleary, half-closed eyes. It seems that on our loch the sound of seagulls, either feathered or mechanical, is the recognised morning chorus!

*　　*　　*

Camping Manners

Remember that camping in the loch area is not permitted just anywhere. Often permission has to be sought. Understandably, the Forestry Commission have enough to do in high summer without campers striking a light in all the wrong, tinder-dry places. If the beautiful surroundings are respected and the correct approaches made, no ill-feeling need be aroused.

Alas, however — nothing can be worse than to trek ashore, laden with gear, to find a mound of rubbish and sodden newspapers (not even yesterday's) littering your proposed base. We are all, to some extent, guilty, but large polythene bags are nothing new and can easily be emptied in one of the many concrete lochside litter bins. Better still, rubbish can be burnt upon breaking camp.

Finally, remember that it is little use camping out with all the man-made benefits I have mentioned if a search party has to be roused to find you: accordingly word should at least be left with the dog — unless you have taken him with you, in which case your next of kin will do!

11
Notes in Boats

A "Daymare"

WHAT would normally be referred to as a nightmare, I have altered to what, I regret, seems a more appropriate word — a *daymare*. Ideally, there should be another word covering a full 24 hours, since the entire affair gives me the same feeling of horror, night and day!

It is only mildly consoling to reason that no true angler worth his salt can go through a lifetime of fishing without a day of complete and utter disaster. The twist to most of these sad tales is that had everything gone right, instead of wrong, the victim might have become some sort of national hero, not the abject article who emerges in a drippingly morose way.

I, and the reader in turn, must be spared every graphic little detail of my own pet daymare. Years later I still cannot admit to seeing the funny side, in any hilarious fashion. At best, I am permitted a slight whimper. It happened one spring morning off the Kitchen, a little crannog jutting out from Clairinch and, to this day, I tend to look away from the spot lest more tears cascade on to the floorboards. The sky was overcast with shimmering black furrows of wind disturbing the surface nicely and, mercifully, as it happened, there was not another boat in sight. Two baits were fed out and the third rod placed in its rest, one of the clamp-on type secured by wing nuts. Everything, I swear, was secure. As I was backing towards the transom seat, a thud followed by a tremendous screech caught me unawares, in a sort of crouched position of neither one thing nor the other. Before time for a rapid prayer, the rod, reel and rest were yanked with great force completely off the gunwale!

As it left for ever, I formed an unforgettable picture of the surging bend in that rod (pure elastic!) and behind the boat a mighty salmon of some 20 lb crashed out of the water, tossing the red sprat skywards, before its great escape.

I should have retired there and then. Instead, I repaired to the boatyard at Balmaha where Jimmie, the boatman, kindly supplied a sound greenheart rod and reel, wiping his tears dry, as I sped out to the fatal spot again feeling curiously dispirited and excited at the same time.

The second salmon seemed well enough hooked. It was playing well when a third fish arrived at the "poker" bait. They both came off — *quietly!* It appeared I was in amongst a proverbial "nest o' fish", with nothing to prove it. The mounts and hooks were checked and, resorting to the smaller sprats remaining, I tried to ignore the empty feeling within. Four more salmon arrived, one at a time and completely indifferent to the smaller bait, seizing them before departing at different stages of the battle. The action, for what it was worth, gradually ceased and to be honest it came as something of a relief. Perhaps I was near to a new world record. I cannot, however, leave the story to end just like that or no-one bothering to read on will bother to row out . . . ! Some days later, miles from the fatal spot, one solitary salmon bothered me at 7 p.m. in an evening wind. It seized the red sprat solidly, did not steal any gear, and weighed exactly 21 lb. I thought then that the previous not so "magnificent seven" would be forgotten. They *never* are.

Since then, I have had many consoling talks with fellow anglers who have suffered along the same lines but, although a few tales run parallel, none have quite matched mine for quantity and rapid times of departure. It still plagues me that *seven* salmon took the baits and still came off. I can only reason that they (obviously) did not take them correctly. Perhaps fresh fish, gathering as they do in a close-knit, excited pack, are too nervous to do the job properly, and "nudge" the bait rather than taking it up and across in true taking fashion.

In retrospect, I have to wonder just what bait would, or could, have converted failure into at least partial success. Quite often, switching up or down a size in baits stops *any* response. Many seasons, much suffering and seven more grey hairs later, I will now reveal what these cute, restless and extremely clever salmon *will* take — something they will accept solidly and with complete abandon: *nothing*.

Still Water

Although Loch Lomond occupies most of my angling thoughts, I have often benefited from reading of other waters. I once read of the huge King Salmon, off British Columbia, which took the Kynoch Killer (or "Lucky Lou" as the Canadians call it) when trolled *very* deeply in the briny. Reading about this caused me to ponder the subject and I evolved a multicoloured Kynoch which competed with the Rainbow for glow and effect. It killed fish after fish, and the odd thing is that I didn't use a paintbrush, but applied streaks and smudges with my fingertips. I could never, naturally, repeat the killing blend of colours thus evolved and alas this particularly lucky bait stopped working for me when it vanished mysteriously from the end of my line when trolling one day. I had no way of telling when or where we parted company. Reeling-in to go ashore for a drum-up, I found the cherished bait had just gone. Knot failure was ruled out, the nylon having been cleanly cut several inches above the bait position. If it was taken by a fish or got lodged in a stony crevasse below the surface, my slumber at the tiller must have been heavy, since the reel gave no audible signal. The Kynoch floats and, so highly did I rate that particular bait, I searched many miles of foreshore for it, but to no avail. I sat staring at the floorboards for ages, possessed of a lonely and insecure feeling. My pal had gone. It was time for a good greet.

I've also read about fishing in Norway, and I should go there. Only major reasons prevent this, but in reading about fly fishing their thunderous rivers, you can't help but pick up a few pointers to improve your casting, and wading in general.

There was a time when you could freely fish the dry fly on the Endrick Water, and this fact prompted me to read a book on tactics applied to an idyllic little English river, as different from the Endrick as could be. Some dry flies were pictured in this book, so I tied up several. All but one failed and even it didn't compete with the old Greenwells or Wickhams, until the trout had nibbled off the upright wings. Thereafter, it was gorged.

I'd forgotten the whole matter until raking through an old fly box, when the same fly dropped out of the dusty innards of the box. It was trying hard to be noticed and I duly tied it on size 6 and 8 hooks and flung it into the loch — and a fair number of sea trout took it away with them, returning it to me each time in the boat! Still in its simple infancy, the "Blue Label" did well on hard, "steely" days.

Fishing seems to be made up of hundreds of wee bits and pieces, gleaned as described. As someone (a Lomondite I guess) once said, "There's more to fishin' than jist goin' oot in a boat!"

I used to fish for sea trout at night on the River Endrick, a little before it became completely impossible, or almost, to do so satisfactorily. The response then was good, by any standards, since not so many fished the river — or at least that particular stretch — during the day, and fish were given a good resting before nightfall.

Well prepared, I quietly entered the neck of the pool, casting a measured amount of line, calculated by previous experience. The far bank had, to my knowledge, never been fished much, but to my surprise there were muffled voices and then the sudden thrashing of a fish. Due to an overhanging bush, and the darkness, I couldn't make out much, but presumed someone had got lucky with the fly. The second and third time it happened made me think they had *really* got lucky, and I retired fishless to the car, and thence home.

Next day, I passed the spot again and, curiosity winning, waded across to where I guessed they had been fishing. There, in front of me, was the complete evidence and proof that I had been fishing too small the night before. It appeared that the fish were being taken with bigger hooks than mine, and very sparsely dressed. Still dangling from a short piece of rope was their stout "cast" and an enormous rusty treble hook. Beside lay the heads and tails, guts, etc of the lamentably caught fish. I still think they might have obtained permits!

I once left my car at the Blane Bridge and strode across the field to fly fish the "Meetings" pool, where the rivers Blane and Endrick unite. It used to be well worth fishing but, since the incident in question, I have not returned.

The waters were in good flow and I started casting with good spirit and high hopes. Something white caught my eye ahead and, as I neared it, a slight wriggle confirmed it to be a fish. But it was upside down. Reeling-in, I came out of the water and climbed the bank whereupon I was able, regrettably, to see one or two more fish, either floating, dead, or in the death throes. Round the corner, in slack water, was an even more pitiful sight. About three dozen fish, a mixture of salmon, grilse and sea trout, were breathing their last.

Agitated and mystified, I concluded that some kind of disease had struck and made to return to the car in the hope that another angler might have arrived, to confirm my suspicions. Propping my rod against the road fence, I saw the most welcome sight approaching, mounted on a scooter, in the shape of one of our water bailiffs. Together, we sped across the field and I am sure, from what I had told him, he had already made the right deduction. "Poison — cyanide!" he said.

It seemed that my day was over and his just about to begin.

The same day, a man who could not run fast enough with the sackful of fish he bore, was caught up with and removed to a place of safety.

The pool, of course, has long since recovered, and many thousands of fish have safely passed through it. But sadly, to me, it was never to be the same again. I decided to fish harder (and more often) an area of water nearby whose very magnitude would pose the poacher immeasurable problems. It has, needless to say, provided me with more than a few too... legally at that!

I often wonder who gives places their names. We should certainly thank you, dear romantic (whoever ye be) for so aptly choosing the name "Balmaha" for our little lochside haven on the eastern shores. Perhaps one reason for its attractiveness is that few place-names end in the letter "a": those that do have a magical aura... Shangrila, Casablanca, Utopia, Balmaha...

There are three letters "a" in the word, which maybe explains the eccentric speech of a dear old lady I met on the shores, about ten years ago. On the first occasion I met her, despite intensive coaching from me, she found the name an impossible tongue twister and settled for her own unique version: Balamahaha! There were no shortages of "ha-ha's" in response.

"Yes," she would say, "what a nice spot Balamahaha is!"

She was English when I first met her but, lately, she seemed to have both changed her accent and got Balmaha, at long last, right. Curing this fault, however, produced another. She now had a better substitute for the word "nice". Anything, and absolutely everything, became "bonnie"! Her last "talk-in" went, "What a bonnie day.. Oh, that's a bonnie fish... Bonnie, isn't it?"

I had to bonnie agree.

Always on a Friday

Once upon a time, we had a blissful set-up in Balmaha in the shape of a small caravan sited in the wee field, behind the present-day

207

petrol station. Each Friday a wife and child (mine) were snatched from home and finally freed, after a non-stop drive, at the steps of the van. Before the car door had closed, I was half way across that field, bristling with rods and gear, heading for the waiting boat.

An amazing run of good fortune followed. On five consecutive Fridays I caught salmon with almost indecent speed within five to ten minutes of being afloat. Two took the fly just off the boats, at the Mudflats, two came off the pier, on the troll, and another from the shore rocks before Manse Bay. There seemed to be some truth in the saying "Never spit on your own doorstep".

The part-owner of the shop and garage, at that time, helped me in a frenzied rush one Friday by carrying the outboard motor to the boat and I could see him watching, pipe in mouth, as I played a fish in lovely conditions of soft, filtered sunshine, just off the moored boats. Success has seldom been so quick, or regular.

The funny and true sequel to this tale was related to me by a friend at a later date when he overheard two newly arrived visiting anglers lament about their prospects, after a blank Wednesday. "We're wastin' oor time gawn oot again the morra'," said one, "We'll wait tae tea time oan Friday — when yon bloke comes doon."

"How?" asked his mate.

"That's the only time these fish take doon here."

And he was serious!

A speedy capture in 1978 upset the pattern. It happened on a *Monday*, at just after 10 a.m., in the first week of June. (Given a choice, I think most regulars would favour this day, since the loch gets a little bit of rest on the Sabbath, at least from the many trolling and fly fishing boats.) The boat was slowed just off the last of the mooring buoys, prior to the pier, and the treble of the first bait unclipped from the reel. A 1 oz Gold Toby, to suit the "poker", had only just been slipped into the wake of the slow-moving outboard when a few loops of nylon sprang up from the spool, giving a slight overrun. It was easily freed but, somehow, I had lost contact with the bait. The cause of the stoppage, to my great delight, was a 15 lb salmon and he entered the boat — via the net — at the side of the pier. I doubt if the Toby was in the water more than 30 seconds, as it fluttered out in the wake of the boat.

A man who had been watching the whole affair from high above, on the pier, shouted, "Is that your first?"

I am, as I was then, speechless, and still pondering what he meant — my first ever or my first that day? The cheek of some people — *spectating should be banned!*

12
Fin

PERHAPS, being so hypnotised by Lomond, I do the rest of the angling, if not sporting, world an injustice. I have loitered in some lovely places where the sport has taken second place (almost) to the scenery. Some rugged parts of Scotland, where the loch fishing has been truly "wild", and some unforgettable Irish loughs with their own particular charm: all have left their imprints in my mind. My fascination with Lomond is partly due to its composition, the contrast between the tap and bottom end, the ingenious layout of the islands, the many different fish species and the variety of the shoreline contours; these and many more attractive features have all contributed to my imagined feelings that someone took a wee bit of beauty from everywhere else and combined them all in the masterpiece we see today.

We all feel our own way about our own fishing, but I have long ere decided that when I lose that electric feeling of anticipation as the boat sails out past Balmaha pier into a steady soft wind coming from the right direction, when there isn't a slight shakiness in tackling up, when the drive down seems unduly slow or there is no great heave of delight at leaving behind the big city, then something will have gone which epitomises, for me, what the angling game is all about.

Curiously unlike many other sports, nervous reactions brought about by the promise of that "big day", fortunately happen when they can cause the least damage. Rhythm, once out on the loch, is soon restored to the angler wielding his fly rod from a lazily drifting boat, and his attention is soon riveted upon the cast of flies and the work they are doing. There is no audience: no spectators to witness your better feats or more customary mishaps. It's just you, the fish and the surroundings. To those of us who prefer the challenge of big lochs, angling upon them becomes an almost intensely private affair — but something you want to share with everyone else!

In looking for the *exit*, then, I would much like to thank the loch for not always staying still, the wind for blowin', the rain for pourin' — both at the right time — (like sometimes twice a year) and the hundreds of dedicated poor souls like me. The fish, too, deserve thanks and encouragement for attending our meetings in more respectable numbers once again. Inevitably, some did not see eye to eye with us and left in an agitated hurry. Others created the usual disturbance in our waters. Most of them, though, supported our great need for excitement and I met a few pleasantly active groups in the nicest wee corners of the loch (and mouth). They were keen to co-operate. Fish members, in general, are against complete union with us and we have even heard reports of certain bodies not sticking firmly to the right channels of approach. It is the angler's duty to report erratic behaviour of this sort to the nearest boat committee who can intercept these wayward culprits (even though they hide) and question them about their demands. If we are to remain on the right lines, using the right methods, we will need all the new fish members who are bound to join us, even if it does mean some of the older "craturs" retiring. They have scoured the loch for long enough. Like me.

Loch Lingo – A Glossary

LET'S DO THE BANK! . . NO LET'S DO IRELAND

GIMME A PRIEST!. . . . . THAT'S A BALLANTINE

IT'S COVERED IN LICE ! . . . . CLEAN LIKE US!

WHERE'S THE TAP END? . . . . . . UP THE ROO

PASS THE POKER . . . . TOOK A TOBY

THAT SEAGULL'S CHOKED! . . . WHAT A KYPE

THESE FISH ARE RUNNING . . WATCH THAT BOB

SEE THE LADIES POINT? . . . . TWA PUN!

STRIKE! WHAT ME ? . . . . . IT TOOK ME WELL

ANYTHING DOING? . . . . HEE — HAW!

LET'S HAP UP . . . NO. LET'S DRUM UP

LUCKY TWO

AA I earnestly hope that this book will assist with angling problems encountered on Loch Lomond. It does not cater for car troubles or beverage difficulties en route. The letters stand for Angling Areas, as shown on the maps.

BACK-END When the curtain comes down on the angling season around September/October, we have reached the back-end. The fish then prepare for spawning and, years hence, we will welcome their offspring in what should logically be called the front-end, but is better known as spring.

BAGGOT You will seldom encounter this fish in the loch, but if you do, the poor thing should be handled with great care, and gently returned to the water. It is usually of the salmon family, but is coloured, with a bulging stomach and inflamed vent from which oversize, stale eggs are often expelled on to the floorboards. The baggot has failed to deposit her eggs on the redds, through late arrival coupled with an unexplained malfunction. The fish then languishes and in continuing its feeble existence returns to the sea, passing, no doubt, fresh springers on the way in. Like most things in the fishy world, it is all a matter of timing. No-one, apparently, told the baggot.

BALLANTINE The local whisky distillers, Messrs Ballantine, have a way of rewarding almost total abstinence. Fish the loch incessantly, avoiding hostelries like the plague, and search every known hiding-place for a sea trout of about 7-12lb. Catch it straight away on the fly, weigh and witness it, tell Ballantines, and you will get some bottles of their lovely beverage — *free!*

BANK, THE The Bank of Scotland, locally, means the half-mile stretch of sandy shallows from Balmaha to the Net Bay. Bars of silver (*Salar*) lie there, but are difficult to withdraw. Local anglers will often be heard to say, "We'll go out and do the Bank". Do not 'phone the police. Follow them!

BAY There are hundreds of bays on Loch Lomond, but the one referred to throughout these tales is at Balmaha.

BLACK NEBS In spite of their being silvery, this is the local name for young adult sea trout to about 1½lb. Also known as finnock. Great wee fish which join you freely, if mistakenly, when wiser fish avoid your same old flies.

BLACK ROCKS A very good salmon lie near Balmaha, being the rocky point between Manse and Millarochy Bays. Every year there are fish taken here on the troll by everyone but me. Apart from three or four salmon and a few sea trout on the fly, the residing fish have heard me coming. It is netted at stipulated times in the season.

BLOWLINE   See *Floss*

BOATPACKING   Packing a wee lightweight tent, sleeping bag, etc, aboard the boat for an overnight stay on the loch. This delightful pastime could, however, be brief if permission in certain areas is not assured. A great number of the islands and the Endrick Bank, for example, are protected by the Nature Conservancy Council, and camping is forbidden. The good angler and boatpacker will never associate himself with litter of any kind. Our loch must remain as untouched as possible, since we hope it will continue to provide us with enjoyment for a long, long time yet.

BOB   This is the name given to the uppermost fly on the cast, the one which surfaces first upon retrieval.

BOTTOM END   All fishable water from, say, Rowardennan downwards.

BROWNIE   Widespread, affectionate term applied to brown trout, our non-migratory residents. Few fish on the loch specifically for them and they are caught usually in the course of fly fishing for salmon and sea trout. Loch Lomond brownies are truly wild and a welcome bonus when they appear towards the back-end.

BUM JOY   Anything comfortable to seat you on a thwart. An inflated Mini tyre inner tube is useful, and can also act as a lifebelt should you bounce off it. Sheets of closed cell foam, stuck together, are probably better and safer.

BURTON   Going for a Burton can be a disaster for a fish. It is a well-known loch pattern fly.

CAPER   A huge bird, the capercaillie (pronounced *cappercailzi*), largest of the wild turkey family. It is more than a match for you if surprised and can floor victims with its enormous wings. Many times when I have been ashore for a drum-up, one has appeared on the ground, under cover of trees, and emerged at great speed to give me all the symptoms of a heart attack. If you like fir cones, you will enjoy the flavour of this bird. Heavy artillery required to obtain them.

CHUCKIES   Wee stones, or droves of jackdaws which fly endlessly from Balmaha to Inchcailloch and back.

CLACHAN Often referred to in parched tones when the fishing is not so good or even, desperately, when it is! A quaint little pub in Drymen, used as angling headquarters by many.

CLEAN When an angler returns the same way as he went out, fishless, he is said to be clean, and there are many spotless anglers about. A clean fish smells of the sea, when fresh in, and this term also applies to practically any fish caught which has not spawned and has become a kelt.

COLOURED This adjective applies to a fish which is advanced in the spawning state, when it loses its beautiful silver sheen for a duller, pinkish coating, developing a kype in the process.

CRIN, THE Inchcruin.

DAP If you mention this word to an angler and he simply runs away, it's safe to assume that he has shared a boat with someone who has used this highly entertaining method of fishing. Huge bushy flies, resembling nothing on earth, are stotted and/or danced upon the surface of the water by means of blowline, or floss as it is better known, in dry-fly style.

The flies should be well soaked in floatant and allowed to dry out before use. The method provokes frustrations in both the fish and the angler, so that if you are stumped for an excuse to fall out with your crony, persuade him to dap and your problem is over.

Unable to stand the sight of the waltzing monster cavorting above them, many fish seize the dap fly fiercely, and only then does it appear a sound and sane method. Even so, I have known both the angler and captured fish stare at each other in puzzlement over their presence together in the same boat!

DARROCH A most beautiful islet, off Inchfad, which I sometimes feel gets a little weary of the large numbers of anglers in boats who pass it or linger ashore. For all its size, an incredible drift given the peace it requires.

DAYMARE When my boat passes certain areas of the loch, tears cascade to the floorboards, as a variety of fishing disasters come to mind. The particular disaster which led to the coining of the word is described in Chapter 11. All honest anglers will have their own private daymares.

DISEASE, THE Angling fever is a pleasant enough disease, but the one referred to has haunted our game fishing scene for what seems like an eternity. For the past ten years or so, there has been an outbreak of the affliction of ulcerated dermal necrosis (UDN). Fishing at the back-end can be a penance, as the fish develop a white, fungus-like covering, often accompanied by loss of sight and eventual death. It spreads like wildfire when the water temperature drops acutely, and little if anything has been put forward as a cure other than Nature and her wondrous ways of restoring the balance in the end.

DOLDRUMS, THE Not a good fishing spot I have omitted from the text, but a state of mind brought on by a windless loch, a broken engine, escaped fish, over-fishing or under-eating. The immediate cure is to land a fish between 1 and 20lb. Some days even a kelt will do!

DRIFT You will not succeed with the fly if your wind-assisted boat does not *drift* over good fish-holding water. A short drift would be little Darroch, a long drift from Inchgalbraith to the area of Inchcruin/Inchfad. Care should be exercised in setting up the boat at the start of a drift and, since fish do not, regrettably, lie in a straight line, the oars will be needed to make corrections in depth and direction. The maps show the various ins and outs of the better-known drifts. Avoid spoiling the whole drift, by careless use of the engine, for boats about to fish the water you have covered. The Loch Lomond permit states, "trollers should give way at all

A drum-up. Note the hand-carved table and choice china

215

times to boats engaged in fly fishing, by at least 100 yd". There may be slight conflict on this point from time to time, due entirely, of course, to the metric conversion!

DRUM UP Possibly the most distinctive term used by all and sundry who fish the loch. Should you lose your fishing bearings, look for a boat or small group of boats drawn up on the shore. They will be having a drum-up, which is a lochside brew of tea, prepared in a charred kettle and unequalled the world over. The anglers will usually be seated on old tree stumps, or the like, swapping tales, teaspoons and Tobies.

ENYTHIN' DOOIN'? Loch anglers rarely talk to each other. They learn more by immediate, sometimes furious, cross-questioning. I have never clearly understood what these two words really mean, but no matter, it befits the newcomer to have many alibis ready or simply reply, "No, there's nothing doing." Alternative answer: "He-haw —", which inexplicably also means nothing.

ESOX LUCIUS Latin name for the pike.

FAD, THE Inchfad.

FISH, A As a matter of somewhat smug angling pride, some do not rate a fish of under 1 lb as a real fish, preferring to call it a "wee thing". This clearly shows how spoilt a breed we are on Lomond. Rarely have I seen one put back, however!

FLOATANT A greasy substance or liquid in which the dapping fly is soaked to enable it to float on the surface film. I find that the mucous from the mouth of a brown trout soon destroys the buoyant qualities of practically any compound, whereupon I change the fly at once. A waterlogged dapping fly with sinking tendencies rarely provokes the result you seek.

FLOSS Also known as blowline. It is a gossamer-light line, usually of synthetic material, that catches the wind, enabling the dapping fly to be fished on the surface water a respectable distance out from the drifting boat.

FRY Tiny offspring, about 2 in long, quite complete little fish which form a shoaling instinct early in their careers for self-preservation. In summer thousands of perch fry and the like gather under the shade of the moored boats in the bay. They are eagerly sought by practically every predator but the angler. He has to wait a while!

216

GEGGLES Well-known area of sandy, shallow water between the islands of Inchmoan and Inchcruin.

GREET In Scotland, especially angling on Loch Lomond, we don't cry. We greet. A fishless angler, therefore, is often described as "greetin' faced".

GRILSE I know an old chap who still can't get the word right. "Any gristles today, Mr...?" They are salmon which have spent but one winter in the sea before returning to fresh water. They are usually slender fish (though some I have landed have been distinctly hump-backed) with small, neat heads and acutely formed wrists to a tail which is decidedly more forked than that of an older fish. Such is their supreme sport on the fly, there is little chance of confusion with a kelt. The loch gets a good run of grilse when the leaves and fields are at their greenest.

HAPPIN' UP The hap is the shaped canvas, or similar material, used to cover the boat when moored. This term simply means fastening it down, and many tales are swapped between anglers when happin' up after the day's fishing. I most strongly advise a hap for your boat, since incessant rain has caused many a boat to visit the bottom of the bay. A hap and ridge pole to match is a worthwhile investment.

INCH A small (usually Scottish) island. On Loch Lomond, the larger island names are preceded by "Inch", e.g. Inchmurrin. Most, but not all, of the smaller islands have "inch" at the end of their names, e.g. Torrinch. Some tiny islets, of great angling significance, like Darroch and Aber, prefer to remain aloof to any such classification, as if to intimate their great independence.

IRELAND, THE This menacing little rock lies between Inchfad and Inchcruin, and is far from an emerald isle. It is clearly marked by a white pole upon which always sits a gull, or perhaps it is a stuffed imitation. Small as it is, the area is of great angling significance — like Ireland.

KELT This is a spent fish, thin and usually big-headed. It is an offence to kill one, so if you are in any doubt at the beginning (and often the end) of the season, put the poor creature back. Some years ago I hooked *twenty-three* in one day, one a salmon kelt weighing 26lb, that I would rather have met the year before.

KYPE Some queer things happen to men during courtship. A male adult fish is no different. Nature alters his face slowly, throughout the season, until at spawning time it has become a positive eyesore. The tip of the snout and bottom jaw develop into bulbous knobs so that the jaws cannot close properly. Many reasons have been advanced for the "facelift", but only two remain fairly acceptable to me. I discount the one most commonly heard, that the hen fish finds her mate attractive, so adorned. During spawning, many small fish present themselves near the hen. The now ugly cock fish snaps at them, but is unable to grasp their little bodies due to the large gap in his jaws. I'm sure the wee chaps have great, tantalising fun swimming in and out of the brute's mouth, safeguarded by Mother Nature's facial alteration to the adult male. The second reason, not to be taken too seriously, results in the angler's fly passing through the gap in the jaws hundreds of times, leaving the fish safe and the hunter demented! There may be an ill-balanced twist to this latter suggestion since there are almost too many cock fish present, ready to fertilise the ova, and a good number of them could be caught without causing great losses (if any) in the numbers reproduced. Regrettably, and all too often, it is the hen fish, heavy with eggs, which is taken and can be ill spared. The hen, alas, should have had the big kype.

LADIES POINT A good fly drift for salmon and sea trout along the south-east tip of Inchcruin. Just before the point lies a very large boulder on the shore (not put there by a lady I'm sure), which virtually marks the most concentrated part of the drift, ending at the shallow tip of the island.

LICE Ordinary people tend to start scratching on hearing this word. Not anglers, though, who recognise these little parasites as the finest sight possible on a fish. Sea lice are small, brown, tadpole-like creatures, which adhere to the flanks and head of fish by means of a suction base, and I believe they keep the fish free of other, smaller, unwelcome parasites. They die and fall off within hours of the fish entering fresh water. Slingers are lice with the long tail sacs still attached, when fish may then be only minutes out of the tidal water. Rumour has it that the Japanese are making plastic stick-on types of lice so that we anglers can lie better still!

LOCH TROUT Often known locally as yellow trout. These are crafty, long-lived cannibals who grow to a fair size in the loch. I have caught several, up to $12\frac{1}{2}$ lb, at the back-end, when they temporarily lose their cunning as the excitement of spawning approaches. Throughout Scotland they are better known as *Ferox*, usually deep, heavy fish with pike-like jaws and teeth. True to form, I don't find our Lomond Loch trout all that ugly. Some I would claim to be quite handsome, depending on what else you might have in the boat with which to make a comparison!

LONG POINT   If you see boats, armed with fly rods, heading for Ichmoan island, they will almost certainly fish both of the "hot spot" points. The Long Point is renowned for salmon and sea trout and can fish all day, in certain conditions, given quiet treatment by drifting boats. See also *Short Point*.

MIDDLE FLY   Fishing three flies on the cast, this is the one between the bob and the tail.

MOAN   Inchmoan.

MULTIPLIER   A type of reel, used mostly in sea fishing, which is mounted uppermost on the reel seat. For every turn of the handle there are many revolutions of the spool. I use the fast-retrieve type for trolling, so that the two "idle" baits can be rapidly reeled-in before engaging with the fish on the taking rod. There is now a trend towards multiplying fly reels, which should benefit me greatly when my next fish wishes to visit Luss in a hurry, and I want it back — quick.

OVA   Female fish, on the redds, lay their eggs, which are known as ova. A 10lb fish might lay as many as 6,500 ova and, although they are like tough little rubberised balls, many perish through predators, birds, floods, eels and the like. About half-way through the incubation period two small black dots appear on each egg. It is then that the ovum becomes "eyed", albeit still defenceless in its shroud. All it is likely to see so early in its career is what is swallowing it!

OVERRUN   This does not, alas, mean far too many fish arriving. On the contrary, it is a complete angling disaster. Should the reel check be set too light and a lively fish dives or leaps suddenly, loops of line or nylon spiral out from the reel, resulting in a seizure of the revolving spool. It has happened to all of us, from time to time, but only when a very large fish *was* attached.

PARR   A beautiful stage in the life of small game fish, about a year old. They are about 4-6 in long, with spots and barred markings

A 6 lb grilse caught in a light "zeephr" of wind. Rowardennan Pier, now renovated, and Ptarmigan Point (off which the fish was caught) can be seen in the background

along their flanks. Salmon parr are easily recognised by several distinctive heavy blotches, like fingermarks, on their sides. Suicidal feeders, they must be handled with great care and not thrown back forcibly. They may swim away speedily enough, but handling injuries or a ruptured swim bladder soon causes death. Quite the most attractive little fish to be found anywhere.

PETROIL Most outboards are two-stroke and need the addition of predetermined amounts of special oil to low-octane petrol. A good many modern engines work on the remarkable ratio of 50:1 or 100:1, which is very little oil, testimony to the very fine engineering tolerances achieved by the makers. Specific oils are often recommended for particular engine makes and it pays in the long run to stick to the maker's directions. I would again issue fair warning that plenty of petroil should be aboard. On the eastern shore, for example, Balmaha is the last chance for a fill-up. Rowardennan, at the end of the same shoreline, has no facilities in this respect but, should you run out of juice, the local hill walking is wonderful!

POKER Three rods are normally used for trolling. On Loch Lomond the centre one, which fishes a short line out from the stern, is

220

known as the poker, due to its short and (quite unnecessarily) stiff qualities.

PUN This local play on words means that no matter if your fish weighs ten pounds, it will rapidly be changed to "ten pun"! Likewise, "twa pun", "hawf a pun", etc.

REDDS When salmon and sea trout have completed their long and ardous journey to the rivers of their birth, they eventually mate and spawn in clean, shallow water. The hen fish lay her eggs (ova) in carefully prepared furrows in the gravelly bottom before the cock fish fertilises them with milt. The fish are at this stage said to be "on the redds".

RISE Fish are said to be "rising" when they break the surface, no matter how slightly. There are many reasons for this, the most common being to a natural fly or your imitation.

ROO, THE Rowardennan Hotel and district, port of call for our cherished paddle-steamer the *Maid of the Loch*, with a beautiful youth hostel and ample opportunities for hill climbing on the Ben above. Also the end of the road on the eastern side of the loch.

RUN, A A good head, or shoal, of fresh fish entering lochs or rivers. Also, when a fish leaves the area of the boat at extremely high speed or takes a trolled bait before becoming unstuck.

SALAR King of Fishes, the salmon.

SALMON LEAP Our locally famous salmon (and sea trout) leap is at the Pots of Gartness, on the river Endrick, where it flows through the tiny community of Gartness on the Glasgow/Drymen/Aberfoyle road. When in spate, the fish can be seen — almost touched — as they ascend the "Pots", a series of small waterfalls, to the river pools above. Tense anglers there await them. There are very few stages, it seems, in the fish's long and torturous journey home when their complete safety is guaranteed. Another Salmon Leap, a well-known licensed hotel and rendezvous for anglers, is located in Drymen.

SCISSORS It may puzzle the novice to hear an angler proudly exclaim, "Aye, hooked right in the scissors!" It is a common enough angling expression and, relating to fly fishing, say, means that the rise has been well timed with the fish completing its turn and the fly lodging in the junction of the jawbone, at the very side of the mouth. This area is known as the "scissors", and a pair should then be needed to remove the well-embedded hook.

SCUNNER An exquisite old Scots word, given much scope for use on the loch. There is really no satisfying substitute for the word, which means a combination of sickened, disillusioned and disheartened. Losing fish can make you "fair scunnered".

SEAGULLS Our seagulls on the loch are fed a mixture of petrol and oil! Hardy birds, you might assume, but they have to be on such a big water, covering many miles per day. I refer, of course, to the well-established British Seagull outboard motor, fondly used on all big lochs for rugged trolling duties. A new model has now arrived, which doesn't need wee bits of rope, having a recoil start, and it goes backwards and forwards too. I feel that the main Glasgow distributors, Clyde Chandlers in Great Western Road, should supply a large placard to anyone changing to the new model and likely to use it on Loch Lomond. It will save us all from shouting, "Hey! That engine canny do that!"

SHORT POINT The equal, in angling merit, of the Long Point on Inchmoan. Busy drift from summer onwards, holding both salmon and sea trout.

SMOLT Since salmon and sea trout eventually head for the sea and its rich feeding grounds, Nature sees to it that when the parr is around 6 in or so in length it dons a silvery, protective coating. It will have spent 2-4 years in fresh water, this period varying somewhat in Europe. Our smolts are usually about two years old and make their exit down the river Leven into the salt water of the Clyde estuary, thence to choice feeding spots — salmon to Greenland waters and sea trout perhaps not quite so far. This migration of smolts happens around May each year, when the temperature of the rivers and tidal water is about the same.

SPRAT A small fish which we put into, rather than take out of, the loch. Used as an early-season trolling bait in gold or a variety of dyed colours.

SPRINGER Early-season salmon, the first usually being caught on the River Leven as they ascend to the loch.

TAIL FLY The bottom fly on the loch cast of three, fishing deeper than the other two.

TAP END All fishable water from Rowardennan up the loch.

THWART A spar seat in the boat, and also what fish expertly do to you.

TICK   This little parasite deserves *no credit*. A minute bloodsucking insect which burrows into the flesh of sheep, cattle and dogs. An excellent dog collar is now available which impregnates the coat against most crawly, obnoxious pests.

TOBY   If you have never seen one, stop the first fellow you meet in the street who wears a deerstalker, and chances are he will produce it from deep in his Harris tweed pocket. In return, you will be expected to stand in the pouring rain listening to tales of grief. It really is about the best-known fishing bait in Europe today, and hardly a trolling boat on the loch would be complete without one, from early summer onwards. From $\frac{5}{8}$oz to the smallest size in fickle conditions, it seldom fails.

TREBLE   A three-pronged hook with barbs, usually standard on trolling bait mounts, lures and spoons, etc. Also, the somewhat rare feat of capturing three fish in the one day.

TROLLING   There's trawling and trolling. The first is usually done by sea-going crews who fish by dragging nets along the sea bed. Hence trawl, trawlers, etc. Trolling (or trailing) concerns us more since it is a fairly common technique for fishing big lochs. Rods and lines are used with deadbait, spoons, plugs, etc, for baits. These are fished behind the moving boat on different lengths of line and, often, at different depths. On bad Loch Lomond days, when you are trolling you might wish you were trawling! If you are trolling and see another boat, you simply say to yourself, "There's another boat." If you are fly fishing and see the same boat you will say, "There's a troller." Note the different viewpoint. The whole matter can be taken too far and one fellow I knew (who couldn't troll) would decline to visit an entire shoreline, with the fly, if he found out that a troller had been over it a week past on Thursday! A bit much, perhaps, but on bad fly days he would point out trollers whom I couldn't see. In angling, more than any other sport or pastime, excuses *must* be found. None of my friends are poorly equipped in this sense.

VOLCANO   A unique type of loch kettle, much used on drum-ups. It utilises a hollow bottom for both kindling and stoking.

Existing Records

BEFORE I was born — but not much — were caught the two salmon which, to the best of my knowledge, remain local records to this day.

In 1927, Women's Lib. took hold and so did a 36½ lb salmon! A Mrs Leckie-Ewing, who fished out from Luss with her husband, an ex-Army Major, tolerated a fearsome gale off the north-eastern tip of Inchfad and was duly rewarded with this sizeable prize. I do not know the fly she used and think it matters little, now. So much has changed since then. Salmon routes, lies, type and size of fly have all altered with time and perhaps, as the years have gone by, our salmon have got fussier for smaller flies and finer gear. There were fewer anglers then and possibly more takeable fish.

Ian Wood, as mentioned in Chapter 4, used his Turkey and Gold flies to great effect. Ably supported by his boatman Bobbie McLean he had many fine catches on the loch, including seven salmon to 77½ lb and five to 67 lb in 1952.

Great catches have come in since then, particularly to Balloch and Balmaha, and every other year a few in the 30 lb class fall to the troll, mostly, and the fly, more occasionally.

The record on the troll should inspire even the most miserable pessimist. Age is no barrier to fame, because Mr Edward Cochrane, of Paisley, was *83 years old* when he caught a salmon of 44½ lb, on 15th April, 1930. It snatched his blue and silver minnow off the Stables, at Ross Priory on the Claddich shore.

I am indebted to Mr Harry MacVinish, of Messrs John Dickson & Son, Exchange Square, Glasgow, for the picture of "Teddy" Cochrane and the record fish. It is a joy to behold the general neatness of the composition — the fastidiously-dressed gentleman, the lovingly cared-for greenheart rod and the perfection of the great fish itself. For its size, I cannot find a single fault.

Oh, that we could return to catch figures of the twenties. As a matter of interest (and great envy) I give below brief details of the

Association catch figures for 1927, since this year yielded some particularly heavy salmon to the fly and troll:

460 salmon, total weight 6,545½ lb

828 sea trout, total weight 1,303 lb

425 brown trout, total weight 400¼ lb

The sea trout and brown trout figures are, if anything, well below normal for that period, catches of a thousand of each species being not uncommon. The salmon figure, though, is mind-boggling when you relate the numbers of fish caught to the total weight. Sample catches included in the figures are 3 of 21½ lb, 7 of 22 lb, 2 of 22½ lb, 2 of 23 lb, 8 of 24 lb, 10 of 25 lb, 2 of 25½ lb, 3 of 26 lb, 1 of 26½ lb, 1 of 27 lb, 2 of 28 lb, and one each of 29 lb, 31 lb, 34 lb, 35 lb, 36 lb, 36½ lb and 38 lb, the last fish being caught by the late Mr J.M. Britton, of Alexandria.

Perhaps the depression felt by many who absorb these mighty figures can be offset, no matter how slightly, by the fact that the river Leven has welcomed in the eighties some impressive salmon catches, a few exceeding 30 lbs in weight. Given the right conditions, therefore, the loch angler should be debating the size of his net. Large as it might be, befitting the "regular" loch man, I make no apologies for repeating that *yours* will be too small — so at least carry a tailer!

My own biggest salmon can be any weight that I or my crony in the boat care to make it since, in the end, it escaped without revealing its poundage, after a 35-minute battle royal. It was hooked, taking like the "tweak" of a small perch, off the pier at Balmaha in a strong northern wind, and was finally brought to the net near the Claddich shore — a rapidly-covered distance away. It took a dark green Kynoch Killer, of my own concoction, and the tears have not dried up yet. We both *now* reckon it was well over 40 lb, yet it started off as 35 lb, in 1967! I can see it yet, lying completely "dead" on the surface, with only the treble hooks safely in the net. It seemed a complete waste of time to start fishing again. Imagine coming in with a mere 20-pounder!

Nowadays, there are many fly fishing competitions on the loch. The biggest is organised by the Loch Lomond Angling Improvement Association, and because of a long series of flat calms in previous years, during high summer, the event is now held nearer autumn. Local club outings are fairly common and at Drymen the Salmon Leap Hotel annually sponsors a well-attended contest.

As far as I'm concerned, every time you go out *it's a competition!*

There should be a record for the heaviest sea trout (or salmon) caught on the loch on the dap. I don't know what it is. My own personal best is a sea trout of 12lb, and a salmon a pound heavier.

I think it fit to record that, although it did not come from Loch Lomond, the biggest sea trout caught on a loch (I am aware of one of 21½lb from the *River* Ailort, since the war) was enticed by the dap, on Loch Maree, in September 1951. If I am wrong, I will surely hear about it. The fish weighed 19½lb and was caught by Mr David C. McNaught, on a Black Pennel, of the inverted umbrella type, hook size 1/0, salmon scale. The rod was 15ft of built cane and the reel very old. No backing was used, just a continuous line of stranded, mercerised cotton.

Should this record ever be broken, I've often said (backed by some monsters risen) that Loch Lomond must have a chance. Just give it one.

A few years ago a man with a name well kent in Glasgow died. Tommy Morgan does not sit on the top of the present-day Records List, although he rightly earns that place. In 1945, he removed from Loch Lomond a pike of 47lb 11oz, but the British Record Fish Committee, when they reviewed records in the late '60s, saw fit to reject the fish for lack of enough verified evidence as to its weight.

How then, has it always been mentioned with the weight taken to ounces? There is a long story about the events of the weighing and it must be kept in mind that the outlook of the angler then was a bit different from his modern counterpart. It was simply "a brute o' a fush".

I clearly recollect mention of the great pike being taken to Agnews the Fishmonger, in Duke Street, in the East End of Glasgow, for what I think was a second weighing. Are a fish-monger's scales likely to underweigh?

I have much respect for the great battle which Fred Buller, a renowned pike expert, put up for Tommy Morgan's pike. I reckon Tommy can rest easy. *We* all know it weighed *forty-seven pounds and eleven ounces*, and, records or not, it's the target to beat!

On a wall of Messrs Robertsons tackle shop in Glasgow, there is a miniature art gallery of historic Loch Lomond matters. The "Teddy" Cochrane picture of the record fish on the troll comple-ments an original cast of two flies preserved on the cast which took five salmon to 60lb, just prior to Ian Wood's record-shattering weeks when he twice broke records with the fly. The reader might feel as I do when he scrutinises thickness of the gut (no nylon then) and the size of the flies. There is no doubt that they worked then, but I trust I have illustrated in the text the great changes in fish behaviour and angling practices in general. Also shown are several salmon flies, about $3\frac{1}{2}$ in long, which were used on the River Clyde over 100 years ago. Were fish caught on such heavy tackle today, I doubt if this book would be needed. Just the same, I would hesitate before trying to obtain this kind of ironmongery over the counter of first-class tackle shops nowadays.

Books Worth Reading

BOOKS on angling are plentiful. Volumes on techniques, tackle and general information abound on the bookshelves. The majority of works, I find, however, cater for the river angler, or for reservoir and similar still-water fishing, with sea angling taking its place. Big lochs are given scant mention, hence my own effort on the biggest loch of them all. Perhaps the reason other lochs are not given fuller treatment is their very much smaller size.

I list below just a few books I would recommend. Some are thought to be dated, and one somewhat romantic. They nevertheless contain information I have found most useful, some of which I have put into practice, in a limited way, on Loch Lomond. The *Vade Mecum* is available from Messrs Dicksons, in Glasgow and Edinburgh, to name but one stockist. The book by John Colquhoun is a treasure beyond words as far as the Lomond of yore is concerned.

The Fisherman's Vade Mecum by G. W. Maunsell (A. & C. Black)
Loch Lomond – A Study in Angling Conditions by Henry Lamond (Jackson Wylie & Company) 1931
Lake and Loch Fishing, Salmon and Sea Trout by W. A. Adamson (A. & C. Black)
The Scottish Lochs by Tom Weir — for general information — (Constable)
Pike by Fred Buller (Pan)
The Art of Sea Trout Fishing by C. C. McLaren — advocate of the light line — (Oliver & Boyd)
Two Hundred Popular Flies by Tom Stewart (Ernest Benn)
Sea Trout Fishing by Hugh Falkus (Witherby)
Nature Detective by Hugh Falkus (Gollancz)
The Moor and the Loch by John Colquhoun
Fisherman's Knots and Wrinkles by W. A. Hunter
Going Fishing by Negley Farson (White Lion)

Announcements of Interest to Readers

Prize catch.

The Ballantine's salmon and trout angling competition offers prizes for the best 12 fish caught in each of three classes every month between April and October. That's quite a catch.

You'll find entry forms in fishing tackle shops and hotels throughout Scotland.

Ballantine's

The smooth Scotch with the memorable taste.

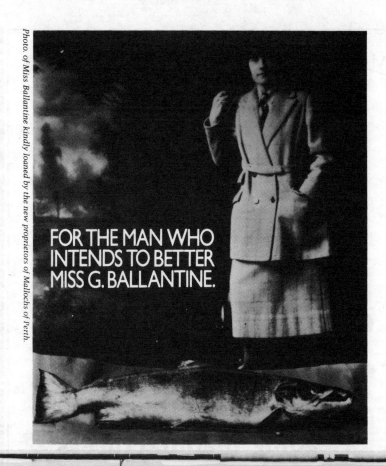

FOR THE MAN WHO INTENDS TO BETTER MISS G. BALLANTINE.

THE 'UNBREAKABLE' UGLY STIK SALMON FLY ROD-14ft. AFTM 10.

Though the good lady's 64-lb, British record has lasted since 1922, it's generally accepted that bigger salmon do exist. For the man who believes in these fish and his ability to handle them, given the chance, we have produced the Ugly Stik fly rod. Utilising our exclusive Ugly Stik blank, with a continuous spiral of 100% carbon fibres sheathed in butt-to-tip lengths of fibreglass, it's unbreakable in normal fishing. There's simply no way a man pulling against a line can snap it.

It also generates enormous power for casting big tube fly flies on big rivers. Yet, allied to all this, it offers an action and fighting curve like that of the best traditional salmon rods. The fittings are, naturally, all you would expect – ceramic butt and tip rings, chrome bridge intermediates, lock-ring reel seat, cork butt and foregrip.

Of course, even all that doesn't guarantee you a record fish! But, what it does guarantee you is the pleasure of using a superb rod that will handle any fish you hook.

Shakespeare Company, P.O. Box 1, Redditch, Worcs. B98 8NQ.
Republic of Ireland: Truetackle Ltd., 13 Main Street, Blackrock, Co. Dublin.

Ugly Stik *Shakespeare*

Go fishing with the world's largest tackle range.

Wishing You all the Best on Loch Lomond
We Buy Your Fresh Salmon!

We serve meals from 12 a.m. to 10 p.m.
Salmon Trout Chicken Pork Lamb
Home cured Ham and fresh Sea Fish
Pub food at its best
Children are always welcome with Dad

Mr & Mrs John *Proprietors FREE HOUSE*

DRYMEN STIRLINGSHIRE
Telephone: Drymen 357

36 MAIN STREET DRYMEN
Telephone Drymen 788

Come and see our extensive range of saddlery and riding wear. We also have a large stock of casual wear ideal for any outdoor sports — jeans, cords, shirts, boots, water proofs and TOG jackets — the perfect jacket for warmth and style worn by all outdoor fanatics.

Open 7 days a week
MON-SAT 9-1, 2-5.30; SUN 2.30-5.30

New from Barbour!

The Northumbria

Made from a new high quality material, in rustic brown with a dry finish oil proofing, giving better all-weather performance and durability. Eight pockets — including 2 lined hand warmers, waterproof inside wading strip and a solid brass easy-action two way zip.

It had to be good!

Barbour

For details of the full Barbour range write to: J. Barbour & Sons Ltd., Simonside, South Shields NE34 9PD

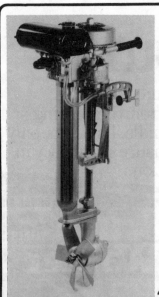